DESI

MANAGEMENT

USING DESIGN

to

BUILD BRAND VALUE

and

CORPORATE INNOVATION

BRIGITTE
BORJA DE MOZOTA

ALLWORTH PRESS
NEW YORK

DMI

DESIGN MANAGEMENT INSTITUTE

07 06 05 04 03   5 4 3 2 1

Published by Allworth Press
An imprint of Allworth Communications, Inc.
10 East 23rd Street, New York, NY 10010

   Cover and interior page design by Jennifer Moore, Brooklyn, NY
   Page composition/typography by Rosanne Pignone, Pro Production

   ISBN: 1-58115-283-3

Library of Congress Cataloging-in-Publication Data
Borja de Mozota, Brigitte.
   Design management: using design to build brand value and corporate innovation /
      Brigitte Borja de Mozota.
      p. cm.
Includes bibliographical references.
      ISBN 1-58115-283-3 (pbk.)
      1. Manufacturing processes. 2. Design, Industrial. I. Title.
TS183.B56 2003
658.5'752—dc22   2003020913
   Printed in Canada

TABLE OF CONTENTS

ACKNOWLEDGMENTS

I WOULD LIKE TO THANK for their early and continuing support, my friends and members of the Design Management Institute board:

Timothy Bachman
Jean Léon Bouchenoire
Bonnie Briggs
David Carvalho
Vincent Créance
Maguy Gabillard
Fennemiek Gommer
Lee Green
Yo Kaminagai
Judith Klappen
Sanjeev Malhotra
Ron Newman
Mark Oldach
Paul Porter
Earl Powell
Robyn Robins
Gérard Vergneau
Gianfranco Zaccai

I would also like to thank Andrea Levy, who worked on the translation of Chapter 4, and, my beloved family: Maxime, Aurore, and Rodrigue.

FOREWORD

THE DESIGN MANAGEMENT INSTITUTE (DMI), since its founding in 1975, has literally built the foundation of the design management profession. DMI is an independent, non-profit organization with members and constituents, as well as education and research programs around the globe. From this independent position, DMI works with a variety of institutions and organizations to help design managers become leaders in their professions and business managers effectively utilize design for business success.

Our publishing partnership with Allworth Press is an important opportunity to further the Institute's commitment to continuously advancing the profession and the understanding of the crucial role of design in business. Because *Design Management* is the first book to bring together the theory and practice of design management, it is a perfect project for the Institute to help make available to readers. We are pleased indeed to be the copublishers of this invaluable resource.

—Earl N. Powell, Doc. Letters (Hon.)
President
Design Management Institute
www.dmi.org

PREFACE

THIS BOOK SHOULD HAVE BEEN TITLED *33* in tribute to the thirty-three companies that agreed to be researched during the 1997 European Design Prize competition. Although all were well known for the excellence of their product design, the research revealed that they were not managing design in the same way. Out of the methods of all these thirty-three companies, a model was devised: the three-level model for design success that constitutes the backbone of this book.

The first part of the book describes the field of design: the difference between design as a process and the output of that process; the skills designers possess, and what can be learned from the history of design; and, finally, because "good design is good business," the importance of design relations, company performance, and design management.

The second part of the book explains how design creates value in an organization when the organization follows the model for value creation: design as differentiator; design as coordinator; and design as transformer. Theories, concepts, and studies relevant to this area of design management are developed in detail.

Design as differentiator. When design strategy aims to create a better brand, improving product, packaging, or service performance, it increases the financial value by boosting sales, exports, and customer-perceived value.

Design as coordinator. When design strategy aims to manage change in the innovation process, it acts as an efficient tool for the management of new product development. Design creates value because it helps coordinate functions and avoid conflicts, encourages cross-disciplinary teams, and improves communications among the designers in a project team. Design is linked to company process management and customer-oriented innovation management.

Design as transformer. When design strategy creates value by improving the relationship between the company and its environment, anticipating a clear vision of future markets and competition, creating new markets, and forecasting trends, it generates substantial strategic value, which can have a direct effect on the organization's positioning. Design contributes to the management of change and to the learning process in organizations.

Part 3 is practical and professionally oriented. It develops design management tools that marketers, business managers, and design managers can use in their decision-making processes when managing design projects. This section covers how to develop a design project in terms of its operations (operational design management), how to manage a design department (functional design management), and how to develop a design strategy (strategic design management).

In sum, this book explains the different ways companies can implement design to be successful. Thanks to the thirty-three!

PART I

THE FUNDAMENTALS

of

DESIGN MANAGEMENT

CHAPTER 1

THE FIELD OF DESIGN

I N ORDER TO RENDER DESIGN COMPREHENSIBLE TO NON-DESIGNERS, a number of interrelated issues and questions must be considered. First, we must describe the nature of the design profession, the diverse areas in which design is practiced, and the various methods designers employ in their work. We can then assess the relevance of design to the science of management, and discover what we can learn from the creative process. Finally, we need to evaluate the impact of design on organizational performance in order to determine what managers can gain from it.

In this book, the term "design" is used to designate the profession as a whole, and "designer" refers to the person who practices it.

"ALL MEN ARE DESIGNERS. ALL THAT WE DO, ALMOST ALL THE TIME, IS DESIGN, FOR DESIGN IS BASIC TO ALL HUMAN ACTIVITY."

—Victor Papanek

THE IDEA OF DESIGN

THERE ARE MANY DEFINITIONS OF DESIGN. In the broadest terms, design is an activity that gives "form and order to life arrangements" (Potter, 1980). Before choosing an authoritative definition, let's look at the etymology of the word. The word "design" derives from the Latin *designare*, which is translated both as "to designate" and "to draw." In English, the noun "design" has retained this dual meaning. Depending on the context, the word means: "a plan, project, intention, process"; or, "a sketch, model, motive, decor, visual composition, style." In the sense of intention, "design" implies an objective and a process. In the sense of drawing, it signifies the achievement of a plan by means of a sketch, pattern, or visual composition.

The word "design" in English, then, has retained the two senses of the Latin word ("to designate" and "to draw") because these two meanings were originally one and the same, "intention" being equal to "drawing" in a figurative sense. An etymological analysis of the word, then, leads us to the following equation:

DESIGN = INTENTION + DRAWING

This equation clarifies the point that design always presupposes both an intention, plan, or objective, particularly in the analytical and creative phases, as well as a drawing, model, or sketch in the execution phase to give form to an idea.

DEFINITIONS

ONE FREQUENT SOURCE OF CONFUSION is the fact that design can refer to either an activity (the design process) or the outcome of that activity or process (a plan or form). The media tends to add to the confusion by using the adjective "design" for original forms, furniture, lamps, and fashion without mentioning the creative process behind them.

The International Council Societies of Industrial Design (ICSID), an organization that brings together professional associations of designers worldwide, offers this definition:

> Aim: Design is a creative activity whose aim is to establish the multi-faceted qualities of objects, processes, services, and their systems in whole life cycles. Therefore, design is the central factor of innovative humanization of technologies and the crucial factor of cultural and economic exchange.

> Tasks: Design seeks to discover and assess structural, organizational, functional, expressive, and economic relationships with the task of:

> * enhancing global sustainability and environmental protection (global ethics)
> * giving benefits and freedom to the entire human community (social ethics)
> * supporting cultural diversity despite the globalization of the world
> * giving products, services, and systems, those forms that are expressive of (semiotics) and coherent with (aesthetics), their proper complexity.

> Design is an activity involving a wide spectrum of professions in which products, services, graphics, interiors, and architecture all take part.

The advantage of this definition is that it avoids the trap of seeing design only from the perspective of the output (the aesthetics and appearance). It emphasizes notions of creativity, consistency, industrial quality, and shape. Designers are specialists who have refined the ability to conceive form and who have multidisciplinary expertise.

Another definition brings the field of design closer to industry and the market:

> Industrial design is the professional service of creating and developing concepts and specifications that optimize the function, value, and appearance of products and systems for the mutual benefit of both user and manufacturer.
>
> *(Industrial Designers Society of America [IDSA])*

This definition insists on the capacity of design to mediate between the industrial and technological worlds and the consumer.

Designers working in design agencies that specialize in package design and graphics for organizations and their brands tend to prefer a definition that underscores the links between *brand* and *strategy*:

- Design and branding: design is a link in the chain of a brand, or a means of expressing brand values to its different publics
- Design and corporate strategy: design is a tool for making a strategy visible

The question of whether design is science or art is controversial because design is both science and art. The techniques of design combine the logical character of the scientific approach and the intuitive and artistic dimensions of the creative effort. Design forms a bridge between art and science, and designers regard the complementary nature of these two domains as fundamental. Design is a problem-solving activity, a creative activity, a systemic activity, and a coordinating activity. Management is also a problem-solving activity, a systemic activity, and a coordinating activity (Borja de Mozota, 1998).

Design entails thinking about and seeking out the consistency of a system or the intelligence of an object, as French designer Roger Tallon has put it. The designer conceives signs, spaces, or artifacts to fulfill specific needs according to a logical process. Every problem posed to a designer demands that the constraints of technology, ergonomics, production, and the marketplace be factored in and a balance be achieved. The field of design is akin to management because it is a problem-solving activity that follows a systematic, logical, and ordered process (see Table 1.1).

KEY MANAGEMENT WORDS

UNLIKE THE ARTIST, THE DESIGNER CREATES FOR OTHERS as part of a multidisciplinary team. The designer functions as a coordinator, and takes into account all of the components of the project. Therefore, design plays a role in the management of innovation as well as in conflict management.

Some designers prefer to emphasize the artistic and cultural dimensions of their profession. The techniques of design involve innovation, aesthetics, and creation. To these ends, the designer acquires cultural and artistic knowledge. The designer is an innovator and a trendsetter who tries to initiate change, to make a leap of imagination, and produce an idea. He considers the world a reality to be interpreted. Design is a "cultural option." The cultural and imaginative dimensions of design are related to the strategic business goals generated by a company vision, as well as the building of a corporate identity.

Design also departs from the realm of pure aesthetics to create objects that serve human needs. Design reflects human needs and wants, as well as the dominant ideas and artistic perceptions of the time. The designer must accommodate economic, aesthetic, technological, and commercial constraints and arrive at a synthesis. He is a "creator of form" who understands creation in the context of predefined imperatives established by other professionals, and places human values over technological ones (Bernsen, 1987).

Design, therefore, is a process of creation and decision making. It is not a substitute for other activities. Rather, it supports other activities and partners creatively with the field of marketing, endeavoring to strengthen and broaden its techniques and capabilities.

THE DISCIPLINES OF DESIGN

THE DESIGN PROFESSION IS ACTUALLY A FAMILY OF PROFESSIONS that developed around the conception of different forms (Forty, 1994). There are four types of design that correspond to the key domains through which the profession is integrated into society, and which describe its possibilities of entry and interface with the different functions of the firm: environmental design, product design, package design, and graphic design.

Environmental Design

Environmental design encompasses the planning of a space for a firm, and the creation of all of the spaces that physically represent the firm—industrial sites, office work areas, areas of production, common spaces (cafeterias, welcome zones), commercial spaces (boutiques, kiosks, corners of department stores), and exhibitions and stands (trade shows). Creating the work environment for a firm plays a fundamental role in the quality of the production, the building up of a culture, and the

DESIGN CHARACTERISTICS	DESIGN DEFINITION	KEY WORDS/TERMS
PROBLEM RESOLUTION	Design is a plan to manufacture something that one can see, touch, hear." —Peter Gorb	planning manufacture
CREATION	"Aesthetics is the Science of Beauty in the domain of industrial production." —D. Huisman	industrial production aesthetics
SYSTEMIZATION	"Design is the process by which needs of the environment are conceptualized and transformed in instruments to satisfy these needs."—A. Topalian	transformation of needs process
COORDINATION	"The designer is never alone, never works alone, therefore he is never a whole." — T. Maldonado	teamwork coordination
CULTURAL CONTRIBUTION	"The profession of designer is not that of an artist nor an aesthetician; it is that of a specialist in semantics."—P. Starck	semantics culture

Table 1.1. Design Characteristics

communication of its strategy. Environmental design can work also for commercial spaces, chains of franchised boutiques, stores, shopping malls, and supermarkets. Competition between stores entails an investment in brand differentiation, and therefore, a demand for design. Environmental designers also create new concepts for entertainment centers and restaurants.

Example: The Glass Innovation Center for Corning (Design by Ralf Appelbaum Associates)

Product Design

This is often the only publicly known type of design. The general public knows of this type of design through the creations of designer "stars" in furniture, fashion, and automobiles. The image of product design is fashion and avant-garde oriented, often because the press privileges this star system of design. But product design is not limited to furniture, lamps, carpets, fashion, and cars. Product designers intervene in practically all sectors, including:

- Engineering design, particularly mechanical engineering.
- Industrial design as concept design, which aims to elaborate on an original solution for a system (assembly-line machines in a factory, for example) for an existing function, or for a new function. (Often the work of design students, concept design consists of conceiving shapes that offer radically different approaches to existing products, or innovate to solve a problem.)
- Industrial design as adaptation design, which implies adapting a known system to a new task and requires original designs for parts or components.
- Industrial design as variation design, often called "restyling," which aims to vary the size or arrangement of certain aspects of a system without modifying the function and its principle.

Examples: Apple iMac, IBM ThinkPad, OXO Good Grips, and the Herman Miller Aeron Chair.

Package Design

Although less known than product design, package design constitutes most of the business for the design profession. The conception of packaging for manufactured products is part of brand development in consumer goods, cosmetics, and medicines. The designs serve to protect these products during handling, storage, transportation, and sale. Package design sometimes is not to be dissociated from the product, as with dairy products, canned foods, frozen foods, mineral water, sauces, etc.

Package design facilitates the recognition of products in stores and simplifies their use for the final consumer. It takes advantage of the idea of distribution through self-service. Packaging, then, began as simple protection and became an important element of information and communication for the product.

The package is the first visual contact the consumer has with the product. Amidst the multiplication of brands and manufactured products using relatively similar package designs, this creates a competitive advantage.

Package design is integrated into three different areas of design:

* Graphic design, in which a designer modifies or creates the graphics of a printed surface, such as a printed label (a work in two dimensions).
* Product design, or volume-oriented packaging, in which the designer improves the functional qualities of the packaging, improving or simplifying, for example, how the product is used by the consumer.
* Three-dimensional design, which is a conceptual level of package design that can transform all aspects of the product, such as modifying the shape, materials, or the interface system of a product.

Graphic Design

The graphic design field works with graphic symbols and typography to represent the name of a firm, its brands, or its products. The graphic designer is integrated into different areas of design:

* The designer creates a graphic system or complete visual identity for an item (whether it is letterhead, packaging, a calendar, an invitation, or signage), and updates that system or identity periodically.
* The designer realizes the brochure for a product, stationery with a logotype, graphic symbols for a store or shopping mall, a poster for an event, or a financial report for a firm.
* Graphic creations for a complex product, such as the control panel of a car.

Graphic design is fashionable. Who doesn't have a logo today? Cities, regions, humanitarian associations, television chains . . . nothing escapes "logomania."

Example: Route 128 in Boston, "America's Technology Highway."

2-D Design	3-D Design	4-D Design
Graphic Design	Furniture Design	Digital Design
Information Design	Fashion Design	Interactive Design
Illustration	Interior Design	Web Design
Textile Design	Industrial Design Environmental Design	

Table 1.2. Types of Design Disciplines

Even personal branding is essential to professional success today. Because branding is everywhere, graphic designers have to go beyond the creation of a visual identity: they design a promise of value. This area of design aims at conceiving complex systems of visual identity that fit with the company's internal systems of signage and communications. In its external communications, the company differentiates itself by a specific graphic and verbal language and applies these messages according to its different publics. Computer software makes the development of graphic design more flexible, and design templates more user friendly.

Web design, or multimedia digital design, evolved from the upsurge of information technology. No firm in the new economy can operate without the input of a professional Web site designer. These Web designers tend to have either a product or graphic design background. Whether for e-commerce or for intranet communication, the designers work as partners with the company.

The least known of all the types of design, information design seeks to represent the maximum information in a minimum amount of space while optimizing the message. This type of design presents figures, numbers, or geographical data. It has developed a universal language of pictograms, which is used by companies to improve decision processes and document flow.

ANGELA DUMAS AND HENRY MINTZBERG, 1991

"We are familiar with the debates that have raged over 'form' (styling) versus 'function' (engineering) and have added a third dimension. We shall call it 'fit' and suggest that it concerns the linkage between form and function and the user (ergonomics)."

Design activity can also be classified according to the dimensions of the created product: two dimensions (2-D) or three dimensions (3-D) (see Table 1.2). This typology includes a new dimension, four dimensions (4-D), which adds the dimension of the user interface as it appears in design processes that are driven by new information technologies. Multimedia design creates the graphic interface (intuitive navigation, icons) in software, games, or multimedia applications, such as databases on the Internet or an interactive information center. An effort is made to improve the ergonomics and the conviviality of the interface as an object that bypasses external visual output to include the virtual dimension of its relationship with the user.

DESIGNERS' SKILLS

The Design Tree

The diagram of the design tree imagined by David Walker (Cooper et al., 1995, p. 27; see Figure 1.1) helps to understand the diverse types of design and the relationships between them. It roots the design profession in the handicrafts and its key areas of expertise: perception, imagination, dexterity, visualization, geometry, knowledge of materials, sense of touch, and sense of detail.

1. The roots of the tree represent the immersion of design in different handicraft techniques and its insertion into the creative community. It assures the transfer of this knowledge to the firm, and distributes this expertise within the firm by a process of cross-fertilization.
2. The trunk of the tree represents specific areas of handicraft expertise, including calligraphy, pottery, embroidery, jewelry, drawing, modeling, and simulation. It represents the permanence of design expertise in its material form.
3. The branches of the tree represent different design disciplines' valorization of the different areas of expertise, and form a synthesis of market needs and design expertise.

TERENCE CONRAN, DESIGNER AND ENTREPRENEUR

United Kingdom, 2001

"What ten qualities must a designer have to succeed? Intelligence, imagination, creativity, common sense, perseverance, market awareness, determination, skill, sensitivity and a thick skin, self confidence."

The design tree shows how a designer builds his or her knowledge through education and practice. Researchers have recently described these skills as "applied" and tacit "processing" skills (Bruce & Harun, 2001) (see Table 1.3).

Design Schools:
What's in the Curriculum?
Another way to understand design skills is to look at a design school curriculum. Most design schools combine:

- General training, which includes both experimental sciences and social sciences
- Specific training in the field of design and in a chosen design discipline
- Theory courses
- Practical courses, which include doing projects using workshops, laboratories, and advanced computing tools
- Participation in real projects by means of an agreement between the design school and private companies or public institutions, and in design competitions

Figure 1.1. The Design Tree

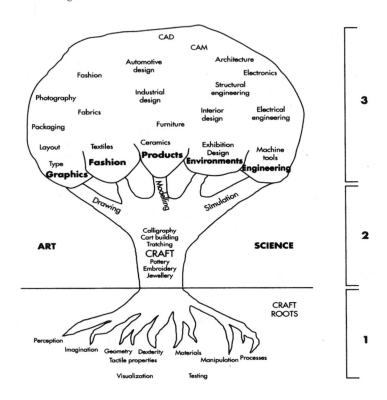

Design schools can be found on either engineering campuses, such as ELISAVA in Barcelona, or in a more cultural background, such as Art Center in Pasadena, California. There are three degrees available in design education:

- ❧ Bachelor of Arts (B.A., three years)
- ❧ Master of Arts (M.A., five years)
- ❧ Doctor of Arts (D.A., a postgraduate degree, eight years)

The courses offered by design schools cover design disciplines as well as other fields, such as art, photography, and film. Some schools specialize in engineering and industrial design, fashion design, or communications design. Other schools, like the University of Art and Design (UIAH) in Finland, offer fashion design and textile design as well as product design and film. In U.S. schools, designers tend to specialize in a field of design at the undergraduate level, whereas in most European schools, they specialize in their third year.

Designers are educated in four-year university programs in which they study sculpture and form, develop drawing, modeling, and presentation skills, and gain a basic understanding of materials, manufacturing techniques, and finishes. Industrial designers receive additional exposure to engineering, advanced manufacturing, and fabrication processes, as well as common marketing practices.

Applied Skills	Knowledge	Processing Skills	Values/Perspective
Practical design skills	Process	Visualizing	Risk taking
Creativity techniques	Material	Researching	Originality
Commercial skills	Market	Analyzing and prioritizing	Anticipating future trends
Presenting and report writing	Technical	Scenario building	Proactive in developing relationships
	Commercial	Adapting and inventing	Managing uncertainty
		Presenting and persuading	
		Synthesizing	
		Understanding and balancing stakeholders' requirements	
		Intuitive thinking and action	

Table 1.3. Types of Design Skills

A degree in design is generally organized in two cycles. The first cycle is similar for all students.

1. In the first year, students acquire key scientific, technical, and expression tools in drawing and illustration—such as volume, perspective, and color—which are required for designers. Students also gain an introduction to design projects, social sciences, art, humanities, and culture.
2. In the second year, students study drawing and creativity tools more deeply in various workshops, while working on basic project work and the mastering of particular key tools, such as technology, information graphics, and oral and written expression, and new elements in social sciences, the artistic culture of the object, and observation skills.

   Second-cycle students specialize in specific subjects: graphic, packaging, communications, product, interior and retail, or Web design. They develop knowledge of computer-assisted design.
3. In the third year, students are assigned applied design projects. They are introduced to wider and more complex concepts related to technology, social science, and professional areas.
4. In the fourth year, studies are more professionally oriented. Students work on quality, value analysis, industrial culture, corporate strategy, organizational

behavior, fundamentals in management and accounting, professional ethics, marketing, and branding.

5. In the fifth year, students usually work on a final project that requires a command of all the stages of a design project, taking into account all areas of creative, strategic, and technical innovation.

When asked about design skills, managers ranked them in order of importance: (1) imagination and sense of detail; (2) quality of dialogue; (3) sense of materials; (4) quality of perception; (5) the capacity to manage a project; and (6) the ability to synthesize. A designer's personal communication skills, coupled with his or her craftsmanship and holistic mind-set, constitute the tacit value of design (Borja de Mozota, 2000).

The Matrix of Design Integration in a Company

All organizations are systems of forms. These forms can be classified according to each design discipline.

- Environmental design: work spaces, welcome areas, factories, stores, exhibition spaces
- Product design: machines, commercial products
- Package design: commercial products, promotional material
- Graphic design: stationery, notices, invoices, files, reports, computer screens, publicity, signage, trade names, and technical documentation

The management of a design project differs according to the typology of the shape to be created (see Table 1.4).

The doors of entry into design are:

FUNCTION/ DESIGN	GRAPHIC DESIGN	PACKAGE DESIGN	PRODUCT DESIGN	ENVIRONMENTAL DESIGN
CEO	Corporate identity		Innovation	Work spaces/ Factory
CORPORATE COMMUNICATIONS	Corporate identity			Event/Trade show/ Welcome area
R&D PRODUCTION	Technical documentation	Logistics packaging	Innovation	Factory
MARKETING	Brand graphics Web site	Packaging product/ Promotion	Product range	Trade show/Store

Table 1.4. The Matrix of Design Integration in a Company

- CEO: When the project is getting settled on a new site or launching an innovation project, or when the strategy of the firm entails a modification of its identity, as in a company merger.
- Corporate communications: For everything that concerns the visual identity of the organization, on- or offline, creating events, or participating in professional trade shows.
- Marketing: When the design is charged with creating new packaging to improve a product, creating or valorizing a brand, or organizing the promotion on a point of sale.
- Production research and development: For an innovation project.

Design adopts different courses of entry in order to be integrated into an organization. The variety of design applications, however, must not hide the fact that there are some common structures among these different management perspectives. The three most common structures for design entry are:

1. Corporate communications and branding policy
2. Product and innovation policy
3. Retail space and retail brand positioning

Design as Process

DESIGN IS A PROCESS THAT HAS FOUR ESSENTIAL CHARACTERISTICS—the 4 Cs (like the 4 Ps of marketing) (Walsh et al., 1992):

1. Creativity. Design requires the creation of something that has not existed before.
2. Complexity. Design involves decisions on large numbers of parameters and variables.
3. Compromise. Design requires balancing multiple and sometimes conflicting requirements (such as cost and performance, aesthetics and ease of use, materials and durability).
4. Choice. Design requires making choices between many possible solutions to a problem at all levels, from the basic concept to the smallest detail of color or form.

Designers have a prescriptive job. They suggest how the world *might* be; they are all futurists to some extent. The design process is essentially experimental; yet, it is not purely ideational: it produces sketches, drawings, specifications, and models.

Holt (1990) identifies three types of design processes:

1. The analytical design process, used when there is little uncertainty about the alternatives, and the outcome is only a modification of something already existing.
2. The iterative design process, which is best suited to medium-risk projects such as radical improvements and adopted innovations.

3. The visionary design process, in which the problem cannot be defined precisely and is, perhaps, vague at best.

These three types of design process differ depending on the degree of freedom given to the designer in the design brief, often associated with the degree of risk taken by the organization.

Design as a Creative Process

Whether analytical, iterative, or visionary, the design process follows different phases (which can be reduced in number if the design brief is only a modification of existing products). These creative phases are identical no matter what the design discipline or design project is. These phases are also similar to the creative process existing in other cultural fields. But the design process has a unique character, because the final goal of every phase is to create a visual output.

For design professionals, creating means there is a problem which first has to be identified to solve. Once the problem is identified, the designer follows a logical process that he applies to every phase of the project. This process is a learned skill that corresponds to techniques, not a creative talent mysteriously inherent in someone. The process is the same whether the firm chooses to work with an external agency or develop a built-in design service.

There are three main phases: an analytic stage of widening the observation field, a synthetic stage of idea and concept generation, and a final stage of selecting the optimal solution. The creative process corresponds to five phases, each of which has a different objective and corresponds to the production of more and more elaborate visual outputs (see Table 1.5).

Preliminary Phase 0: Investigation

Phase 0 is a prospective phase in which an opportunity or potential need is identified and ideas are generated to see if that need can be turned into a design concept. This phase aims to widen the field of investigation in order to identify a problem that can be solved by design. This phase exists in a more- or less-developed manner depending on whether the brief is fixed or not, and the degree of freedom offered for creation.

Phase 1: Research

The designer looks at a brief that identifies the problem and the objective of the design project. He then inquires about the opportunity and the importance of the project for the firm, and asks the different people responsible to better understand the data the firm used to make its decision to launch the project. He proceeds to analyze the positioning of the product or graphics in its competitive market and explore the technical and functional parameters of the project. This analysis often leads the designer to make complementary studies and to accumulate documentation on the "environment," or context, of the project. The

PHASES	OBJECTIVE	VISUAL OUTPUTS
0. INVESTIGATING	*IDEA*	*Brief*
1. RESEARCH	*CONCEPT*	*Visual concept*
2. EXPLORATION	*CHOICE OF STYLE*	*Roughs of ideas, sketches* *Roughs of presentation* *Reduced-scale model*
3. DEVELOPMENT	*PROTOTYPE* *DETAIL*	*Technical drawings* *Functional model* *3-D mock-up for visual correctness* *and working capabilities*
4. REALIZATION	*TEST*	*Documents of execution* *Prototype*
5. EVALUATION	*PRODUCTION*	*Illustration of the product*

Table 1.5. The Design Process

objective of this phase is twofold: to draw a diagnosis of the project and to define a visual concept (or to create a script or verbal and textual definition of the project).

Phase 2: Exploration

After understanding the problem in its totality, the designer employs all of his creative resources to concretize the concept by making presketch drawings of the different possible shapes the project can take. These drawings help to disclose the axes of creation and discover the different product architectures, graphic signs, and style choices that might be of help to the design.

Those creative directions that stand out will be presented to the client in "roughs," or drawings of different solutions and proposed perspectives. The exploration phase ends with the selection by a committee that includes the client of one or two creative directions. This selection is facilitated by a diagnosis of the various solutions in relation to the hierarchy of desired functions defined in the design brief.

The committee presentation allows the reactions of the different people responsible to be analyzed and a dialogue established about the concrete, visual elements of the project. This dialogue helps to improve chosen creative directions. Solutions are examined according to an analysis of the aesthetic, functional, and technical constraints. This phase ends with the selection of one or two solutions to be developed in phase 3.

Phase 3: Development

It is now time to formally represent the chosen solutions in three dimensions. This 3-D version is indispensable because it allows for judgment of the shape's quality in space. A life-size model is made, which can also be functional. The designer makes technical plans of the pretest prototype. These drawings allow him to verify the technical constraints in assembling the product. This model can also be used to perform marketing tests. After various tests, the final model is adopted and the creative phase of the process ends.

Phase 4: Realization

In phase 4, the designer works on the realization of a prototype for the project. He creates documents of execution and a plan that defines the materials used, surface treatment, and color for the different elements of the product or sign. This is a time-consuming phase because it requires the collaboration of different departments—the manufacturer and external suppliers.

Phase 5: Evaluation

Tests are launched in three different directions:

1. Technical control: tests of conformity to norms of use, security, and durability
2. Calculation test: preparation of production programs
3. Marketing evaluation: appropriateness of the design solution to brand values, target market, and market share objectives. (Although this market evaluation can be conducted earlier, consumer preferences and behavior can be assessed during prototype testing.)

Figure 1.2 The Design Mission at Renault

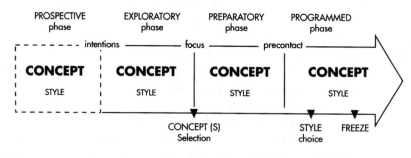

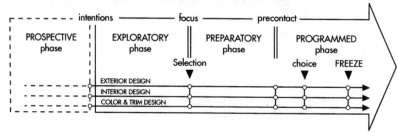

In this last phase, the designer is generally only responsible for follow-up. But he can also play the role of artistic director, in which case the client will ask him to realize illustrations, product views, and communications documents (such as press reports), and choose the photographers. (In the fashion industry, the creative process after the prototype phase divides in two: the realization of the technical documents for manufacture and the production of sales documents, such as catalogs, and the development of the advertising campaign with the marketing department.)

IDEO

Shopping-cart concept redesign. To demonstrate the process for innovation for an episode of ABC's late-night news show, *Nightline*, IDEO created a shopping-cart concept. The show concentrated on recording while a multidisciplinary team brainstormed, researched, prototyped, and gathered user feedback, turning the concept into a working model in four days.

The Web Design Process

The Internet transforms information into an interactive communication system. Today, our ideas are part of the Information Age, but the execution of them still takes place in the Industrial Age.

The architecture of a Web site is just like that of any design object. Like a product, a Web site has different functions. This has given rise to an increasingly non-linear knowledge base, creating new models of conduct and interaction. Designers are now confronted with a network of unprecedented stakeholders (shareholders, of course, but also suppliers, clients, etc.).

The complexity of reconfiguring users' experiences has transformed the design process. The "problem" that must be solved in designing a Web site is that the site must be viewed as an object that has many semantic levels and wide interactions to consider over time. Design has shifted its emphasis to graphic user interfaces (GUIs) that are supposed to generate user-friendly, interactive graphics, thus allowing for more user/Web site transactions. This is compelling designers and graphic designers to learn about transactional processes, technical infrastructures, and new ways to visualize information. By decentralizing access to information and promoting individual empowerment, digital technology is wreaking havoc on established business practices (Mok, 1996). Professional boundaries between design disciplines are falling as fast as the digital economy is growing.

Design as a Management Process

The design process is an identity process. It defines the company for itself, its customers, and its investors. It differentiates a firm from its competitors and is at the heart of the firm's success. Design provides a key identifier for the company to the public, hence the great necessity for design managers to take proactive positions in design process management (Anders, 2000).

The design process begins with a brief that defines the nature of the problem to solve. It ends with a result—a product, packaging, or service—in answer to the brief, which is distributed and evaluated by the firm. Therefore, the creative process is much like the processes used by management in new product development and the innovation process. Often, "design" and "innovation" are interchangeable words to describe two creative activities.

The creative design process, therefore, has a multidisciplinary and iterative character. The creative process goes further than the simple production of visual outputs because design is inserted into many areas of management decision making. Thus, design is an internal management process that integrates market research, marketing strategy, branding, engineering, new product development, production planning, distribution, and corporate communication policies.

KARL ULRICH AND STEVEN EPPINGER, 2000

"In 1996, the new Motorola StarTAC design emerged from a product vision to be 'more wearable' than previous cellular telephones. . . . StarTAC sales have reached into the millions. Success can be attributed to several factors: the small size and weight, performance features, superior ergonomics, durability, and ease in manufacturing the appearance.

"The StarTAC development team included different engineers. However, without the contribution of industrial designers who helped to define the size, shape, and human factors, the StarTAC would never have taken its innovative form. . . . In fact, the Motorola team could easily have developed just another phone. Instead, a revolutionary concept generated by the industrial designers turned the project into a dramatic success."

As an example, see how these processes are integrated into the definition of the automobile manufacturer Renault's design mission (Figure 1.2), where design is a management process rather than only a creative process. The creative design process fits into a "total design" process (Hollins & Hollins, 1991) so that design is:

- A creative internal process
- An external process of production
- A management process
- A planning process

Finally, the design process is a knowledge process, through which a design is acquired, combined, transformed, and embodied. Design knowledge has a tacit nature, and instead of presenting the design process as a vertical, sequential model, it might be wiser to represent it as a wheel, which illustrates the cyclical nature of any organization. The creative process must internally apply technologies, concepts, and production methods and externally satisfy the needs of a large environment of users and stakeholders.

Peter Gorb says design is not a creative process, although it entails some creative people. Design is a thermostat for innovation, a process that modulates, controls, and encourages creativity in the company. The designer's profession is similar to that of the entrepreneur.

BONNIE B. BRIGGS

Corporate identity & communications manager
Caterpillar Inc., USA

Briggs attended the University of Wisconsin and is a graduate of the prestigious Art Center College of Design in Pasadena, California. Prior to joining Caterpillar, Briggs held design director positions in California and Illinois.

Briggs's brand awareness initiatives at Caterpillar have changed the way employees perceive the role of corporate identity and helped employees to accept their own personal responsibility for building the brand. Briggs speaks extensively on voice and identity in Asia, Europe, Great Britain, and North and South America, and has published numerous case studies and business journal articles.

"Operating within a decentralized company, I see my role as one of integrator, influencer, teacher, and facilitator. I've worked for Caterpillar Inc. for thirty years in a variety of positions. All of the positions involved creativity of one kind or another. None of the positions existed before I had them. My title is Manager, Corporate Identity & Communications, and the position resides within the Global Brand Management Group, which reports to a Group President. The work (if I must call it that) involves brand strategy, communication strategies, and education.

"Brand management/strategy has at its foundation a fundamental grounding in design principals. Those principals come into play as we look at new ways to apply our brand or trade dress; influence the quality and visual effectiveness of our communications; and challenge our organization, suppliers, licensees, and distributors to continuously improve and innovate.

"My work involves extensive worldwide travel because Caterpillar's 680 manufacturing, marketing, and service support employees reside in every continent. And 210 Cat dealers, with a combined total of 900 employees, represent the brand, selling and supporting equipment, with a presence in every country around the world.

"My team functions as a critical resource to anyone who is driving new businesses, making choices that affect the Caterpillar brand, or communicating on behalf of the brand. The Global Brand Management Group has access to all operating units and is involved in every brand decision initiated worldwide.

"Developing a common language and understanding what our brand stands for was a five-year process—and continues today. The concept of communicating with one voice was the result of a grassroots initiative that began following the company's decentralization in 1992. I led a team effort that drove a comprehensive assessment of our values, competencies, attributes, and communications positioning.

"Through that information, we were able to create a more objective set of tools for evaluating all brand-related decisions. We then created an education program to show people how to use the tools. Over time, the concept of 'One Voice' spread throughout the organization. Now, it's very much a part of our corporate culture. Employees, dealers, and suppliers are familiar with the term and respect its meaning.

"I love what I do . . . and I've never had a dull day."

CONCLUSION

* Design is a process that creates a form, an artifact involving unity between structural, functional, and symbolic constraints.
* Design is a profession that can be practiced across different disciplines. The disciplines of design are: environmental design, product design, package design, graphic design, and Web design.
* Design enters an organization through different functions: CEO, corporate communications, research and development (R&D)/ production, and marketing.
* Design generates visual or formal outputs in every phase of the creative process.
* Design is a creative *and* management process.

CHAPTER 2

THE HISTORY OF DESIGN: PORTRAITS OF ENTREPRENEURS

DESIGN HISTORY REVEALS THE DIVERSITY in the forms created by designers as well as the variety of their opinions on the role of the artifact in our society. Exploring the different phases of design history helps us understand the basic values of this new discipline, values that a firm might want to integrate into its management system. This chapter describes the different periods of design history and discusses the ways in which history can be useful to the understanding of the links between design and society at large.

LANDMARKS IN DESIGN HISTORY

Precursors (1850–1907)

The "prehistory" of design begins in England with the emergence of the standardization of production, which dissociated the conception of an object from its manufacture. Until this time, these two operations were embodied in the skill of one person: the craftsman.

Examples: Wedgwood pottery in the mid-eighteenth century, the Crystal Palace in London in 1851, and the Thonet Bistrot chair of 1830 prefigure the new approach in the conception of an object.

ADRIAN FORTY

Objects of Desire, 1986

"Among the reasons for Wedgwood's exceptional success were the rationalization of production methods in his factory, his imaginative marketing techniques, and his attention to details. He attached great importance to the appearance of the pots . . . Much of Josiah Wedgwood's own interest in pottery lay in technical discoveries and innovation. Experiment and innovation were, therefore, as important to him as entrepreneurial activity and commerce; what made him so exceptional was that he was talented in all of them. . . .

"The development of forms that both suited the methods of manufacture and satisfied the tastes of the market was the work of design. The achievement of Wedgwood modelers was to arrive at forms which satisfactorily fused the requirements of both production and consumption. In this the modelers were occupied in exactly the same task as every subsequent designer."

The exhibition building "The Crystal Palace" was remarkable in its modernity. It was designed by Joseph Paxton, a horticulturist. His project was preferred to more classical architectural ideas because of the modernity of the architecture, which was the synthesis of the creator's knowledge of the techniques of horizontal roofing used for greenhouses, the expertise of a firm that manufactured beams for railroads, and the modernity of the modular construction and standardized production using interchangeable beams, nuts, and bolts manufactured by machine.

Thonet's work was another precursor of standardized production in furniture. For his Bistrot chair, he invented a new process of bending wood by wetting and heating it. It was developed from techniques used by shipbuilders. The shapes designed with bent wood in the Thonet café chair are the result of a technique borrowed from another field and adapted to a new need—a prime example of the transfer of knowledge and innovative techniques.

TERENCE CONRAN, 2001

What is your favorite chair?

"If I really had to choose one, then it would be the Thonet café chair, because it epitomizes all of the principles of design, manufacture, and distribution that I believe in. It was designed for an unfulfilled requirement, for a mass and growing market, and it was economical to manufacture using beechwood, a raw material in plentiful supply in eastern Europe.

"Innovative techniques were used in its manufacture (such as steam bending) and it was designed so that it could be shipped all over the world in a disassembled state and put together on arrival."

The Arts and Crafts movement in Britain was led by William Morris. Morris feared industry would abolish the object made by the artisan and its guarantee of beauty. Different "guilds" of craftsmen that were willing to fight against the moral decline of society formed, taking as their model Gothic art. The first guild was the Guild of Saint George, founded in 1872 by John Ruskin, an art critic, writer, and thinker. Ruskin believed an artifact is an abstract entity, the result of a complex process comprised of economic and social circumstances, relations with customers, and methods of execution that determine the final product.

William Morris put into practice the basic principles of the movement by opening a business in which production, though automated, reflected a willingness to produce artifacts that combined form, function, and decoration. The new element of decoration was the origin of the Arts and Crafts movement, for which ornament was necessary because it represented the free expression of the artist and of the craftsman in relation to the culture of his time.

This movement also had an influence on architecture. Morris's house, the "Red House," is the first example of "total design"—a set of forms conceived like a work of art in which each detail is carefully studied.

The Art Nouveau movement (1890–1905), developed in France, exemplifies similar characteristics:

- A willingness to create unity between the different handicrafts
- The use of ornamentation derived from natural shapes: Lalique, Guimard, Gallé (artist and manager) are the best-known representatives
- A structuring of space following the example of Japanese architecture, which inspired artist Charles Rennie Mackintosh, among others, in Glasgow

The Deutscher Werkbund was founded in Germany in 1906. This association organized industries, artists, and craftsmen. Its founder, Herman Multhesius, who was responsible for the founding of applied art schools, returned from studies in England, where he had encountered the Arts and Crafts movement. His objective was to ally art and industry in the creation of a school of artists and engineers. To this end, he petitioned architects who shared his ideas—in particular, those architects who were already using materials such as steel, glass, or concrete: Peter Behrens, Walter Gropius, Le Corbusier, and Mies Van der Rohe.

In 1907, Behrens became the first official designer of modern times for AEG, a German electricity firm. He was responsible for the construction of a factory, the conception of electric products, the creation of packaging, catalogs, prospectuses, stationery, and posters, the interior decoration of the stores and exhibits, and even the building of city lodgings for the workers. This innovative and highly unique experience is the first example of a global approach to visual consistency within a company.

The Functionalist Movement (1910–1930)

Modern design was born in Germany in 1919 with the apparition of the Bauhaus school and movement of ideas. The Bauhaus movement developed the idea that art could be functional, thanks to artists whose vocation was to create universal forms for the industry under "masters" like Walter Gropius and Johannes Itten (Droste, 1990; Whitford, 1984).

The Bauhaus designer aimed to aesthetic perfection, induced by a total confidence in functionalism and a distrust of distortions introduced by the human psyche in the conception of a design object. Objects created by Marcel Breuer or Mies Van der Rohe often took innovative shapes, though through a process of abstraction and an infusion of utopian ideals that made them difficult to understand

23

by anyone except a small group of avant-garde individuals. Only some of the objects passed the prototype stage and were manufactured in a series. Several of the objects became eternal, such as the tubular chair, which has been manufactured since 1922.

The Bauhaus School closed in 1933 after some difficult years, due to the political and economic context, but the Bauhaus had a considerable influence in the world through its diligent, pedagogic methods. Its approach was founded in practice through a variety of workshops: bookbinding, pottery, printing, wood, metal, and textile work, in which prototypes were developed. Training in craftsmanship was conducted through courses in "basic design" directed by "masters of form," painters like Johannes Itten, or sculptors. Important to Walter Gropius, the founder of the Bauhaus, this conception of art and handicraft was seen not as two different activities but as two branches of the same activity; hence, the emphasis placed in the Bauhaus on the study of form and color. This educational method assimilated fundamental theoretical courses with practical work in workshops, and became the model used by design schools throughout the world.

TERENCE CONRAN

Designer and entrepreneur, United Kingdom, 2001

"I went to Bryanston in Dorset, a school that had a rather unconventional system, where I was greatly influenced by masters like Handley-Read, who taught art, and Don Potter, who taught pottery, metalwork, and sculpture.

"I then studied textile design at the Central School of Arts in London. Central opened my eyes and introduced me to exciting new ideas about art and design.

"At Central, many of the teachers modeled their courses on Bauhaus methods of design instruction and some had even studied under former Bauhaus teachers and artists.

"Before I went to Central, I had been heavily influenced by the Arts and Crafts movement, which emphasizes the importance of craftwork and the role of design in improving life not merely for a few but for everyone. I call it my William Morris period. . . . At Central I realized that mass production could be used in the same way and that industry had the potential to bring intelligent design to a wider audience, not least because prices could be kept at an affordable level."

The impact of the Bauhaus is illustrated by the personalities and philosophies of its founding members. Centered around Walter Gropius, they developed a strong image and a true identity based in a philosophy of aesthetics and form: the notion that by finding a universal answer, one is able to solve complex problems within an ideal artifact. This philosophy was transplanted to the United States, where many Bauhaus founders, including Gropius, emigrated in 1933. Their influence extended beyond the Bauhaus through their teaching at Harvard University and at the New Bauhaus in Chicago, and culminated in the development of American vertical architecture.

Architects like Louis Sullivan and Frank Lloyd Wright designed buildings whose exterior appearances were dictated by their internal components: an architectural "machine aesthetic" that privileged scientific knowledge and fought against ornament. In this sense, the architecture dominates and the furniture becomes only the natural extension of the building, following the symbolism of the machine. This is similar to the architecture of Le Corbusier and his "Esprit Nouveau" in France.

At the same time as the industrial and scientific revolutions in Europe, a cultural revolution was taking place. Avant-garde painters were inventing a new language, an art independent from the representation of objects. Precursors of Italian Futurism—painters like Picasso, Braque, and Mondrian, the movements of Dadaism and Russian constructivism, the creations of Kandinsky, Klee, and Moholy-Nagy, and the preeminent educators at the Bauhaus—were the leading players in this new world of plastic arts. All of these artists had an influence on each other and met in major movements, such as the De Stijl, with Van Doesburg as founder. Works by the architect Gerrit T. Rietveld provide concrete examples of tenets of this movement.

The Emergence of the Design Profession (1930–1945)

Design became a profession in the United States in 1930 as an indirect consequence of the 1929 stock market crash. In the context of an economic crisis, manufacturers quickly became aware of the role product design played in commercial success (Woodham, 1997). This new consciousness encouraged the emergence of industrial designers. The first industrial designers, who were consultants to industrial organizations on the conception of products, worked freelance for large companies and came from various backgrounds: graphics for Walter Darwin Teague, decoration for Raymond Loewy, theater or publicity for others.

These men, accustomed to teamwork and conscious of the necessity of adapting their creativity to commercial constraints, realized the encounter between the industrial and art, and between functionalism and pragmatism. Design became an independent profession, and the first agencies and aesthetics consultants appeared. Because these agencies did not fundamentally question the structure of the artifact, but limited their work to making changes to fit the trends and style of the day, their work was referred to as "redesign" or "styling."

Differing from the Bauhaus, which created prototypes for industry without reference to the market, the American styling of 1930 considered design a team effort that aimed to relaunch a product by giving it a form better suited to consumer needs. The first businesses to feel the need to take aesthetics into consideration were those that produced in large quantities, such as the automobile industry. In fact, the opening of the first "styling department" happened at General Motors in 1928, where Harley T. Earl was named stylist.

These first designers developed a streamlined, aerodynamic style, and applied to other industrial sectors the symbols of the fledgling commercial aviation industry. This style was synonymous with dynamism and modernism, a synthesis of aesthetics and technology, and fascinated all types of creators, who applied it to railroads as well as cars. The public at large appreciated this trend toward aerodynamic shapes, and, eventually, the cult of speed was abused by a proliferation of rounded, friendly shapes (such as the Coldspot refrigerator of Raymond Loewy). The "streamliners" had a process of conception completely inverse to that of functionalism. They worked on the external surface without questioning the function of the product.

RAYMOND LOEWY

La laideur se vend mal (Ugliness doesn't sell), 1963

"There is much written on function and aesthetics. The common theory is the following: 'All things that function well are visually harmonious,' or 'If the function is respected, then the harmony of forms will materialize automatically.'

"In fact, it seems that there cannot be beauty without order. The threshing machine performs in a marvelous fashion, each of its parts designed perfectly, though the whole isn't much to look at. Why? Because a machine gives the impression of being complicated.

"That is, I believe, the true response to the theories of the 'industrial designer.' It seems that, more than the aesthetic Function itself, Simplicity is the deciding factor in the aesthetic equation. 'Beauty from Function *and* from Simplification.'

"Moreover, in its tribute to beauty, industrial design pays in another way as well. It constitutes a wise investment because it favors what will sell."

During this period, graphic design emerged with varied realizations. Graphic designers simultaneously developed typography and new alphabets. In this domain, the Bauhaus again played a precursor role with Moholy-Nagy at Dessau in 1925, although the leaders in typography were in the United States, mostly working for advertising agencies.

Around 1930, the first system of visual identification appeared: the graphics of the London underground, originally created in 1916, were revised under the direction of Frank Pick. Since 1933, a unified look of vehicles, buildings, and decorations (on the posters hung in the stations as well as on subway maps) has continued and is still in effect today.

Examples: The Shell logotype (1927), by Swiss designer Max Bill; the new Lucky Strike cigarettes packaging (1940), by Raymond Loewy.

Some firms encourage individual talents and develop long-term collaborations with one or several designers: in the U.S., Charles Eames with the Herman Miller Corporation; Marcello in Italy, Nizzoli with Olivetti. National promotion of design emerged in Britain with the creation of the Council of Industrial Design in 1944, which distributes design awards and organizes exhibitions.

The New Pluralism of Design (1950–1975)

During this period, the new design profession juxtaposed different styles in practice, and organized and internationalized itself. The cultural debate between partisans of rational design and functionalism and partisans of symbolism remained. Those who felt design is not an art, but functional, rational, and based upon eternal, practical principles came up against those who believed that design influences and is influenced by "transitory aesthetics," aesthetics that are based on the beliefs and artifacts of the particular era.

Examples of rational design include:

- The Modern Artist Union (UAM) in France, with Charlotte Perriand and Jean Prouvé, and the "formes utiles"
- The Ulm school (Hochschule fur Gestaltung) in Germany, defending functional design, whose classic example is Braun Design with Dieter Rams
- The engineering design movement in the United States, creating convenient, vital, and eternal products, particularly for the army, such as the Jeep in 1941 and the Ranger in 1942

Developments that upheld "free" design are:

- The development of American Pop Art, and a mass culture that linked music and the new "jean attitude" with hybrid design
- The realization of the Independent Group in London, which emphasized colors, decoration, surface, and pop fashion
- The revival of "crafts" in London with the Biba store and the rebirth of an Art Deco style
- In Italy, the Radical Design and Archizoom movements, inspired by Pop Art and Indian mystical culture

The American professional model was exported through the creation of design agencies and design departments in large corporations. The relationship between design and the corporation also developed out of famous pairings between star designers and the companies they worked for: for example, the pioneers Olivetti and Herman Miller with designers like Mario Bellini and George Nelson. New organizations took the same route: in Denmark, Jacob Jensen with Bang & Olufsen; in France, Roger Tallon and SNCF; in the U.S., Eliot Noyes and IBM. Noyes was hired by Thomas Watson, president of IBM, who appointed him chief of design in 1956; he stayed in this position for twenty years as corporate design director, working with Paul Rand in graphics and Marcel Breuer in architecture.

Graphic design also became internationalized, and designers structured themselves around large design agencies (as well as large projects, such as the Olympics logos):

- In the United States, Henry Dreyfuss, Paul Rand, Saul Bass, Ivan Chermayeff, Tom Geismar, Herb Lubalin, and Milton Glaser

* In France, illustrator André François, and in Italy, Bob Noorda
* In Germany, Anton Stankowski and Willy Fleckhaus
* In Switzerland, pioneers of Zurich Max Bill, Hans Neuburg, and Richard Lohse became the international representatives of the Swiss school of graphic design

The Return of Ornamentalism
(1975–1990)

Eventually, design invaded all domains of business activity. In 1977, the Studio Alchymia gathered around the personality of Alessandro Mendini, using furniture design for ideological ends. In the same way, the Pentagon Group in Köln created design symbols of an "aesthetic of dissuasion."

In furniture design, the Memphis (1981) group of Italian designers celebrated the decline of the functionalist dogma in their aesthetics, privileging the symbol over function. Totem in France and NATO in Britain took the same approach.

This period saw the revival of handicraft through, for example:

* Alessi, who, in 1980, asked famous contemporary architects (Michael Graves, Aldo Rossi, Richard Sapper) to design domestic products
* Issey Miyake, the Japanese fashion designer who sculpted fashion textile
* WMF (design by Matteo Thun), the design of the "lifestyle product," such as the Madonna table settings
* The trend "En Attendant les Barbares," by Elisabeth Garouste and Mattia Bonetti, which reinvented the baroque with Christian Lacroix haute couture in France

Product design continued to have its stars: Giorgetto Giugiaro in the automobile industry, Andrea Branzi and his collections of "neoprimitive" furniture, Philippe Starck in France, Luigi Colani and his bio-design with Canon in Japan.

Architecture developed a postmodern style around the slogan "Less is a bore." It signified the rebirth of ornamentation, with realizations of Michael Graves (in the U.S.), Ricardo Bofill (in France), and Norman Foster and Terry Farrell (in Britain).

The social vocation of design emerged with such creations as the kitchen utensils for disabled people by Ergonomi Design Gruppen in Sweden, and subway station signage, comprehensible even to the illiterate, by Dreistadter in Germany.

Graphic design was enlivened with the same debate between partisans of a functional Swiss ethic and partisans of a free style. The development of information design aimed to improve the quality of documents to make complexity accessible and permit better visualization of the problem (Tufte, 1983). Design agencies such as Pentagram and Wolff Olins developed complex visual identity programs and diversified environmental design departments to create greater consistency between the graphic signs and the architecture of commercial spaces.

Table 2.1. The Chronology of Design

	1850–1910	1910–1930	1930–1945	1950–1975	1975–1990	1990–

U.K.	· Arts & Crafts
	· John Ruskin
	· W. Morris
	· C. Rennie
	  MacKinstosh
	· Wedgwood
			· Council of
			  Industrial
			  Design
			· F. Pick
			· London
			  Underground
				· Design Center
				· L. Ashley
				· T. Conran
				· D. Mellor
				· M. Quant
				· Pentagram
					· R. Arad
					· Seymour /
					  Powell
					· NATO
					· N. Foster
					· R. Rodgers
					· K. Hammet
					· V. Westwood
						· Pentagram
						· W. Olins
						· Neville Brody

France	· Lalique · Art Noveau · Gallé · Guimard	· Art Deco · G. Chanel	· Le Corbusier · Esprit Nouveau · C. Dior · Grès	· CCI · Formes Utiles · C. Perriand · J. Prouvé · R. Tallon · Y. S. Laurent · P. Cardin · Courrèges · T. Mugler · Grapus	· J. P. Gaultier · C. Lacroix · Putman · R. Bofill · Les Ateliers · P. Starck · VIA	· Naço Studio

Germany	· Deutscher
	  Werkbund
	· AEG
	· P. Behrens
		· Bauhaus
		· W. Gropius
		· J. Itten
		· M. Breuer
		· Mies Van der
		  Rohe
		· Moholy-Nagy
				· ULM School
				· Braun
				· D. Rams
				· Rosenthal
				· O. Aicher
					· Pentagon	· Frog Design

U.S.A.	· Shakers
	· Ford T
	· Tiffany
		· School of
		  Architecture,
		  Chicago
		· F. L. Wright
		· C. Eames
		· Bel Geddes
			· Streamlining
			· R. Loewy
			· New Bauhaus
			· IBM
			· E. Noyes
			· Cranbrook
			· Knoll
				· Pop Art
				· H. Dreyfuss
				· Albers
				· S. Bass
				· M. Cooper
				· M. Glaser
				· V. Papanek
					· Branzi
					· Post-modern
					· M. Graves
					· R. Venturi
					· Apple
					· Greiman
					· Media lab
					· Mogggridge
					· I. M. Pei
					· P. Rand
						· Digital Design

Italy		· Domus
		· M. Nizzoli
		· Olivetti
				· Compass
				  d'Oro
				· Archizoom
				· Cassina
				· R. Sapper
				· E. Fiorucci
				· G. Giugiaro
					· Memphis
					· E. Sottsas
					· Alchymia
					· G. Pesce
					· Alessi
					· G. Armani
						· Domus
						  Academy

Netherlands		· De Stilj · G. Rietveld		· Jacob Jensen · B&O · Total Design	· G. Dumbar	· Total Design
Scandanavia	· Kosta	· Aalto · G. Jensen	· T. Wirkkala		· Ergonomi · Design Gruppen	
Others	· A. Gaudi	· Lissitsky		· Issey Miyake · Kenzo · A. Frutiger	· Sony · R. Kawakubo · S. Kuramata	· Swatch

Examples: Fitch Co, Michael Peters, and Minale Tattersfield in Britain; Landor Association in the U.S.; Total Design in Amsterdam.

PHILIP KOTLER
"Design: A Powerful but Neglected Tool," 1984

"One only has to look at current U.S. products to acknowledge the lack of good design. Yet its potential rewards are great. Consider the dramatic breakthroughs that some companies have achieved with outstanding design: in stereo equipment the Danish company Bang & Olufsen, in the sports car market Datsun designing the handsome 240Z, in the hosiery market Hanes by using packaging design, catapulting the L'eggs division to the position of market leader, in the kitchen furnishings market Crate & Barrel designing environments.

"Each company has to decide on how to incorporate design into the marketing planning process. There are three alternative philosophies. At one extreme are the design dominated companies which allow their designers to design out of their heads without any marketing data. At the other extreme are marketer dominated companies which require their designers to adhere closely to market research. An intermediate philosophy holds that designs need not be market sourced but at least should be market tested."

Freestyle graphic design introduced humor or a "smile" factor: Studio Dumbar in the Netherlands; Neville Brody in *The Face* in London; and the collages of Cranbrook Academy in Michigan. These designers often recommended a design with a mission and social responsibility. In France, the group Grapus worked as a cooperative. The American designer April Greiman allied herself with Swiss rigor, invention, flexibility, and software possibilities.

Design Since 1990

The most important evolution since 1990 has been the relationship between design and technology (Dormer, 1990). The designer can now play with the outside appearance of an object without being subjected to its internal structure. Constraints have been softened by new material and progress in electronics. As electronics has replaced mechanics, design has gone from "hard" to "soft," with form liberated from function. The dogma of functionalism has been questioned, and one now speaks of product *semantics*: "Form follows fashion" (the British agency Seymour Powell), or "Form follows fun" (the German Frog Design), or "Form is 90 percent emotion and 10 percent technology" (Naço Studio in France).

New technology has allowed artificial objects to possess organic aspects. New materials can manage complexity, and the artifact is the product of its material qualities. Innovative fashion design has created laser impressions in cloth and on surfaces that vary according to light or temperature. Auto-repair services are now able to increase the longevity of a product by controlling its deterioration.

The product designer must adapt her creative process to a general tendency toward abstraction, immateriality, and complexity. Technical knowledge has become transversal. In order to know "what the consumer needs," the designer must be able to guess "with whom to make contact and communicate." To paraphrase Edgar Morin, the designer must have "a knowledge of the knowledge." The physical shape of these new, intelligent objects is not the issue. The issue is the design of our relationship with the shape and how this relationship makes an impression on our brains. This is called Interface Design or Experience Design.

Mass production has shifted toward one-to-one customization. The automobile industry, for instance, has greatly increased its options for market niches. The computerization of the creative process with CAD (Computer-Aided Design) software and computer assisted manufacturing has facilitated the integration of design into a company's innovation process.

Design now faces the cultural challenge of interactive hypermedia. Interaction and information design treat, first and foremost, functional design problems. Graphic design has helped to transform the Internet from an academic data pipeline to an "information highway." Interface design functions as a door giving access to information. Since new media is not a physical presence, it is necessary for design to be invisible: it creates the service, the experience. In this way, multimedia design has become a new branch of product design that aims to create the "architecture" of virtual information environments.

Designing for Sustainability

Designers now participate in the challenge of the new millennium—how to be sustainable both environmentally and economically. Most who strive to reduce environmental impact are induced by government legislation and public relations. Designing for sustainability is not about cleaning up after you have made a mess but, rather, about designing waste and mess out of the system in the first place.

Often called "green design," sustainable design takes a holistic approach. The issues are:

- Making a complete assessment of site conditions (site design)
- Applying energy efficiency and conservation strategies
- Using materials wisely
- Reducing, refusing, and recycling at all levels (the three Rs)
- Linking the project with the larger community while creating a greater sense of community

Example: An advanced design and development group at GE Plastics developed strategies and tools for sustainable design as early as 1991.

Design Rules

1. Use recyclable and compatible materials only; avoid toxic materials; maximize use of all materials through recycling and reuse.

2. Minimize the number of parts; minimize the disassembly surface; design for z-axis assembly and disassembly; improve disassembly access; maximize part symmetry; avoid separate fasteners whenever possible; drive toward modular design; provide standardized, easy identification of all materials; simplify, integrate, and standardize the fit and interface of reusable components; reduce part size, product size, and material count; minimize waste in production; use clean fastening and bonding techniques; use clean packaging.

Life Cycle Analysis

1. At each step of the "life cycle": raw material; material conversion into parts; product assembly and finishing; product used by final consumer; recycling and reconstitution; final disposal.
2. Consider the environmental impact: air emission, heat, water emission, solid waste.

Examples of sustainable design: GE Generation 2 Battery Charger; The Body Shop refill policy; NMB Bank in the Netherlands; Novopen 11 insulin injection system by Danish manufacturer Novo.

STEPHANSO MARZANO

Director, Philips Design, 2000

"Because of their privileged role as interpreters and communicators between people and technology, designers are able to develop ideas for the new consumption patterns such as accessibility versus ownership, reparability versus substitution, sharing versus individual use."

Universal Design

Another direction for sustainable design is the designer's ability to design for all. Universal design is not about producing specialized "elderly" or adaptive products. It is about designing all products to accommodate the widest possible spectrum of users regardless of age. For example, transforming the myths of aging—senility, disability, homogeneity, poverty, lonely isolation, dependency—into a new dignified "silver market."

Examples of universal design: OXO international "Good Grips" by Smart Design offer special handles designed to be comfortable and easy to hold; Fiskars soft touch scissors that assist individuals who have low hand strength; Nike women's walking shoe and men's outdoor training shoe; Herman Miller Sarah reclining chair and accessory furniture; Metaform personal hygiene system by Design Continuum (Pirkl, 1994).

LESSON FROM THE PAST:
THE DESIGN MARKET AND ITS ACTORS

DESIGN HISTORY DEMONSTRATES THE COMPLEXITY AND VARIETY OF FIELDS that constitute the design market. It explains how each of these fields came to be and how they came to a consensus about what "good design" is. History is what designers all over the world share as a common culture. Myths, schools of thought, design gurus, and products that are examples of design excellence all help us to understand how good design has developed up to the present.

The four fundamental characteristics of the design market are:

1. It is international: Creativity does not follow countries' boundaries.

   The Bauhaus School and the international impact of the Italian Memphis group demonstrate that designers are well aware of trends and ideas outside their own country, while they still thrive on their own cultural and national heritages. This is still true today, and it is a part of the intangible value of design for companies that want to internationalize their trade.

2. It can be divided into two spheres: internal and external.

   The internal sphere concerns the projects and the agents active in the process: the designers, their clients, and the intermediaries that help maintain the success of the relationship (agents, design promotion centers, etc.). The external sphere is where good design is valued and recognized. This sphere has many different guardians: design schools, design awards, competitions, movements of thought, museums, design collections, design journals, and design professionals.

3. The "design contagion process."

   The following is fundamental advice for a company aiming at design leadership in its market:

   ※ Design plays a unique role in our society. Designers teach consumers taste through various complex channels. The good design infusion process explains why design is an actor in the broader economy and the world of consumer trends, not simply in the designer-client project relationship.

   In a design management context, one tends to think only of the relationship between the design consultant and the client. But design is a big part of our society, and even CEOs are consumers outside of their working hours. They shop at IKEA for their country place, dress themselves in Armani suits, and drive designer BMW cars.

   ※ The design profession is made up of entrepreneurs. Designers run or create a variety of entrepreneurial organizations and institutions: design consultancies, retail chain stores, and manufacturers.

4. A "bundle of entrepreneurs."

Designers are also entrepreneurs in an economic sense. They are much like economic thinkers (such as Schumpeter or Hayek). When a designer creates a new form, he or she aims to transform its environment, to create new productive combinations and new markets.

The designer also makes decisions in a context of uncertainty, in which routine methods and known processes are useless. Design, therefore, assumes a function of organization and coordination by bringing new factors and past factors closer together. Design becomes a function transforming information in society.

The designer challenges the static models and fits into an evolutionist vision of society and business. Design history teaches us the unavoidable evolution of form and the existence of masters who have inspired the designers of their generation and future generations. Every period in history generates its own style.

THE SUPPLY FOR DESIGN

IN SCHOOL, DESIGNERS CHOOSE A DISCIPLINE while working on real projects, from traditional disciplines to new ones, such as "sound design." They also choose the way they want to work as designers: on a freelance basis, in a design consultancy they create, in design agencies as junior employees or executive and senior staff, or as staff in the design department of a company.

THE "GO-BETWEEN" ORGANIZATIONS

WHEN A DESIGNER IS PARTICULARLY ILL AT EASE with marketing himself, he can choose to sign a contract with an agent, a situation much like that of a competitive

DESIGN "PRODUCERS"	*Design schools* *Designers (freelance, design consultancies, in-house designers)* *Trend styling agencies*
DESIGN "MANUFACTURERS"	*Segmented according to design input in product/service strategy*
DESIGN INTERMEDIARIES	*Designers' agents. Recruiting consultants* *Advertising and corporate communication agencies* *R&D consultancies*
DESIGN PRESCRIPTORS "DESIGN CONTAGION SYSTEM"	*Press media* *Architects* *Design museums* *Design awards*
DESIGN DISTRIBUTORS	*Design galleries and showrooms* *Retail stores created by designers or segmented according to their specialization in design*
CONSUMERS	*Segmented by attitudes toward design*

Table 2.2. The Different Actors of the Design Market

athlete. (In France, for example, the agent bureau Kreo has an exclusive agreement with some of the rising stars of the profession, such as the brothers Ronan & Erwan Bouroullec and Martin Szekely.)

Consultancies specialize in selecting the right designer, whether it is for a design center in a national organization, or for a private firm recruiting or auditing the project. They help organizations find the design competency the project requires.

THE DEMAND FOR DESIGN

THE DEMAND FOR DIVERSITY IN DESIGN is not the result of the latest trend in marketing research. Manufacturers have always made distinctions between designs on the basis of different markets. In the past, for example, different textile designs were printed for different social classes. In this way, a nineteenth-century clothing catalogue can represent a particular time in society. The same is true today, when the abundance of designed products and services gives us an image of our society, as well as a sense of the power of branding and differentiation by design.

ADRIAN FORTY

"The history of soap shows design being used commercially to create demand in a particular class market. In 1884 W. H. Lever realized that to increase his sales to working-class customers he had to advertise. For this he needed a distinctive product with a distinctive name.

"He introduced the name 'Sunlight' for all of the bar soaps he sold. To distinguish it from existing types of bar soaps and to draw attention to the brand, he sold it in one-pound tablets, ready-wrapped in imitation parchment with his name and 'Sunlight' printed on it.

"The role design played here was merely to create a commodity which was sufficiently distinctive to be advertised effectively."

The high demand for design is the result of three forces: the manufacturer's quest for diversification, the generation of new needs through innovation, and the desire of designers to express their creativity and artistic talent. Designers' clients tend to be manufacturers and distributors.

Manufacturers

There are different categories of manufacturers in relationship to design:

1. Companies that could not exist without design, whether they are editing designers' concepts, or manufacturing designers' creations under their name
2. Companies that have integrated design at various levels of their strategy and employ in-house or outsource design services

Distributors

Distributors can be divided into similar categories, in terms of their involvement with design: 1) organizations created for distributing designers' lines; 2) chains of distribution created by a designer; 3) distributors that encourage a total-design concept strategy; and 4) distributors or service industries with designed corporate identities.

TERENCE CONRAN, 2001

"What do you consider to be your greatest achievement?"

"Habitat. The first Habitat opened on Fulham Road on May 11, 1964. It was far from an impulsive venture. I'd spent the previous decade trying to get my work in front of the public and had come to the conclusion that the direct approach was the only way. In those days Fulham Road was off the beaten track, which made the rent rather attractive. We put in a huge shop window and converted it simply with white walls and a quarry-tiled floor. The shop was stocked with our own furniture and fabric designs and with dozens of household products.

"I remember some of our staff being quite mystified by my insistence that the crockery, cookware, and other items be displayed stacked high as if they were in a warehouse. I was trying to create that irresistible feeling of plenty you find on market stalls. I think that what made Habitat one of the first 'lifestyle shops' was the look, the fact that all the products appeared to have been selected by one pair of eyes. . . . I gained huge satisfaction from seeing my ideas win public acceptance. But my finest moments are really seeing something that I have designed—whether it be a piece of furniture, a shop, hotel, or restaurant interior—in its final form.

"I have always thought that design was 90 percent common sense and 2 percent aesthetics. It's the same for business except that the magic ingredient is vision. Design and business are totally interlinked and one cannot succeed without the other. While we would all wish to run our own creative business as democratically as possible, I'm absolutely sure that a certain amount of autocracy is necessary. After all, a creative business needs to have a house style and somebody has to be the keeper of that style and philosophy.

"Every entrepreneur likes to believe that their business will collapse without their hand on the tiller. However, having come to the sad conclusion that I am not immortal, I have begun the process of encouraging other hands to steer the boat while I keep a close watch on the compass. I believe that the Conran brand will survive as long as there are talented, entrepreneurial, and ambitious people in the business who see merit in the brand and the philosophy behind it."

THE FOUNDATION FOR "GOOD DESIGN"

DESIGN IS ABOUT QUALITY. The value of design is that it reconciles art with industry. "Good design" can be ornamental or functional, according to the times, since designers are both the heirs of craft and of the Bauhaus. Good design is shared and nurtured through the design press, exhibitions, museums, design competitions (such as the Braun Prize), and design awards.

Example: For the exhibition "Design, Miroir du Siècle," the public chose four eternal objects: the Vassily armchair of Marcel Breuer (1926); the refrigerator of Raymond Loewy (1950); the 2CV prototype by André Lefebvre (1936); and the Telephone PTT Universal (1943).

In its December 18, 2000 issue, *Time* magazine voted for the "best of" designs of the century. While insisting on *transparency* as the year's buzzword, with outstanding buildings like the Rose Center (the new planetarium addition to the Museum of Natural History in New York) and the Het Oosten Pavilion corporate building in Amsterdam, it also praised the Tate Modern in London, the Oklahoma City National Memorial, and the Design Culture exhibit at the Cooper-Hewitt Museum in New York, making clear Americans' rising interest in design. On the product side were the HeadBlade's power razor, lifestyle design guru Bruce Mau's book arguing that form is inextricable from message, the Ducatti sports bike MH900e, and the Nike for Web surfers, which lets shoppers customize the sneaker online by selecting the style, color, and lace types, and stamping an ID code.

Good design worldwide shares common criteria (based on a culling of criteria from design competitions around the world). The design excellence awards revealed four core criteria (Demiribilek & Park, 2001):

1. Functionality, efficiency
2. Aesthetics, attractiveness
3. Ease of use, user-friendliness
4. Setting new standards for the world to follow, i.e., "out-of-the-box" thinking

Two examples of design excellence are: the new plastic bottle designed by Ross Lovegrove for the Welsh company, Tynant, and the Apple computer logo, one of the world's best-known trademarks, which is an excellent illustration of the company's identity (the apple, the tree of knowledge, the rainbow with the dream just beyond the horizon, and the anarchy expressed in the missing bite).

Two international design awards of note are:

1. The iF Design Award in Hanover, Germany, which provides a broad range of design-related services, such as an annual list of recommended design firms. iF is one of the most important design competitions in the world, attracting 1,800 entries every year .
2. IDEA (Industrial Design Excellence Awards) in the United States. Industrial Designers Society of America (IDSA) executive director, Kristina Goodrich, and editorial page editor of *Business Week*, Bruce Nussbaum, have worked closely together for the past fifteen years to bring the story of industrial design to the world. Every year, the magazine writes a stirring review of IDEA and design trends. In 2002, 174 hot new designs took the top honors, ranging from new car designs to household and medical equipment.

This peer recognition system also happens in graphic, package, and product design.

For managers, the ability to cast myths into tangible, fashionable forms is critical for commercial success. But do you work with the design gurus or with anonymous partners?

PHILIPPE STARCK

"SubverChic" designer, France, 1996

"We have moved from traditional design—Bauhaus, Loewy, and people fascinated by the object—to the explosion in the last fifteen years of narcissistic design, made by designers for other designers, a masturbatory exhibition of their know-how, of their panache. Designers like me and everyone else! It is a type of design that cannot be innocent, that always ends up with excess. The product is created for the media. The most intuitive designers, who I would hope includes me, realize that it is time to destroy the machine, stop the facility, and talk of 'no design' or 'low design.'

"Hence the situation I find myself in today. I turned 47 last week and I know that my only task is to bring about happiness. Those who believe they are here to make things more beautiful in order to increase sales are either idiots or mercenaries.

"The urgent thing today is not to create a car or a chair that is more beautiful than another. The 'beautiful' is a concept that is obsolete for the time being and does not respond to the urgency facing society today, where barbarity has reared its head again. What we need to do today is to replace aesthetic objects with semantic objects, which results in replacing the beautiful with the good. We must start again from scratch so that these objects and machines serve us, so that the object is good for us, in order to live better."

Design has an avant-garde spirit. While not generating major innovations, the designer anticipates new needs and creates new answers to meet constraints, while integrating progressive technologies. Design is a partner and initiator of change in society. Therefore, it is a partner in the management of change in organizations.

The "trend agency" is a good example of this prospective input. Consultancies that once worked only for the fashion industry have extended their domain into other fields. Employing experts in sociology and philosophy and designers who travel all over the world, the agencies detect emerging trends. Their sociocultural analysis of new consumers' behaviors is a useful marketing tool for anticipating lifestyles. The agencies edit trend brochures and consult on branding in international marketing and market positioning.

Designers are willing to change their environment through their creations, even on a small scale. One can like or dislike the "missionary" or "visionary" aspect of the design profession. To think you can improve the world by simply designing an object can come across as naive. However, it is true that designers challenge us with their creations. Their ideas cross borders, traveling from the frame of reference of the elite to progressively become the property of all.

CONCLUSION

- Design originated in the Arts and Crafts movement in Great Britain and emerged in Germany around 1919, with the founding of the Bauhaus School.
- Design agencies structured themselves in the U.S., and spread around the world after 1950.
- Design has oscillated between functionalism and ornamentalism.
- The designer is an entrepreneur, an authority in aesthetics, and an initiator of change in the society.
- The design market is a complex set of relationships because of the "design contagion," through which different specialists, editors, and award-winning competitions have emerged.

CHAPTER 3

DESIGN AND
BUSINESS PERFORMANCE

THE GOVERNMENT CAN PLAY A PROACTIVE ROLE in setting up a system that sustains the development of design in the economy. In most countries, the government encourages design through financial aid and professional quality certification systems, education, and partnerships between design schools and industries.

THE GOVERNMENT'S ROLE IN PROMOTING DESIGN

THERE IS NATIONAL PROMOTION OF DESIGN STRUCTURES in countries all over the world. The international design center in Nagoya, Japan, established in 1992, is financed by the Japanese government and 103 Japanese corporations, and develops international competitions. Britain and Denmark have active design centers that organize exhibitions, edit publications, or finance research. Korea and Taiwan also have national design policies.

The British Design Council conducted a national survey in 2001 to find out how design, innovation, and creativity had contributed to various firms. Below are listed the percentage of companies that agreed that these attributes had impacted on various aspects of company culture:

Increased turnover	51%
Improved image of company	50%
Increased profits	48%
Increased employment	46%
Improved communications with customers	45%
Improved quality of services/products	44%
Increased market share	40%
Development of new products	40%
Improved internal communications	28%
Reduced costs	25%

The survey determined that in Britain, as of this writing, 76,000 designers are working in 4,000 design agencies.

Design is often supported through national programs. Countries develop policies to support and promote design. Financial subventions through grants are allocated to managers. Exhibitions and design research programs are organized, and support is given to design publications.

Design can be used as a political tool. For example, a recent program in Britain, "Design Against Crime," called for design research aimed at crime prevention and creating a reduction in crime in British companies.

Regional design promotion centers are highly active. They provide expert advice and audit in favor of SMEs. Firms that want to work with a designer can solicit advice from a design management consultant or from a technology transfer innovation consultant.

Many design competitions aim at developing creativity in a particular industry (such as optical instruments, clock and watchmaking, and automobiles). They are also launched by manufacturers who solicit designers to imagine new applications for their technologies, or by firms that are strategic design leaders in their industry (such as Braun).

DESIGN AS A PROFESSION

THE DESIGN PROFESSION ACTIVELY PARTICIPATES IN THE NATIONAL ECONOMY. In the late nineties, agencies recovered growing rates, took advantage of the reconfiguration of their clients, and benefited from their international strategies.

In France, the largest design agencies are Dragon Rouge, CB'a, Landor, D/g* (Desgrippes Gobé), Extreme Design, Architral, and Carré Noir. Most of their consultancies are part of communication groups that allow them to work on an international basis. Seven out of the eight largest design agencies in the world are British, and they gain a significant amount of their business in export markets.

The Design Management Institute in the United States conducted a survey of its professional members (based on questionnaires from 136 design agencies and 114 corporate companies, 195 of which were in the U.S. and Canada, and fifty-five were outside North America), which offers the following information about the design profession:

- Seventy-five percent of the designers were male.
- Forty-eight percent of the U.S. respondents had bachelor's degrees and an annual compensation of between $50,000 and $125,000; 17 percent earned more than $200,000.
- Non-U.S. respondents had the same proportion of bachelor's and master's degrees.
- No respondent under the age of thirty earned more than $100,000.
- Ninety percent of the companies outsourced design to a certain degree.
- Design ability, competency, and excellence of design work were the most important criteria for selecting a design agency. Other criteria were also essential: understanding the brand or the company, cost efficiency, portfolio and references, creativity, and human relations (i.e., partnerships).
- The responsibilities of the in-house design department included communication and marketing materials, new products and redesigns, brand management strategy and corporate identity, preparing all presentations, design management, and interface design.
- Primary expertise was in graphic design, brand identity, and design strategy in both design agencies and corporate companies.
- Sixty-one percent ran the design policy at the corporate division level.
- Design culture was rated as "good" in 34 percent and "excellent" in 15 percent of the companies.
- Design agencies obtained 39 percent of their clients from direct personal contact and 38 percent from referrals.

- Most design consultancies reported to the CEO, vice president, director of marketing, or senior management.
- Forty-four percent of the respondents managed between one and ten people.
- All respondents liked their jobs because they found them challenging and interesting and because they worked with a variety of people.
- Design agencies' expectations for the future were more optimistic than corporate companies', 62 percent to 33 percent.
- The biggest challenges for design were thought to be the downturn of the economy and the maintenance of business during crisis.

(See *www.dmi.org* for more information about this survey.)

Companies that share their design strategies are rare, and the same firms will be mentioned in the business press again and again. The way design is perceived by the press has changed over the years, from design as the "beauty" that helps to gain market shares to design as "the art of innovation" and "the art of waking up the consumer" to a new strategic dimension, or design as good business.

Development perspectives for the design profession are good, since consumers look for differences and for products that mirror the intimate expression of their relationships with others. In their buying behavior, consumers search for aesthetic satisfaction as well as performance satisfaction. Traditionally, functional design in such sectors as electrical or audiovisual products now incorporates semantics, emotion, and pleasure dimensions.

It is difficult to describe the impact of the design profession because a designer's edge is everywhere—in the packaging of our consumer goods, in our mobile phones, in our furniture and fashion, and in the stores we patronize. However, design has always been at the forefront of the avant-garde and its radical changes in forms will be imitated in other fields. "We have finished with industrial design. We want cars with emotions," said the design manager of Mazda. The credo of Hartmut Esslinger, founder of the FrogDesign agency in Germany, is, "Form follows emotion." Design is art as much as it is a marketing strategy. Design is about raising domestic objects to the rank of art objects.

The trend at the beginning of the twenty-first century is toward porosity and permeability between economic sectors. For example, in fashion, a sector in which design is traditionally associated with avant-garde and creativity, designers claim a rational approach to the production process. In furniture, design "stars" develop prototypes, as well as objects for mail-order catalogs. Design reserved for an elite group disappears. Society at large is asking for designers' input.

Companies turn to designers because they capture better than anyone the air of the time: the cosmetics for Nina Ricci by Garouste and Bonetti, for instance. Design is the cultural barometer of postmodern times. Products express the emerging values and aspirations of consumers.

THE IMPACT OF DESIGN ON NATIONAL COMPETITION

IF THE DESIGN PROFESSION IS BOUND TO PLAY a more and more important role, it is because it participates in the development of our economies and is linked to mutations in the international and digital environment. The development of design depends upon intra- and international economics; it is, therefore, dangerous for the profession to disregard macroeconomic issues.

Design has some indirect effects on indicators of international competition—such as technology, research and development (R&D), and the commercial balance of trade—but also on a country's social equilibrium, collective well-being, and consumption levels.

Design develops a demand for impulse and renewal products (such as automobiles and fashion) that stimulates national consumption. Demand in graphic and package design is sustained by the development of multilevel brand concepts: the internationalization of branding and its corollaries in a global marketing policy, as well as the multinational brand and its corollaries in local markets.

Design is a tool for globalization publicity: "Think globally, act locally." A larger European market, for example, multiplied alliances while it also created new strategic marketing programs that generated demand for European brand design.

Mutations in our economies generate a demand for design. Designers are not conscious enough of this macroeconomic determinism. Competition is now on a worldwide scale. Strategies become both national and global, and design agencies are obliged to think globally. They participate in world competition—the global village—which holds that a good concept is good everywhere.

DESIGN AND MACROECONOMIC ISSUES

DESIGN CONTRIBUTES TO THE SUCCESS OF AN ECONOMY on various levels:

- ✽ Design agencies generate profits and tax revenues.
- ✽ The improved performances of manufactured products in the world market sharpen the competitive edge of a country's output.
- ✽ Design agencies develop service industries abroad. (For example, the majority of British design agencies do between 10 and 30 percent of their business abroad).
- ✽ The development of the service sector—bank services and insurance; leisure, including tourism and hotels; transportation; and chain stores—drives the demand for environmental design, retail conception, graphics, and signage.

Every innovation, whether radical or incremental, requires the input of design. Just as any invention generates different formal configurations and successive modifications, the majority of product design is based on past inventions and incremental innovations: In fact, 90 percent of product design is incremental innovation (Rothwell & Gardiner, 1984). Research demonstrates that the evolutionary improvement of past innovations and existing design is a more reliable strategy for success than trying to introduce new innovative products (although as of now, there is a trend toward rediscovering "radical innovation").

Design plays an important role in the secondary phase of innovation, as well as in the concept phase of radical invention (Walsh, 1992) and in the qualitative policy to improve products (Riedel et al., 1996). The degree of innovation in an industry correlates to the degree of design input, just as the management of innovation in an industry correlates to the success of its design (Roy et al., 1986).

MARC SADLER, DESIGNER

"We are the guarantors of technicity and taste, we must master these fields as well as an orchestra conductor: without being an expert of every instrument, we must know them all to give with talent and precision the signal at the exact right instant."

The arrival of a new technology generates a multiplicity of design solutions that later tend toward a common and convergent dominant design. This convergence does not exclude the diverse aesthetic solutions that arise. The integration of a technology into an industry entails changes in forms (Walsh, 1992). When an industrial sector develops itself, the demand for secondary innovations and competitive designs increases.

Technology plays a major role in our societies. It affects production structures and employment, as well as social evolution. Design participates in the innovation and transfer of new technologies, as well as in the revitalization of a region (Lovering, 1995; Guimaraes et al., 1996). The creative process is a precious tool for technology's transfer from the economic sector to the consumer, and for structuring technological channels in the economy (Ayral, 1994).

If designers are not inventors, they diffuse new material and new technology throughout society and accelerate the sociological acceptance of technology. Their creativity stimulates innovation at the cultural level and on the corporate level by inspiring companies to push the limits in new product development.

ANDREW HARGADON, 2001

"Consider the strategic role of design, the emergent arrangement of concrete details that embodies an idea, in mediating between innovations and the established institutions they must confront.

"Taking as an example the prototypical innovation of Edison's system of electric lighting by looking carefully at the relationship between Edison's design decisions and the existing institutions he sought to change, historical analysis generates insights into how the grounded details of an innovation's design shapes both its initial acceptance and its ultimate impact.

"Robust design explains how Edison's design strategy successfully gained acceptance as an innovation that would ultimately displace the existing institutions of the gas industry.

"Edison's design strategy selectively chose which elements of his system of electric lighting to present as new, which to present as old and familiar, and which to hide from view altogether. By doing so Edison designed a technological innovation that was simultaneously revolutionary and familiar, allowing entrepreneurs to simultaneously exploit existing institutions while retaining the flexibility to ultimately displace them.

"The design of the new Volkswagen Beetle is not to replicate history but to allude to it. Design mediates between technologies in the abstract and social systems. When a technology emerges a social process follows. The role of design is then to arrange the concrete details that embody an innovation in ways that construct people's interpretations of novelty from pieces of what are old and familiar to them."

The economic competitiveness of a country is measured by its capacity to innovate as well as to undertake research. Industrial design is factored into R&D budgets. Patents or protected brand names fall under product and package design operations. Investment raised in R&D, for example—and particularly in applied research—explains Japan's economic success: this engagement helped design penetrate industry. The worldwide success of Scandinavian Designs is due to a political involvement in R&D investments to sustain industries in which they could develop a world competitive advantage through design (Walsh et. al, 1992).

Design is not neutral or apolitical: it is dictated by commercial and political interests. Design can be held responsible for products that don't satisfy basic human needs, therefore, contradicts its ideology. Designers are subjected to and influenced by the ideas of the society in which they live. The deviations are not their only responsibility (Forty, 1986).

Author Victor Papanek criticizes industrial design producing toys for adults that make them forget the problems of the real world. He believes it is the design profession's responsibility to put forth projects that are justified in terms of social utility and value. (See his book, *Design for the Real World* [1991], in which he talks about green design, or the spiritual dimension of design.)

The social value of design is part of professional ethics. It emerges concretely in macroeconomic issues in terms of a country's level of well-being. Designers invent solutions for collective lodgings, schools, hospitals, and urban facilities. Design plays a social and collective role by giving shape to human aspirations; it reflects and reinforces social values and can contribute to modifying prejudices in human relations. More and more women have become product designers, which should improve a good portion of the products conceived by men, who are often unaware of the real needs of the final consumer.

The postmodern individual's quest for identity expresses itself in the creation of social ties. Design services have to think of how to give form to social interfaces

(Cova, 1994). Léon Burckhardt speaks of "Design beyond the visible," or of conscious design that considers artifacts and human relations together.

Throughout its history, design has always taken into consideration the evolution of society. Stephano Marzano, design director at Philips, states: "Design is a political act. Every time we draw a product, we make a statement about the direction the world takes." Ezio Manzini of Domus Academy speaks of the autonomous culture of design, which is not the business culture, and must create the "aesthetics of the bearable."

Tables 3.2 and 3.3 (at the end of this chapter) sum up studies made on the macroeconomic impact of design. Table 3.2 analyzes the effect of design on the efficiency of an economic sector. Table 3.3 analyzes the effect of design on exports.

THE IMPACT OF DESIGN ON EXPORTS

DESIGN CAN BE AN OFFENSIVE WEAPON in the international market. Smoby, considered number one in the toy industry in France, has stated that "savoir-faire, savoir être, et faire savoir" ("know-how, identity, and making it known") are the imperatives of industry: design is the capacity to assert know-how and generate brand value with a global strategy of products, packaging, and brand communication.

In France, for example, the ministry of industry goes as far as advising French firms that wish to develop in the Japanese market, reputedly difficult to enter, to make their designs appealing because design speaks to the needs of the Japanese consumer. In Japan, the foreign firm must communicate its values, cultural heritage, and qualities. Design is an adequate tool to adapt to this market (Anselin, 1998).

Competition is high in the world economy. Several economic studies have shown that Europe has endured increased imported goods penetration. Some of the studies blame the poor sales of European-made objects on weakness of design (Corfield, 1979; Roy et al., 1990) or the negative perception of a country's product design in overseas markets (Cooper, 1993). Studying the export and import rate of a country measures the strength of its economy. The general deterioration of European commercial balance in favor of imports from Asia is well known. Sectors of activity where the market share is the most damaged are the automobile and electronics industries. This deterioration can be explained by the lower price of imported products. But it also shows that consumers choose some foreign products because they offer a level of quality and performance that consumers perceive as superior. Therefore, one can see a correlation between the positive commercial balance of trade of an industry and its high degree of design investment (Sentance et al., 1997) or between the export rate and the success of design (Potter et al., 1991; Roy et al., 1986).

The validity of the neoclassical model is contested by the importance in international competition of non-price factors like innovation and quality of service. Countries search for a competitive advantage that permits the production of good products—qualitatively different, more sophisticated technically, and of better design (Rothwell, 1983). Design creates this competitive advantage.

Design has a direct effect on competitiveness concerning price; margin; non-price factors such as performances, originality, appearance, finish, reliability, durability, and security; and service factors such as point-of-sale presentation, packaging, maintenance, and time of development and delivery (Rothwell & Gardiner, 1984; Roy, 1990; Walsh et al., 1992) or semantic product value (Paul, 1999). Competition valorizes creation (Hetzel & Wissmeier, 1991) and the improvement of the product's non-price factors.

A majority of managers consider efficient design management to be of increasing importance on a national level (Butcher, quoted by Gorb, 1988). Since 1996, the Design Council of Great Britain has launched a new strategy that insists on the development of research and education in order to transform design ideas into competitive realities (Dumas, 1996). In 1998, a new action called "Creative Britain" centered around the designer-entrepreneur James Dyson. The objective was to create a nation in which the creative talents of all are used to construct an economy for the twenty-first century in which "one competes on brains and not on muscles."

THE IMPACT OF DESIGN ON BUSINESS SUCCESS

THE SUBJECT OF THE POTENTIAL LINKS between company performance and design generated a varied body of research largely conducted by the Design Innovation Group in Britain following governmental programs on design promotion. This analysis of design and business success articulates four themes (Table 3.4):

1. The economic value of design
2. The integration process of design
3. The importance of top management attitudes toward design
4. The classification of design strategy

Design: A Profitable Investment

Research provides evidence of a correlation between company performance and design management (Walsh et al., 1988). The Design Innovation Group studies conducted in several sectors of the British economy in comparison to international sectors have shown that "design-conscious" firms have better results in terms of sales growth and profit rate (Roy, 1990; Walsh et al., 1992; Press, 1995; Hertenstein & Platt, 2002) and that they do a better job of managing design: for example, they have a formalized design brief and a person responsible for design at the top management level.

Design is a profitable investment because the return on investment is less than three years, with an average period of fifteen months (Potter et. al, 1991; Ministère de l'Industrie, 1995; Walsh, 1995). When a company works with a designer for the first time, it is most likely that the design projects will be launched with success. The impact of design on business performance is measured first by its impact on sales (Sentance & Clarke, 1997; Press, 1995), then on product price or perceived value. There is a correlation between receiving a design award and a potential margin increase and export rate.

48

Companies use design to position themselves in upscale markets (Riedel et al., 1996) or in markets with high added value (Walsh et al., 1992). The success of a design policy is measured by:

    ✳ The improvement of the perceived value of products (Walsh & Roy, 1983)
    ✳ The increase in sales and selling price (Arbonies, 1996)

Companies insist on the contribution of product design in their analyses of the link between design and business performance. Design allows for the penetration of a new market or the increase of a present market share (Walsh, 1995).

The Integration Process of Design

The integration process of design into the business setting can be disturbed by managers' behaviors and power struggles (Kotler & Rath, 1984). Business performance is correlated to the attitude of top management toward design and the decision to encourage simultaneously a design policy and a marketing policy (Hart and Service, 1988). Design is a process that never stops (Roy et al., 1990), and design management is essential to the success of a firm's innovation policy (Walsh et al., 1988; Roy et al., 1986).

Using design generates success, and this success sets up an integration process in three ways:

1. The functional integration of design in product development
2. The visual integration of design in the culture and creation of a company brand identity
3. The conceptual integration of design in business strategy and the company mission (Svengren, 1995)

CHRISTOPHER LORENZ

The Design Dimension, 1986

"Towards a new era: design, marketing, and technology as equal partners"

"In these circumstances where interdepartmental friction, time, cost, and risk must all be minimized, the synthesizing, integrating, and communicating skills of the industrial designer are becoming especially valuable. But the designer can also play a central part in helping the company take the sort of risks which are increasingly imperative in today's ultra-competitive environment. Here it is the industrial designer's imagination, as well as the skill to make connections, which is of paramount importance."

DESIGN MANAGEMENT ISSUES

The Differences in Design Management Styles

Firms differ in their design management policies according to their position on four key variables: identification of design responsibility, design experience, strategic positioning, and design integration:

1. Design responsibility: One key issue that affects the quality of a company's design management is whether or not that company has a person who is responsible for design, as well as responsible for implementing design training programs (Press, 1995).
2. Design experience: Depending upon the amount of experience it has with design, management sees design as a resource to develop in the future, or as a resource without engagement in the future, or is undecided (Price et al., 1995).
3. Strategic positioning: When the company's strategic positioning is reactive, the market determines the company design policy; when proactive, the firm is able to influence the market and views design as a tool to create new demand, which entails some organizational change in the management of innovation (Hart et al., 1989).
4. Design integration in the company's value chain: design as economic competence (its effect is on the firm's primary functions); design as managerial competence (its effect is on the support functions); design as strategic competence (its effect on the external value chain) (Borja de Mozota, 2002).

Measuring Design Management

Design management performance is measured by financial and nonfinancial measures (Hertenstein & Platt, 1997). The financial measures are the company turnover and the product and product development costs. The nonfinancial measures of design performance are customer satisfaction, creativity, and innovation.

Research establishes a relationship between design and strategy that goes beyond the link between design and product. This demonstrates the existence and importance of efficient design management in companies.

In conclusion, different companies have different opinions about design, whether they use them or not (Walsh & Roy, 1983). A gap exists between the meaning of design for those companies that use it and the way it is perceived by the nonuser companies.

The differences in perception above illustrate the fact that design has an identity problem. Successful implementation of design can only take place if certain core

What does design mean?	To companies *without* a design policy	To companies *with* a design policy
Shape or visual appearance	100%	63%
Ergonomics or adaptation of use	66%	75%
Increase in product value (rise in sales or profit)	22%	63%
Efficiency of production or materials used	24%	50%
Fashion and coordination of the product range	17%	25%
Durability	12%	25%
Security of use	7%	25%

Table 3.1. The Perception of Design Experience (Walsh & Roy, 1983)

objectives are pursued, such as quality of products or diversification of the product range. The integration of design in companies can be compared to the development of R&D as an integrated function.

VIVIEN WALSH, 1986

"The major period of takeoff of R&D [research and development] as a specialized, integrated function in the firm was complementary to the widespread adoption of the highly structured and functionally differentiated M-form. This made the organization of R&D more complicated. Some multidivisional firms have specialized R&D laboratories in each division, while some have a central corporate-wide R&D department for the whole enterprise, and others make some kind of hybrid arrangement with elements from both.

"This makes the institutionalization of R&D somewhat more complicated but still relatively clear-cut as a specific in-house function compared with design."

Designers are also responsible for some of the opposition design meets in companies. There are often conflicts between designers on how to design; some, for example, want to create products for an ideal world, where all objects are perfectly "designed" and market imperatives and "bad taste" do not exist, which comes across to many as too utopian (Gulmann, 1987).

Designers are sometimes tempted to confound the strategic character of certain design projects with the conviction that they can be the strategists of the firm. In order to make the strategy visible, which is the objective of their profession, they need to know the strategy in depth. This often results in the firm going back to a renewed consciousness of its fundamental values. Designers help the firm to conceptualize these values and, therefore, work in the company's ideation process. But that does not mean they are able to take a leadership role in the company.

It is obvious that industry executives will have difficulty choosing their design partners (Anselin, 1998). Though design education is changing to include marketing and strategy courses, most designers are not prepared to work with management. Creative individuals often cultivate an "ego" but, paradoxically, lack confidence and communicate badly. They create multiple barriers between themselves (for example, between graphic, product, and environmental designers who are not of the same professional organization)—barriers that are invisible but very real, so that one form of design rejects another.

The fact that there are few reliable professional statistics, as well as a lack of design management courses and research policies with long-term design missions, helps explain the difficulties design has in being implemented into a company.

The design profession is still young, with a small library of references, and designers often don't communicate their methodologies with specificity, thus making working with design somewhat fuzzy. Even though these characteristics have become less and less true, the mentalities remain. Managers need strong reference

Table 3.2. Design and Macroeconomic Performance

OBJECTIVE	METHOD	RESULTS

STUDY:
Ayral, S.; 1994 (France)
L'intégration du design dans les stratégies de développement des industries de matériaux polymères ("Design Integration in Plastic Industries")

OBJECTIVE	METHOD	RESULTS
Can design be managed by the plastics industry and integrated into polymer development strategies in the building sector?	Regional analysis: Oyonnax Plastic Valley Representative sample of sixteen plastics firms (out of 118) Analysis of the building sector	Analysis of the plastics industry—poor integration of the sector and dependence on both the large chemical groups—and of the demand in materials of different user industries. Design contribution: in a situation where there are multiple materials to choose from, creating value by differentiating the product to avoid market saturation, and the role of coordination between actors. Typology of practices of design management: · Firm with in-house design: design for economy of cost and improvement of product quality. · Firm managing design at top level: design communication power between functions, strategic design mission, creation of concepts. · Firm outsourcing design: design plays subsidiary role in improving profitability of production tool. Building sector: Introduction of polymers uncertain because of inertia between the two sectors of construction and manufacture. Strategies of the missing linkages or innovating structures of polymer industrials to create interfaces. Designer and architect well placed to fill this role of innovation and diffusion.

STUDY:
Lovering; 1995 (Great Britain)
Corporate design management as an aid for regional development

OBJECTIVE	METHOD	RESULTS
To prove the role of design in revitalizing a regional economy	SMEs South Yorkshire Art & Design Research Centre, Sheffield Hallam University case study	· Find new uses for recycled glass: glass prototype and ecological composite cement. · Development of an innovation program on gas energy in a mining region that suffers from unemployment. · Conception of a cultural bridge between the heating industry and the center of design research. · Center of research becomes coordinator of the project.

STUDY:
Press, M.; 1995 (Great Britain)
From mean design to lean design and a smarter future

OBJECTIVE	METHOD	RESULTS
Facing the competition from imports: Is design a weakness?	Ceramic industry. Arts of Table Survey: Eighty manufacturers, North Staffordshire, Thirty-six answers	The British ceramics industry has a weakness concerning design: limited investment and lower status are given to design management. However, for the firms: · Design judged pertinent. · Design, a process that helps maximize firm efficiency. · Design, a problem-resolution process.

(continues)

Table 3.2. Con't.

OBJECTIVE	METHOD	RESULTS
Do differences in design management entail differences in companies' performances?	Complementary interviews by certain firms that manage their design or give design a key role	• Design, a bridge between production and marketing functions. • Design, a key for success. Firms speak rightly of design but don't recognize the links between design and management. *Example: Firms judge that it is important to diffuse design throughout the organization but only six offer design training.* Typology of design management (number of firms in sample): • Design-led (three): employs a design manager, educates in design, foresees employing a designer. • Design-managed (six): Design manager, little training. • Unmanaged design (five): Unsure about the role of design, no design manager, no training. Relation between design management and firm performance. Firms that manage design have three times more sales increase than those that don't manage design, and forty times more export sales. Future: the "lean design model": • Reduction of design staff but better managed. Change from design induced by processes to a design induced by creativity. More coordination of design with functions. • Exploration of new market opportunities by research based on design. University as partner.

- -

STUDY:
Ministère de l'Industrie ; 1995 (France)
Les PMI françaises et le Design ("Small and Medium Industries and Design in France")

Research from experts and survey	Research from experts Survey of 672 Small and Medium Industrial firms (SMIs) 565 questionnaires sent to firms using design or not	About 1,000 design consultancies in France: 70 percent established 10 years or less. Design practice: • One small or medium-sized industrial firm out of 3 uses design, but only 16 percent use it regularly. Design penetrates more in the domain of consumer goods. Firms that regularly use design are those that create more new products. • The SMI's use of external design (75 percent), in-house design (35 percent), hybrid (10 percent). • CEO greatly implicated in the product-development process. • Firms using design regularly charge design costs to R&D or a special design account (1/3).

(continues)

Table 3.2. Con't.

OBJECTIVE	METHOD	RESULTS
		• The more you practice design, the more design is integrated early in the development process. • The average budget per year for design is about 70,000 euros for regular design users (16,000 euros for the others). Perception of design by management: • Design gives a competitive advantage. • Design participates actively in company culture: image improvement and an incentive for teams. • Design is a profitable investment: return on investment comes after less than three years for 65 percent and less than one year for 20 percent. Sales increased on French market and on export (60 percent). Profitability superior for companies regularly using design. Eighty-five percent of the SMIs think design will help them penetrate new markets. • Design, an investment for pleasure: design brings a part of vision and identification and reduces uncertainty. What companies want from the state for design: • Financial aid: (for 70 percent of companies using design) and aids for enrollment of designers (30 percent). • Labels for design schools and definition of the designers' rights in the design/company relationship.

STUDY:
Walsh, V.; 1995 (Great Britain)
The evaluation of design

OBJECTIVE	METHOD	RESULTS
The commercial impact of the design project	Sample of 221 firms among 5,000 having benefited from a government assistance program in the U.K. Government's support for design and funded consultancy designs Ninety-one interviews 130 questionnaires	Sample: Mostly small and medium enterprises (SMEs) since they were the target of a governmental support program. Types of design projects: product design, 49 percent, product repositioning, 27 percent, graphic or packaging design, 22 percent, feasibility study, 2 percent. • Average investment about $120,000. • Non-merchandise projects, $16,000. • Projects imply design engineering costs were most expensive. Results of projects: • Success in commercialization: 50 percent, partial success, 10 percent. • Generate losses: failure/success, 21 percent, failure, 19 percent. About 65 percent of these projects were launched on the market: • 82 percent graphic design, 57 percent product design, 43 percent design engineering projects. • On the 120 merchandised projects for which financial information exists, 89 percent were a success.

(continues)

Table 3.2. Con't.

OBJECTIVE	METHOD	RESULTS
		• On ninety-one projects, average return on investment period is fourteen and a half months (less for graphic design projects, at 11.5 months).
		• Increase in export sales: rate 19 percent (on forty-seven answers).
		• 28 percent entry on a new market.
		• 30 percent rise of market share.
		• 21 percent domestic sales on market with high import rates.

STUDY:
Price et al.; 1995 (Australia)
Design users' view of their design experiences: some Western Australian data

Industry attitudes toward design	Sample of manufacturers and services firms	Three variables pertinent for multivariate analysis:
		• Organizational satisfaction with design: positive appreciation of the experience in design.
	Questionnaire of eighty-one questions, Likert scale, 163 answers	• Design as a valued asset: designer plays an important role in the success of the project.
		• Design conviction: commitment toward design in the future but realization of this conviction unclear.
		Factorial analysis: typology of firms in four classes according to the variables studied (experience in design/attitudes facing design).
		• The engaged 26 percent: satisfied; design is a resource they are going to develop in the future.
		• The happy 23 percent: design is a valid resource, but won't commit in the future.
		• The neutral 36 percent: average answers on all factors and uncertain for the future.
		• The undecided 15 percent: improbable future commitment toward design

STUDY:
Riedel et al.; 1996 (Great Britain)
Investment in design: a market analysis using the MADRID map

First phase of a research project:	Analyses of the commercial data of 220 design projects between 1987 and 1990.	Mapping of projects according to two axes:
		• Vertical axis: degree of sensitivity of the market to price and quality.
Market Demands that Reward Investment In Design (MADRID)		• Horizontal axis: driven by market volume or niche, creating four quadrants.
		Results: The majority of projects are in the two quadrants corresponding to market quality and niche orientation.
		• Very few projects in the quadrant that is sensible to price/mass market.
		• Most projects are in the quadrant that is sensible to quality/volume: companies appeal to design to change their market and product range upwards or to increase their sales.
		• No firm appeals to design to change the product range downwards.
		Conclusion: Design project = change upwards and towards quality.

(continues)

Table 3.2. Con't.

OBJECTIVE	METHOD	RESULTS
STUDY: **Guimaraes et al.; 1996 (Brazil)** *Product design and social needs: The case of Northeast Brazil*		

Companies'
relationship
with government
innovation experts;
Integration of
Design in NPD
	Industry of metal
	Industrial sector
	State of Paraiba,
	  Northeast Brazil
	
	Questionnaire: thirty SMEs
	twenty-eight interviews
		SMEs rarely ask for governmental aid: six for
		innovation and twelve occasionally.
		
		• "Unconscious" design: made by designers trained in
		  an informal manner or by the entrepreneur himself.
		• Design seen like an outside aspect of product, useful
		  when technical problems are solved.
		• Integration of design in NPD: build on existing
		  practices such as the ability to visualize and the
		  capacity to make roughs and prototypes.

STUDY: **Paul J.; 1999 (USA)** *The search for performance metrics to measure the value of design*		

To identify variables
to measure the per-
formance of design
	In-house study
	Eastman Kodak,
	R&D
	
	Benchmarking on twelve
	American firms
		• Benchmarking consensus on perception of design
		  even though its place in company structure varies.
		• Implicit value of design.
		• 75 percent pretest of customer satisfaction/design
		• 80 percent design as a key for competitive advantage.
		• Two-thirds design reports to marketing.
		• Design value for the firm: performance of products.
		• Design value at product level: value for the end user,
		  according to semantic scale on emotional levels,
		  including cognitive, connotative, and associative
		  (measure of appearance and ease of use).

Table 3.3. Design and Macroeconomic Performance: Design's Impact on Exports

OBJECTIVE	METHOD	RESULTS
STUDY: **Corfield, K.G.; 1979 (Great Britain)** *Report on Product Design, National Economic Development Council*		
To analyze the British industry and its perform-ances in terms of product design	Five case studies that are successful in terms of design "perceived"	Better design would have a tendency to improve British economic performance, increase exports, reduce imports, and improve productivity.
STUDY: **Rothwell et. al; 1983 (Great Britain)** *Design and the economy*		
To show effects of design on economy	Macroeconomic approach; case studies	Price is not the only criterion for international competitiveness. To succeed, it is necessary to make good product; selection of critical points in order to integrate design.
STUDY: **Rothwell & Gardiner; 1984 (Great Britain)** *The role of design in competitiveness*		
Analysis of purchase factors for agricultural equip-ment and cars Comparison of performance between Great Britain and foreign attitudes	Survey on 150 British farmers: comparisons of opinions between English and foreign material Comparison of performances of two ranges of cars: British Leyland and Ford Cortina between 1960 and 1975	· Design plays a central role in determining competi-tiveness of exported manufactured products. · Factors such as durability, flexibility, performance, and reliability of use are more important than price. · Integrating design very upstream in NPD entails a high degree of feasibility. · Studies on industrial innovations that are centered on radical innovations are focused on technology and neglect design aspects. · Other omission: these major innovations will be followed by many incremental innovations that will have a more important economic impact than the radical innovation itself. Example: car industry.
STUDY: **Unghanwa & Baker; 1989 (Great Britain)** *The role of design in international competitiveness*		
Evidence of international com-petitiveness factors and the role of the design in industrial competitiveness Impact of design on the British market	Questionnaire sent to sample of 138 firms among a popu-lation of 2,092 firms having received Queen's Award between 1966 and 1985 Relationship between macro- and microeconomic dimensions	Authors distinguish three levels of analysis: · The "variables of design": finality, product resistance, technical sophistication, product performance for use. · The "variables related to design": quality of post-sale service, efficiency of delivery, advertising, and promotion. · The "variables influenced by design": innovation, value analysis, aesthetics, ergonomics, TQM (Total Quality Management) circles management style, TQM methods attention given to users' needs. Authors demonstrate how these variables correlate and influence industrial competitiveness and, therefore, success for exports of manufactured products.

(continues)

Table 3.3. Con't.

OBJECTIVE	METHOD	RESULTS

STUDY:
Roy; 1990 (Great Britain)
Product design and company performance (see also Winning by Design by *Walsh et al., Study B)*

OBJECTIVE	METHOD	RESULTS

Role of design in the competitive-ness of companies	Long-term study (seven years) comparing forty-two GB firms with nine foreign leaders of the same sector: electronic, office furniture, heating
	
	Comparison of the key factors of success
		Design has an influence on price and non-price factors in international competition.
		   Commercial success seems based on differences on the importance given to the following variables:
		· Value rather than price.
		· Technical performance and design quality.
		· Marketing: quality of service and brand loyalty.
		
		Design definition: for 53 percent, aesthetic and appearance; 52 percent quality and performance; 49 percent satisfaction of user needs; 42 percent creativity.
		   Design leaders have superior performances in profit and return on investment.
		   Firms that succeed employ designers and have efficient design management:
		· Multiple sources of ideas.
		· Innovation by collective decision.
		· More exhaustive brief in design leaders firms.
		
		Responsibility: design, 24 percent; direction, 18 percent; R&D, 8 percent; marketing, 26 percent; interdisciplinary group, 18 percent.
		Integrated design: 21% of the firms, 33 percent in leaders.
		Evolutionary approach of NPD: imitation and improvement of competitors' products of design, sources of ideas.

STUDY:
Potter et al.; 1991 (Great Britain)
The benefits and costs of investment in design

OBJECTIVE	METHOD	RESULTS
Commercial impact of design	Survey proposed by researchers of Open University and UMIST (Design Innovation Group) 221 products from firms having received subvention for design advice; 50% of the firms had never used design	Main results: · 90 percent of projects generate a profit. Return on investment in fifteen months. · 48 percent of projects repay the totality of costs in less than one year. · Average cost of projects that succeed: $120,000. · 40 percent of projects generated sales in exports. · 25 percent of projects allowed entry to new market. Future: 50 percent of the firms developed design function.

STUDY:
Hetzel & Wissmeier; 1991 (France)
L'artiste et l'artisan: une comparaison France /Allemagne des stratégies marketing des entreprises d'habillement ("'The Artist and the Craftsman: A Comparison between France/Germany in the Fashion Textile Industry")

OBJECTIVE	METHOD	RESULTS
Comparison of structures, strategic marketing, and operational marketing of firms	Synthesis of a comparative survey published in Germany (Heidenreich, 1990) and the researchers' work in their respective countries	· Number of firms similar in both countries, but size more important in Germany. · Germany: considerable development of exports. Firms prepared for international development, whereas in France, this was only the case in luxury firms.

(continues)

Table 3.3. Con't.

OBJECTIVE	METHOD	RESULTS
in France and Germany in the textile industry		• Strong rationalization of production in Germany. • Criteria of segmentation: socio-demographic in France, lifestyle in Germany. • Germany more attentive to consumer trends—French demand stimulated by creativity. • Creation of German identity by evolutionary continuity and better brand recognition. • Concentration on trends due to strong integration of the sector in Germany. • Creation conditions very similar but cultural contexts differ. German designers have a Bauhaus tradition: accent on continuity. 　French designers have a Beaux-Arts tradition: accent on radical change. As for the management vision: • Germany anticipates international market; it is the craftsman who sells very coherent product, long-term visibility, conquest myth, product in a lifestyle: clothing follows consumption. • France has international market: product style is strong and educates customer taste; clothing precedes consumption. • Product offer comes from *haute couture*, the artist comes before the market, consumer and manager dream of fashion; passion and seduction myth.

STUDY:
Cooper, R.; 1993 (Great Britain)
Perceptions of design: a study of the attitudes and perceptions among European buyers of the design of a range of products

---

OBJECTIVE	METHOD	RESULTS
Analysis of the perception of British design: ceramic, textile, and small domestic equipment Comparison of purchaser opinions in Greeat Britain and in Europe	300 questionnaires with presentation of product examples Questions on their attitudes in relation to British design compared to best-selling products in the same category	European buyers had some negative attitudes toward the design of British products and were very critical. For the textile and ceramic sectors, differences of perception concerned design variables like color, decoration, shape, and satisfaction of consumer needs. For the domestic equipment, differences existed on factors like brand and customer services.

STUDY:
Sentence & Clarke; 1997 (Great Britain)
The contribution of design to the British economy

OBJECTIVE	METHOD	RESULTS
Center for Economic Forecasting, London Business School Understand the impact of design on the economy	Questionnaire to 800 manufacturers Links between design activity and economic performance	• Design and its activities use 300,000 people: 1.2 percent of employment in Great Britain. • Designers' incomes: 25 percent on abroad advice activities. • Indirect contribution of design exports: sectors that invest in design that have a positive commercial balance, including aeronautics, mechanics, engineering, and chemical industry. • Design disciplines: product design, engineering, technology. • Regional effect: Eastern England, design impact on growth: 1 percent increase in investment in product development increases sales and profit by 3.4 percent. • Design's impact on growth.

Table 3.4. Design and Business Performance

OBJECTIVE	METHOD	RESULTS

SURVEY:
Walsh & Roy; 1983 (Great Britain)
Plastics products: good design, innovation, and business success

OBJECTIVE	METHOD	RESULTS
To compare performance of firms in the same sector in order to put in relation performance and design	In the plastic industry. Two groups: one with eight firms recognized for their effort in design, the other with forty-one companies with no design reputation	The attitude towards innovation of the firms recognized for their effort in design is different from what prevails in the sector. Success explains itself by the fact that design confers more perceived value to products.

SURVEY:
Kotler & Rath; 1984 (USA)
Design: a powerful but neglected strategic tool

OBJECTIVE	METHOD	RESULTS
To try to understand why design is difficult to use	Authors' opinion	Four motives are advanced that curtail design implementation: · Managers don't know what design is. · Budgetary constraints. · Power struggles. · Resistance to change behaviors.

SURVEY:
Borja de Mozota; 1985 (France)
Essai sur la fonction du design et son rôle dans la stratégie marketing de l'entreprise
("The Role of Design in the Firm Marketing Strategy")

OBJECTIVE	METHOD	RESULTS
Does design increase company's profit because of its impact on innovation management or innovation marketing?	Sample of eleven incremental innovation projects in all design disciplines	· Design increases companies' profits. In five out of eight projects, the return on investment came after less than eighteen months. Profit comes not only through sales increases or cost reduction but also through cutting back in communications costs. · Design promotes participative management of innovation. · Design does not improve the management control of innovation. · Design improves the management of ideas. · Design improves the company's image, its coherence, and its differentiation from competitors. · Design improves the innovation performance. · Design improves users' perception of innovation.

SURVEY:
Roy et al.; 1986 (Great Britain)
Design-based innovation in manufacturing industry
Principles and practices for successful design and production

OBJECTIVE	METHOD	RESULTS
To identify and compare practices and success models of product development and, consequently, to improve the educational material for engineers and managers	Surveys thirty-seven British firms and ten foreign sectors: office furniture, domestic heating, computer equipment	Measure of design success: · Firms having received a design award or having been recognized as strong in design by a design council or competitions and competitors. · Interrelationship between information on the market coming from several sources and product success.

(continues)

Table 3.4. Con't.

OBJECTIVE	METHOD	RESULTS
		• Design briefs exist in 84 percent of the firms, and exist in a formalized way in 64 percent of the firms.
		• Foreign firms had a more complete brief, established in a collective manner.
		• Link between brief inserting information on product positioning and success.
		• Design improvement of existing products rather than creation of new products.
		• Importance of the influence of competitors' products: profitable to improve their products, but radical innovation not always path to success.
		• Influence of suppliers on design: 70 percent.
		• Evaluation of prototypes and models by clients: 57 percent.
		• Production constraints considered in the design process.
		• Someone qualified in design to direction committee: 22 percent. Firms that had the best reputation had been created by designers or had some designer in top management position.
		• Firms with in-house designers have more design awards than others.
		• With reservations: interrelationship between the number of design awards a firm receives and the proportion of sales abroad (exports).
		• Firms that received design awards do better in terms of growth and capital.

SURVEY:
Walsh et al.; 1988 (Great Britain)
Competitive by design

OBJECTIVE	METHOD	RESULTS
To specify the role of design in industrial competitiveness. To explain design management put in place in firms that succeed	Questionnaire addressed to about 100 British firms	Many firms disregard design. The most effective companies are those that invest in design and manage their innovation, but that, at the same time, have the design know-how. Design is not an end in itself.

SURVEY:
Hart & Service ; 1988 (Great Britain)
The effects of managerial attitudes to design on company performance

OBJECTIVE	METHOD	RESULTS
To see if there is a link between the attitude and the implication of top management towards design and the commercial performance of the firm	Questionnaire addressed to 369 CEOs of British firms	Authors define seven attitudes toward design: • Table of interrelationship between attitudes towards design and indicative of performance. • Best performances are found when top management encourages design and marketing together, i.e., when design takes into account some market imperatives.

(continues)

Table 3.4. Con't.

OBJECTIVE	METHOD	RESULTS
SURVEY: **Hart et al.; 1989 (Great Britain)** *Design orientation and market success*		
How to develop well-designed products and construct a favorable climate for design integration	Twenty exploratory interviews with firms that employ more than 100 people	· Avoid overinvestment in design: sixteen firms out of twenty. · Contact with consumers is vital: thirteen out of twenty. · Good design is adaptation to use: sixteen out of twenty. · Good design is cost-conscious: fourteen out of twenty. · Importance of outside appearance (aesthetic): fourteen out of twenty. · Product development by team: sixteen out of twenty. Typology of firms in two groups: · Reactive firms (market determines policy): use design if necessary. · Proactive firms (think they can influence their market): design is used to create the demand and design diversity; unconventional ideas are encouraged. These two groups differ also in design management: · Reactive: lack of data on market, whereas the consumer's implication in the process is important for proactive firms. · Proactive: work in common with all functions on product development, team decision process by team. Continuous R&D program.
SURVEY: **Roy et al.; 1990 (Great Britain)** *Design and the economy (rewritten report by Rothwell et al., 1983)*		
To show the role of design in British economy To advise managers who want to utilize design	Case studies of British firms that succeeded or failed	It is because Britain doesn't use industrial design enough that an industrial decline occurs. · Lessons to be learned: A design approach never ceases; it is at the basis of product evolution. When a product is launched, another should be in the concept phase.
SURVEY: **Walsh et al.; 1992 (Great Britain)** *Study A*		
Winning by design	Questionnaires Comparison of forty-one British firms Sectors: Plastic, bicycles, and cars And eight international model firms Design conscious	Performance comparison between British firms and foreign models: · Return on capital: 8 percent Great Britain, 11 percent foreign. · Rate of profit: 6 percent Great Britain, 7 percent foreign. · Turnover growth: 15 percent Great Britain, 43 percent foreign. · Capital growth: 12 percent Great Britain, 19 percent foreign.

(continues)

Table 3.4. Con't.

OBJECTIVE	METHOD	RESULTS
		Development strategy: • Products with added value: 20 percent Great Britain, 100 percent foreign. • Diversification of range: 24 percent, GB 63 percent foreign. • None: 42 percent GB, 0 percent foreign.

SURVEY:
Svengren, L.; 1995 (Sweden)
Industrial design as a strategic resource

OBJECTIVE	METHOD	RESULTS
Industrial design from a managerial perspective To develop a model to demonstrate how design influences strategy; formulation process	Thesis Three case studies of the project Triad Bahco, Braun, Erco, and Ericsson	The author defines three design integration processes: • Functional, or design upstream in the product development. • Visual, or the design in the company identity and culture. • Conceptual, or design to question the company mission. Results: • Firms resort to design to create a competitive advantage with technology and marketing. • Top management supports this strategic position of design. • Communication between departments implied in design process is frequent and continuous. • Design integration is also a process of organizational training: Design as resource for organizational change and company mission development. Typology of the design-oriented firm: • A vision of how artifacts make life and work better, easier, and more fun. • Empathy to understand user interface. • An aesthetic sensitivity physical objects. • Courage to transform these elements into actions.

SURVEY:
Hertenstein & Platt ; 1997 (USA)
Developing a strategic design culture

OBJECTIVE	METHOD	RESULTS
Forty-three variables were used in order to measure design performance	Case studies: eight firms that have an active policy of design management, including: Bissell Black & Decker IBM Kodak Steelcase Thomson Whirlpool	Selection from forty-three variables to measure design performance. Financial measures most used: • Turnover, product cost, cost of product development process, and performance of design group. Firms stress turnover and product cost. What would be better would be to stress economic value, added value, and percentage of sales to faithful customers. Nonfinancial measures: • Customer satisfaction, innovation, and creativity are the most used; at least one is used in each firm to measure design performance. Firms stress customer satisfaction and time to market to measure design performance. Designers would also like to measure design performance by its impact on the firm business strategy.

(continues)

Table 3.4. Con't.

OBJECTIVE	METHOD	RESULTS
SURVEY: **Arbonies; 1996 (Spain)** *Product design and the role of external design consultants*		
What are the key topics of design management in the success of innovation? To identify the role of design in strategic change	Use of methodology of the Design Innovation Group for questionnaire Region: Basque county Survey on twenty-nine design projects and twenty-one firms	In more than 50 percent of the projects, designers' fees are 14 percent of total budget. • Design importance understood only in the majority of businesses at the level of product design. • Firms privilege the relationship between design and R&D. • 76 percent of projects were merchandised. • Eighteen projects were a commercial success: increase in sales (eight), higher price (five) or higher margin (three), design award (one) costs reduction reduction (one).
SURVEY: **Gemser & Leenders; 2001 (the Netherlands)** *How integrating industrial design in the product development process impacts company performance*		
Questionnaire administered by face-to-face session with senior management	Dutch manufacturers' home furniture precision instruments Comparison of two samples of twenty-three firms, each either investing highly or investing little in design	Perceived contribution of industrial design to product performance: similar perception in both industries, but instrument precision industry anticipated higher increase in demand for design expertise. Relationship between investing in ID and company performance correlation strong in precision instruments industry: profit indicators, export sales, turnover. Furniture industry ID intensity not a significant predictor for any performance measure. Validation of hypothesis business performance is positively related to ID intensity, but the impact of design investments on company performance is much stronger in the instruments branch than in the furniture industry. Effect of the ID intensity on company performance dependent on the industry and on the degree of innovation in design.
SURVEY: **Borja de Mozota; 2002 (France)** *Design and competitive edge: A model for design management excellence*		
Are companies excellent in design similar or different in their design management? How does design create value in a firm?	Thirty-three SMEs from fourteen different countries nominated for the European design prize competition in 1998 Questionnaire and interviews with top management	First, the integration process of design was described, showing that the reasons for design entry were: product differentiation, launch of a brand, design leadership, and new technology. Based on Michael Porter value chain and on literature review, twenty-one variables for design's impact on value were analyzed. A factorial analysis validates three levels of value creation; nineteen out of twenty-one variables were grouped into three clusters:

(continues)

Table 3.4. Con't.

OBJECTIVE	METHOD	RESULTS
		· The economic value of design: impact on primary functions.
		· The impact of design on support activities of the firm.
		· The impact of design on the value chain: system design as a factor of change.
		Typology shows that these thirty-three SMEs were all excellent in the design of their products, but had different design strategies:
		· Class 1, design as managerial competence (sixteen firms).
		· Class 2, design as a resource competence (eight firms).
		· Class 3, design as an economic competence (five firms).
		· Class 4, firms indecisive on design role (four firms).

SURVEY:
Hertenstein, Platt & Brown; 2001 (USA)
Valuing design: enhancing corporate performance through design effectiveness

OBJECTIVE	METHOD	RESULTS
Is there a difference in financial performance between design-conscious firms and others?	Fifty-one publicly traded companies in four industries · furniture · electrical appliance · computer · automotive Ranked by an expert panel in design management according to their design effectiveness	Company financial performance was computed using industry-relative financial ratios. Four areas of financial performance were examined using 12 measures: · Growth rates: percentage growth in net sales, net cash flow, and net income. · Returns on sales. · Returns related to assets. · Earnings before interest, taxes, depreciation, and amortization, cash flow from operating activities, net cash flow, and net income. · Total stock market returns: total stock return relative to the S&P 500. Comparisons done over a five-year period. Of these forty-eight comparisons, the results in forty-five instances were in the right direction, i.e., the group of firms with more effective design out-performed the group with less effective design. In twenty-five comparisons the results were statistically significant. Taken as a whole, these results provide strong evidence that effective design is associated with better financial performance.

(continued on page 72) marks, reliable information, and the assurance that they will be able to finance design with security.

CONCLUSION

- ❦ Design quality has an impact on national competitiveness and, in particular, on the rate of exports.
- ❦ Design participates in macroeconomic issues, such as the level of innovation and consumption or welfare of a nation.
- ❦ Design is an asset for business performance.

Different design management models exist, offering paths for different value creation by design.

CHAPTER 4

DESIGN MANAGEMENT

W E HAVE LOOKED AT DESIGN FROM AN ECONOMIC PERSPECTIVE; now, we will look at it from a managerial point of view. Design management is rooted in the shift from a hierarchical, Taylor model of management to a flat and flexible organizational model, which encourages individual initiative, independence, and risk taking. Designers feel at ease with the new, more informal model of management. The new model is based on concepts like customer-driven management, project-based management, and total quality management, which all deal with design.

This shift in the approach to management has created a demand for in-house design management. It is no longer only a matter of giving a visible form to a particular business or marketing strategy, but of contributing to changing corporate behavior and vision. Thus, the designer's "defects"—creativity, initiative, attention to detail, concern for the customer—become strengths that managers can deploy deliberately to sustain the management of change.

In order to be effective, design must be introduced into an organization in a gradual, responsible, and deliberate way:

1. Gradual. An excellent way to bring the entire company to an understanding of the benefits of design is to integrate design into the organization in stages through a number of successive projects: "Begin with a single project and make it a small-scale success. It will help to sell the idea of working with designers throughout the company" (Bernsen, 1987).

2. Responsible. Even if it begins with a single project, the integration of design requires the support of senior managers to demonstrate the strategic character of design and put to rest the idea that design is difficult to manage. Someone from within the company should be put in charge of making design decisions.

PROFESSOR ROBERT HAYES

Harvard Business School

"For a company that has achieved 'world-class' in all other dimensions, the next challenge is design. . . . Quality design and the many contributions it can make to a global corporation as a facilitator, differentiator, integrator, and communicator is, like most strategic resources, not an event but a process."

As for innovation management, projects in the field of design must be promoted by a "champion." An individual with a passion for design can make all the difference (Peters, 1989). We need only think of the impact of managers such as Apple's Steve Jobs, Sony's Akio Morita, or Robert Blaich, design manager at Philips.

3. Deliberate. Design must be managed on all levels, not only in design programs and design projects. Information about corporate values must be communicated to designers; the design group must be supported across all company divisions; and communication must take place between the design group and top management in the company.

THE ORIGIN OF DESIGN MANAGEMENT

DESIGN MANAGEMENT ORIGINATED IN GREAT BRITAIN in the 1960s. At the time, the term referred to managing relations between a design agency and its clients. In 1966, Michael Farr observed the advent of a new function: the design manager, whose mission was to ensure the smooth execution of projects and to maintain good communications between the design agency and its clients. As far as he was concerned, the role could be played either by the design agency or by a manager from the client company, since the objective was to keep communication open.

It was in Great Britain that awareness of the critical role a designer could play in industry and the economy first dawned (Hetzel, 1993) with the joint efforts of London's Royal College of Art and the London Business School's Department of Design Management, headed by Peter Gorb.

In the United States in 1975, Bill Hannon and the Massachusetts College of Art founded the Design Management Institute (DMI) in Boston (see Table 4.1).

THE DEFINITION OF DESIGN MANAGEMENT

EARL POWELL

President, The Design Management Institute Boston

"DMI sees a future where design management will have ever-increasing importance in four fundamental ways. First, as businesses of all kinds deepen their understanding of the role of design in innovation they will look to design management as a powerful resource for innovations that will effectively differentiate their businesses and build sustainable competitive advantages; secondly, as people continue to find increasing choices in the marketplace and become more determined to improve the quality of their lives, they will demand more of what only the effective management of design can provide—good design; thirdly, the shift in attitude from design management to managing for design will unleash design's potential; and fourth, the increasingly important role design will play in building a bridge between the fundamental economic and cultural aspects of individual nations and the world will open the door for design to make an important contribution to healthy, balanced societies worldwide."

Table 4.1. Overview of the Design Management Institute (Boston, Massachusetts)

Vision	Improve organizations worldwide through effective management of design for economic growth.
Mission	Be the international authority, resource, and advocate on design management.
Objectives	• Assist design managers in becoming leaders in their profession • Sponsor, conduct, and promote research • Collect, organize, and make accessible a body of knowledge • Educate and foster interaction among design managers, organization managers, public policy makers, and academics • Be a public advocate for the economic and cultural importance of design.
	The Institute envisions a future in which superlative design improves the world's products, communications, and environments—a future in which design is managed in the best possible way and all industries, organizations, and managers value design as a crucial business tool.
Constituencies	The Institute serves primarily senior design executives and other executives involved in the development of products, communications, and environments. Educators involved in research and teaching in this field also form an important constituency. Finally, DMI strives to improve the general public's understanding of the nature, process, and significance of design.
Background	DMI was founded in 1975 at the Massachusetts College of Art in Boston by Bill Hannon. In 1986, after building its membership and becoming recognized as a leader in the profession through its conferences, DMI became an independent not-for-profit entity. During the following years, it increased its membership by 400 percent and extended its networks to three continents. In cooperation with Harvard Business School, DMI launched the TRIAD project, the Institute's first international research project in the area of design management. In 1989, the Institute launched the quarterly *Design Management Journal*, the leading publication in the field. In 1990, the Institute received the prestigious honor of a special award from the Industrial Designers Society of America. DMI's relationship with Harvard Business School has grown even stronger throughout the 1990s. The institute's Braun case study became required reading for all first-year students in 1991, and in 1995, Harvard Business School Publishing became the sole distributor of DMI case studies.
Structure	The Institute's activities are conducted through a number of programs: Conferences DMI' s conferences, symposia, and professional seminars on strategy, brand, and design management tools form an invaluable educational and networking resource. Senior design executives, policy makers, scholars, and top-level management leave our conferences armed with ideas on how to better harness the power of design. Publications The Design Management Institute Press is the publishing arm of DMI. The press has built up a collection of design management literature unmatched in the world. Publications include: • *Design Management Journal* • Case studies • *DMI News* (a bimonthly newsletter) • Academic review (the best of research) • Conference recordings.

(continues)

Table 4.1. Con't.

Research

The research center organizes and conducts programs on issues of concern to designers and senior managers. There is an International Research Forum on Design Management Research & Education. This forum is held every two years in a different location and is hosted by prestigious institutions. Past locations have included: Northeastern University, Boston, 2002; German Design Council, 2000; Pratt Institute, New York, 1998; ESADE Barcelona, 1996; and Paris ESCP EAP, 1994. This academic forum publishes conference proceedings and an academic review.

The foreign relations program functions through several networks, which represent one of the Institute's greatest resources in the United States, Central and Eastern Europe, and Asia, as well as through partnerships, such as the MBA design management distance learning program at Westminster University in England.

Design management has a twofold objective:

1. To train partners/managers and designers. This entails familiarizing managers with design and designers with management.
2. To develop methods of integrating design into the corporate environment.

DR. JURGEN HAUSER

Interbrand Koln, 1998

"In essence, design management challenges the most popular misperception of design management—that it is basically a contradiction in terms."

Peter Gorb (1990) defines design management as "the effective deployment by line managers of the design resources available to a company in order to help the company achieve its objectives." Design management is therefore directly concerned with the place of design within an organization, the identification of specific design disciplines that are relevant to the resolution of key management issues, and the training of senior managers to use design effectively.

This definition underscores the point that design is at once an end (putting design in the service of corporate objectives) and a means (contributing to solving management problems). Design management is an "asset management" which builds value, as well as an "attitude management," which adjusts a company's state of mind.

Alan Topalian (1986) distinguishes between short-term design management, which involves managing a design project, and long-term design management, or management of "global design." Patrick Hetzel (1993) broadens the scope of design management when he defines it as:

- Managing design—that is, managing the creative process within the corporation
- Managing a company according to design principles
- Managing a design firm

Design management involves more than assigning routine administrative tasks; managing human and financial resources and other administrative duties are part of a design manager's responsibilities but do not exhaust them. The distinguishing feature of design management is its role in identifying and communicating the ways in which design can contribute to a company's strategic value.

DONALD E. PATERSON

Former Ford CEO

"The key issue in managing the design process is creating the right relationship between design and all other areas of the corporation."

Design management is the implementation of design as a formal program of activity within a corporation by communicating the relevance of design to long-term corporate goals and coordinating design resources at all levels of corporate activity to achieve the objectives of the corporation. Design management's role is also to foster an understanding of the relevance of design to fulfilling the company's long-term goals and coordinate design resources at every level of the company. This entails:

- Contributing to corporate strategic goals by developing and auditing a design policy, articulating the design policy alongside corporate identity and strategy, and using design to identify needs
- Managing design resources
- Building a network of information and ideas (a design network and interdisciplinary information resources) (Blaich & Blaich, 1993)

Design management is specific to design activity. The only person who can make the brief clear to the staff is the senior design manager or director in his or her day-to-day interpretations of a design policy.

GARY VAN DEURSEN

Corporate Director of Industrial Design, The Stanley Works

"In the management of design it is critical that the manager be highly skilled in design. It is here that he or she can contribute significantly by critiquing, challenging, and selecting the best solutions."

Design management is the deployment of design within a company to help the company develop its strategy. This involves:

* Managing the integration of design in the corporate structure at the operational level (the project), the organizational level (the department), and the strategic level (the mission)
* Managing the design system within the company. Designers' creations are artifacts: documents, environments, products, and services that have their own unique aesthetic qualities. Companies have a formal design system that has to be managed

This definition encompasses the dual character of design:

* Design is an integral part of company processes and management paradigms. This is the intangible dimension of design
* Design is part of the system of societal forms and design paradigms. This is the tangible dimension of design

Companies vary greatly in the extent to which they devote resources to design activities and to developing design as a core competency. Design is a valuable asset that deserves to be managed with at least as much skill and care as other business activities (Oakley, 1990).

TOM PETERS

Fall, 1989

"Design is only secondarily about pretty lumpy objects and primarily about a whole approach to doing business, serving customers, and providing value."

Courses in design management are now being developed all over the world, as well as MBA programs that have a specialization in design. For example, at Pratt Institute in New York, the topics covered include:

* Marketing professional services, advertising, and strategic marketing
* Leadership behavior simulation and negotiation
* Business and intellectual property law
* Management communication skills
* Design operations management
* New product management and development
* Financial reports and analysis
* Financing companies and new ventures
* Business strategy and managerial decision making
* Business planning and design management case studies

PROFESSIONAL PROFILE

WHAT IS THE CAREER PATH toward becoming a design manager?

Anne Haerle, former student of the University of Westminster MBA distance learning program in design management, worked for her dissertation on the question of describing the career path of a designer. She concluded her preliminary research with the creation of a design management career life cycle model in five phases—each requiring different skills and educational requirements (see Table 4.2).

In France, another study (Vervaeke, 1999) shows that designers work either in design agencies or the design department of organizations. An in-house designer fulfills a more strategic role in new product development. Designing takes between 41 and 100 percent of the work time of a designer.

THE CONVERGENCE OF DESIGN AND MANAGEMENT

SOME FIRMS HAVE SUCCEEDED in bridging the two worlds of design and management. This augurs well for the possibility of a convergence between these two disciplines.

A Comparative Approach to Design and Management

Differences in the cognitive approaches of designers and managers are often cited as the reason companies find it difficult to integrate design. But are their approaches really so different? The mere juxtaposition of the words "design" and "management" can be difficult, especially to designers who do not see beyond the rational and financial dimensions of management. However, an analysis of the fundamental characteristics and concepts of these two disciplines reveals more similarities than differences (Borja de Mozota, 1998).

	JOB TITLE	RESPONSIBILITIES
DESIGNER	*Associate designer* *Assistant designer* *Designer*	*Developing creative solutions to design problems*
DESIGN PROJECT MANAGER	*Senior designer* *Project manager* *Associate design director*	*Coordinating resources in order to deliver a design within a predetermined schedule and budget*
DESIGN STAFF MANAGER	*Creative director* *Studio leader*	*Managing design staff, transferring design strategy into creative briefs, and assembling design teams to meet project needs*
DESIGN ORGANIZATION MANAGER	*Director* *Principal*	*Making operational and general management decisions that drive the development of a design group or organization*
STRATEGIC DESIGN MANAGER	*Chief design officer* *Chief executive officer*	*Developing the organization's strategic business objective, along with the related design strategies that help meet the goals*

Table 4.2. The Designer Career Path

Table 4.3 compares key concepts of design and management. Clearly, most of the concepts are common to both disciplines. Even the cultural and aesthetic dimensions of design have equivalents in management in the areas of consumer preferences, organizational culture, and corporate identity.

Cognitive differences between design and management are thus rooted primarily in the mutual suspicions managers and creative teams have of each other. Because design involves a quest for originality, novelty, creativity, and innovation, it risks finding itself in conflict with classical management styles and conservative attitudes that resist organizational change.

As a rule, the rational model of management is based more on control and planning than creativity. The Taylor model, which, according to some executives, lacks "gestalt," makes it hard to accommodate systemic design activity, but it can acknowledge design as a problem-solving activity aimed at promoting company growth and building competitive advantage through differentiation.

More recent management models, however, recognize the importance of intuition for strategy formulation, and provide a framework for a more "artistic"-oriented manager (Mintzberg, 1994). This informal model lends itself well to the design process insofar as it favors a light, simple structure and a focus on key values, and encourages action and experimentation. The manager's decision-making model thus becomes more intuitive, placing the emphasis on observation and the human dimension, which makes it more appealing to the designer. From the perspective of the informal management model, design and management both represent investigative and experiential decision-making systems with potentially convergent cognitive structures.

Since they share common concepts, the domains of design and management might readily become interfaced. However, practical experience demonstrates the complexity of integrating design into the corporate structure. For certain companies, overcoming this difficulty can be turned into an internal competitive advantage. The ability to integrate design becomes a know-how that is difficult for competitors to imitate, in addition to being a core competency.

If design and management really do belong to two different cognitive spheres, design management must be viewed as an organizational learning process.

DESIGN CONCEPTS	MANAGEMENT CONCEPTS
DESIGN IS A PROBLEM-SOLVING ACTIVITY.	*Process. Problem solving.*
DESIGN IS A CREATIVE ACTIVITY.	*Management of ideas. Innovation.*
DESIGN IS A SYSTEMIC ACTIVITY.	*Business systems. Information.*
DESIGN IS AN ACTIVITY OF COORDINATION.	*Communication. Structure.*
DESIGN IS A CULTURAL AND ARTISTIC ACTIVITY.	*Consumer preferences. Organizational culture. Identity.*

Table 4.3. A Comparative Approach to Design and Management Concepts

Designers and managers are like any other people: they rely on the decision-making processes that they have depended on in the past, and cling to familiar frames of reference. Managers and designers each have their own ways of seeing and interpreting reality.

The cognitive approach of design management accounts for the difficulty in introducing design into the organizational structure. For management, design is unknown information. Further, managers do not readily perceive the need for change; they tend to go with what they know. Finally, managers do not always react in a completely rational manner.

The "Designence" Model of Design and Management

The respective conceptual schemas and paradigms of design and management can serve as a starting point for building a convergent model of the development of design management based on two perspectives: reactive (managerial) and proactive (strategic) (Borja de Mozota, 1992).

The *managerial approach* involves enhancing design by accommodating administrative and management concepts. All management paradigms are examined in order to choose the ideas and methods that will make corporate design more efficient. This can be achieved by linking design with the key concepts of product, brand, identity, and innovation management.

This perspective calls for applications of the different theories of management—scientific, behavioral, situational, decisional, and systematic—and an inquiry into their conceptual and practical relevance for the enrichment of design management methods:

- Scientific: design management seen as a purely logical process
- Behavioral: design management as getting things done by people, centered on relationships, interpersonal group behavior, and cooperation
- Decisional: design management as a decision-making activity
- Systemic: design management as organizing systems with open interaction with the environment and complex interactive subsystems
- Situational: design management depends on circumstances
- Operational: design management includes basic managerial activities like planning, organizing, command, control, and departmentalization

The *strategic approach* involves examining design as a new paradigm in order to arrive at ideas and methods that can be used to enhance the efficiency of management in general, and design management in particular. This requires an understanding of the ways in which design perceives reality and an examination of its methods, such as the shape, color, aesthetics, and sociology of objects, in order to enhance management concepts. A different vision of organizational reality emerges from the "science of design": a management system based on *sign* and *form* that is essentially relational and interpretive and which can contribute to enhancing business strategy and the company's vision.

Design management approach	The objective of design management	Its application to quality management
The managerial approach to design management	Enhance design with managerial methods · design and organizational performance · design/brand, identity, strategy · general management and design management methods	Contribution of "qualiticians" to designers and design managers Data on design's impact on "zero defects" Test of quality perceived
The strategic approach to design management	Improve management with design knowledge Theories of form; design principles Creativity and idea management	Contribution of designers to "qualiticians" Rethinking processes Shared vision, continuous improvement

Table 4.4. A Convergent Model for Design and Management: "Designence"

Design offers specific tools, such as auditing procedures for strategy formulation, competitive benchmarking, idea management, and models and prototypes for innovation, as well as "boundary-spanning" communication tools.

APPLYING THE MODEL: DESIGN AND TOTAL QUALITY MANAGEMENT

WHILE DESIGN IS SYNONYMOUS WITH QUALITY, quality does not mean the same thing for designers as total quality management. Designers are often unfamiliar with the methodology and techniques of total quality management.

Many companies are adopting the total quality approach. Design management can contribute its design competencies to the quest for quality, while enhancing its approach by applying methods derived from this quality certification process.

Total Quality in the Service of Design

Historically, the total quality movement has gone through numerous stages: from the logic of *a posteriori* inspection of quality, meeting specifications and reducing defects, to the final stage of customer-oriented total quality. Nowadays, quality management is an active principle, and its goal is to make individuals aware of their responsibility in achieving a common objective: to develop a product or service that the customer will perceive as superior. Total quality entails all of the successive scientific advances in the field of quality management for the benefit of the company and its performance.

The concept of total quality is a good illustration of the convergence model of design management described above:

- Design management is enhanced by management paradigms—design and design management can be measured and improved by total quality methods
- Design paradigms are placed in the service of management—design processes optimize total quality, and methods are developed to measure perceived quality, which is then incorporated in total quality management methods

We can analyze the contributions of quality management techniques to design management from a scientific, managerial, and human resource perspective. Design already employs some of the scientific techniques of quality management, such as ergonomics, marketing, and value analysis. Design management would benefit from looking at the techniques of quality management to develop design management tools, as well as tools for measuring design effectiveness—such as collecting data on customer satisfaction. The importance of design in the value chain can be evaluated by using quality measurement criteria, such as the impact of design on quality objectives like zero defect, zero inventory, and zero delay, on reducing production defects, and, finally, on the choice of partners and the selection of suppliers.

New proactive management methods, which focus on prevention, shared information, cross-disciplinary teams, and network management, are entirely consistent with the way designers work. Design can, therefore, accelerate changes brought about by quality management. Total quality requires an organization to focus on customers and employees (who are also customers). Design introduces a vision of quality that is not quantifiable: the perceived quality of the product or service. We are moving from the notion of measurable quality to the notion of perceived quality. Designers contribute to creating perceived quality.

Quality improvement techniques are meaningless without employee participation. Motivation studies, psycho-sociology, group dynamics, and organizational sociology are not part of a designer's training, yet the knowledge yielded by these disciplines is fast becoming essential for the design manager who wants to produce results.

Finally, quality has become a key factor in competitiveness, and this applies to the final product as well as the process. Causal analysis—seeking the causes of a problem until the root is found—is a natural tool in the creative process, as well as a method of process improvement. It may be used to improve the way in which design processes are structured, especially when facing the recurrent problem of design integration.

Design as a Tool for "Qualiticians"

Total quality is often described as a radical new way of thinking, a cultural revolution. It represents a shift in management paradigms that brings quality management closer to the conceptual framework of design. Companies concerned with quality must focus on a number of decision-making processes in which design thinking has already acquired expertise.

The achievement of quality requires an ongoing examination of procedures, errors, and defects. By its very nature, the design process tends to challenge routine. Designers like to ask why things are done in a certain way. This aptitude can be deployed proactively as a tool for change within an organization. Quality depends on the will to improve products, as well as the company itself, on a continuous basis. Design is already used as a means of product optimization, but designers can also become active partners in optimizing strategic functions, such as internal communications and human resource management (personnel training and motivation). Design is a horizontal function that can help to create a consensus around quality and inspire a new vision. This process culminates in the incorporation of quality managers into the design department.

Example: At Renault, the car manufacturer, quality managers are involved in design and the direction of design has had its quality certification since 1998.

The Renault Design Excellence report defines design in terms of quality: "Our mission is to contribute to the constant improvement of product quality, both in terms of its cultural, technical, and industrial components and of customer perception, by putting forward innovative concepts whenever possible and compelling styles." This mission is associated with process reengineering and aims at quality certification. It is also related to a total quality and continuous improvement approach, which calls for design department managers to be highly involved.

The issue of quality brings us back to the problem of the transition from an industrial to a postindustrial economy, and of the dichotomy between the functional and creative aspects of management. The idea of quality relates to the struggle against negative qualities: the specification gaps, defects, and deficiencies that constitute the measurable weaknesses in products or services, and which companies try to minimize using rational tools. However, there is another domain: that of positive qualities that make it possible to overtake competitors and exceed the expectations of potential customers. Some positive qualities can be acquired as a result of constant improvement, and others can be gained through creative innovation and intuition (Bucci, 1998).

SOHRAB VOSSOUGHI

President, ZIBA Design, 1998

"Design management is an integration process that gives a company a single voice and conveys a clear message to people inside and outside of the company. Design management requires a delicate balance between art and commerce. To be successful, a design manager must maintain control without limiting creativity. A design manager must reconcile change with consistency.

"The greater the penetration of design, the stronger the company. In great companies like Federal Express, Nike, and Microsoft the greatest contribution of design is not visual. The most important contributions of design are:

1. To focus on the human side of business.
2. To create a passion for the power and magic of getting details right.
3. To communicate a positive vision of the future.

"To be successful design should be everywhere. Successful designers should contribute to every aspect of corporate activity through creativity, innovation, and passion.

"The newest frontier is process design. Designers should look beyond the conventional activities such as packaging, graphics, and product design. Designers have an important role to play in defining how companies use information. How is production information documented and communicated? How are the employees trained? How can the customer experience be simplified and refined?"

Conclusion

* Design management is the planned implementation of design in a company to help the company achieve its objectives. The person in charge of design is the design manager.
* Design and management are mutually beneficial: the "designence" model.

PART II

THE VALUE

of

DESIGN

CHAPTER 5

DESIGN AND MARKETING:
DIFFERENTIATION THROUGH DESIGN

M arketing is the process of matching customer needs with want-satisfying goods and services. This process can be viewed in different ways:

- Marketing as an exchange process. Design can help the exchange by which two or more parties give something of value—a product, service, or idea—to each other in order to satisfy each party's perceived needs. The designer works either to identify these needs or modify consumers' perceptions of value.
- Marketing as a liaison. Exchanges are vital to closing the gaps that naturally exist between producers and consumers. The designer works to improve spatial and perceptual gaps in the marketplace.
- Marketing as a function. The designer works with marketing on logistics and distribution operations.
- Marketing as a creator of utility. Production, marketing, and design are jointly responsible for creating and providing "form utility," and play a vital role in directing the ultimate shape, size, quality, and attributes of products—the core product, the extended product, and the brand product.

Marketing, like design, is a business philosophy focusing on consumer wants and needs. Modern marketing emphasizes customer orientation, requiring coordinated efforts by all departments within the company to provide customer satisfaction as a long-term profit goal.

In theory, design and marketing share the same mind-set of developing an understanding of customer needs and the factors that influence those needs in order to establish healthy customer relationships. In practice, the relationship between design and marketing poses problems that spring from a reciprocal ignorance of the other profession: the designer working with the marketer on product specifications ignores other marketing responsibilities and expertise. The marketer views design as an output (a package or product), not a process. The essential divergence between design and marketing occurs in their different conceptions of "customer needs," and designers often criticize "rearview mirror" market research.

However, design is an efficient management tool for developing a more customer-focused culture in the company. In business, relations between marketing and design are more complementary than divergent. Both work to build a product strategy that differentiates the company from the competition and strengthens its competitive advantage. The designer contributes by creating the differences that are perceived by the consumer as benefits and which have an impact on consumer behavior. Branding is the most frequently used process of differentiation. Brand differentiation and brand management are part of design management.

Design's Impact on Consumer Behavior

A CUSTOMER'S KNOWLEDGE OF A PRODUCT is acquired through her perception of it. A customer's behavior, then, is determined by how she perceives the products and services around her. Design plays a fundamental role in marketing because:

- The visual differentiation introduced by design is perceived by the final consumer.
- The product shape influences the consumer's behavior.

In a 1973 article, Philip Kotler uses the term "atmospherics" to describe the conscious action of organizing a retail environment to generate emotions that are likely to increase the probability of purchase. Environmental retail design—including the ambient conditions, the layout of the space, and its signs and symbols—generates internal responses in both the employee and the customer in terms of cognition, emotion, and physiology, and, therefore, behavior: what they approach, what they avoid, and how they interact (Baker, 1987; Bitner, 1992; Everett et al., 1994).

The "experiential model of consumption" developed by Holbrook & Hirschmann (Holbrook & Hirschmann, 1982) provides a general framework to represent design's impact on consumer behavior. Within this model, the prevailing information processing model is contrasted with an experiential view, which focuses on the symbolic, hedonic, and aesthetic nature of consumption. This view regards consumption experiences as a phenomenon directed toward the pursuit of fantasies, feelings, and fun. This is an enlarged model of consumer behavior, in which the consumer is not making a decision but is participating in an experience.

MORRIS HOLBROOK, 1986

"The consumer's aesthetic responses matter, they command our interest in their own right, and they deserve investigation since these responses are a key component of the consumption experience. There are potentially individual differences in preference structures in evaluative judgment associated with psychological variables:

- visualizing/verbalizing tendency
- intrinsic/extrinsic motivation
- romanticism/classicism."

The "design-form" induces the consumer's behavior according to different approaches to perception and information processing: form translates into cognition, an emotion, a message, and a relationship.

Design as Cognition: Perception and Cognitive Psychology

The fundamental laws of visual perception apply first: vision is instantaneous, orders, and regroups. Taking as an example a document or computer screen, when one looks at these objects, the eye instantaneously orders the luminosity and associates the darkest zones with the most important information. It then regroups those elements closest to one another, according to the law of "gestalt," and, in particular, the law of proximity, and, finally, regroups elements that have common features of luminance, scale, or shape, according to the law of similarity.

A consumer's cognitive interpretation of the situation precedes and determines the emotional reaction (Lazarus, 1991; Markin, 1976):

- A shape induces a mental picture
- A shape is categorized

Shape is cognition. When looking at an object, a mental picture is constructed that is the result of free association and projection. A shape can make us recall a memory, unconscious thought, or belief. Mental imagery might send us back to a personal, internal construction we made in the past in interaction with the environment.

The design-form activates a process of mental imagery through its visual imagery. This is especially critical when competition makes it difficult to differentiate the product from others on the market (Felix, 1994). This cognitive perception of the design-form:

- Affects consumers' beliefs about products and brands (Morrow & McElroy, 1981; Zweigenhaft, 1976; McElroy et al., 1990; Bellizi et al., 1983), retail spaces (Linquist, 1974; Zimmer & Golden, 1988), and businesses
- Affects consumers' evaluation of quality, durability, and dollar value, and their propensity to buy at a higher price (Dodds et. al, 1991; Grewal & Baker, 1994; Grossbart et al., 1981; Weners, 1985; Evans et al., 1980)
- Affects consumers' interpretation—both functional and aesthetic— of information. The design-form is the first contact through which the consumer experiences and values the product or idea. (Parasuraman, 1988; Spies et al., 1997; Nussbaum, 1993)

A shape activates cognitive as well as sensory stimulations (Grossbart et al., 1975). The consumer learns through perception, and what he learns influences his future perceptions (Markin et al., 1976).

Consumer response to a design-form is determined by two different styles of information processing: the cognitive and the preferential. Research on the differences in individual consumer behavior primarily incorporates measures of consumer verbal response. Further research expands the examination to include a holistic look at the consumer's visual information processing. Visual processing—particularly mental imagery—is a strong facilitator of information acquisition. Mental imagery is an internal learning model, individualized by each consumer, who can attest to her particular mental imagery by an explicit verbal or graphic response (Childers et al., 1985).

Individuals tend to choose between visual-image and verbal-discursive information processing:

1. The individual with visual skills opts for a more holistic style of information processing (in support of holistic processing, gestalt psychologists argue that an object is perceived as a whole).
2. The individual with a verbal tendency uses a more analytical style of information processing (his reactions to the design-form are based on atomistic perceptions).

Individual imagery capabilities are measured by:

* Imagery vividness: the clarity of the mental image an individual evokes
* Imagery control: the ability of the individual to self-generate a mental image or to perform certain manipulations of it, such as a mental rotation
* Imagery style: the willingness to habitually engage in imagery versus verbally oriented processing

Another aspect of cognitive psychology is the process of *categorization*. Every design-form is categorized. An individual's mental imagery points to the fact that there exists a stock of shapes or objects that act as referents or "prototypes" for each individual. Cognitive processing typecasts a shape to fit a product category and proceeds by making comparisons between the new shape and preexisting knowledge of that category. This visual routine outlines the cognitive path of information processing (Loken & Ward, 1990; Sujan & Dekleva, 1987; Bloch, 1995).

This method of typecasting, or "typicality," is usually defined as the degree to which an item is perceived to represent a category. Family resemblance is an example of typicality. It is measured by the degree of similarity between the attributes of two or more objects. Typicality is linked to:

* The consumer's attitude in his assessment of an object: familiarity determines both typicality and attitude
* The consumer's preferences: the most typical objects often have more value (Loken & Ward, 1990)

The importance of *familiarity* (the number of experiences a consumer has with a product) and *expertise* (the capacity to successfully accomplish the product functions) creates the distinctions between the product categories that are perceived differently by consumers.

As a designer, it is useful to know that:

- Rather than leaving categorization to chance, designers should adopt a proactive approach by using prototypes with target consumers to determine whether the intended categorization is successful.
- If the product is radically new, categorization can be difficult and frustrating (Cox & Locander, 1987).
- Consumers prefer goods that are only moderately different from existing products (Meyers, Levy, & Tybout, 1989). The distinctiveness is clear enough to warrant further processing, yet the product can still be easily categorized.
- A brand is a mental image, structured knowledge, and a range of associations.

A consumer usually prefers to choose products perceived as typical of the brand. In some cases, however, atypical designs are preferred, either because of the appeal of variety or because these products are more salient.

The best strategy for design is to move away from the stereotype in order to increase the impression of novelty while moving toward an ideal that increases the harmony, elegance, and symmetry of a design, which is to bring the stereotype closer to the ideal (Del Coates, 1997).

Design as Emotion: Perception and Emotional Psychology

Product design is associated with positive effects and pleasurable experiences. Its goal is to elicit positive reactions in consumers who encounter its creations rather than negative reactions. These affective responses might be to the overall form (or "gestalt processing"), or they might relate to individual design elements.

The intensity of the emotional reaction to a design is a function of the intrinsic elements of the perceived form (Levalsky, 1988; Veryzer, 1993; Gröppel, 1992). It encompasses strong attention and involvement.

BERND SCHMITT, 1999

"Experiential marketing differs from the traditional approach because consumption is viewed as a holistic experience and the customer as a rational and emotional animal.

Experiential marketing incorporates all types of customer experiences:

- sense: sensory experiences
- feel: appeals to the customer's inner feelings
- think: appeals to the customer's intellect by engaging the customer creatively
- act: enriches the customers' experiences by showing them alternative ways of doing things
- relate: creates experiences that relate the customer to a broader social system."

The schemes for emotional classification are conceptualized by:

1. The Mehrabian-Russell model (1974) or the PAD paradigm: the three dimensions of pleasure, arousal, and dominance (control). Emotions are classified around three axes: pleasure/displeasure, excitement/torpor, ascendancy/passivity. For example, the arousal stimulus potential suggests that factors such as novelty and complexity of visual patterns interact to evoke pleasure.
2. The eight basic emotional categories by Robert Plutchik (1980): fear, anger, joy, sadness, acceptance, disgust, expectancy, surprise. Research explaining these emotion classifications analyzes the possible differences in consumer experiences. For example, one can predict purchase behavior by looking at the characteristics of the design environment. Researchers (Donovan & Rossiter, 1982) criticize studies that insist on the cognitive component of attitude (price, localization, assortment, quality of products). They suggest that a consumer's behavior is, above all, an emotional response. A sense of pleasure for the customer increases the intensity of her interaction with the staff, as well as the likelihood of a purchase (Donovan et al., 1994; Dawson et al., 1990).

The emotions classified under the Mehrabian-Russell model entail a type of behavior: attraction or repulsion. Positive/negative emotional responses to design can be considered along an approach/avoidance continuum. Consumers who have positive psychological responses engage in approach activities such as extended viewing, listening, or touching.

Avoidance behavior is an outgrowth of negative feelings. The stronger the positive/negative responses to a product's form, the greater the propensity to approach/ avoid the form.

The attraction behavior demonstrates a desire to stay in the retail environment or explore the product or packaging visually or tactilely. There is an interrelationship between the feeling of pleasure and attraction behavior (Russel & Pratt, 1980; Csikszentmihalyi & Robinson, 1990). If the consumer is really attracted to the product, he will continue his approach behavior after he gets the product home, displaying it prominently and maintaining it carefully.

The PAD consumption model defines new criteria to measure this emotional response:

- The introspection process of the qualitative experience: the consumer tells how the product is consumed and how he interprets his experience of consumption
- The consumer's description of his negative or positive feelings when confronted with the design form (as one would do for a publicity campaign)

The pleasure a product can give to a consumer can come from the aesthetics of an object without any relation to its function. It is not uncommon, however, for aesthetic and utilitarian value to occur together. The most successful products offer both benefits to the consumer.

Other research has investigated the emotional impact of a design-form variable, such as the visual, auditory, olfactory, or tactile sensations it invokes. Light and color are more frequent themes of this type of applied research:

- Light is an element of attraction and attention for the customer (Schewe, 1988) and can provoke impulsive purchasing (Birren, 1969; Rook, 1987). Retailers can influence the time passed in a store by the selection of lighting levels (Bitner et al., 1987; Markins et al., 1976).
- Color generates biological reactions (Evans et al., 1980), provokes emotional states (Danger, 1969; MacNeal, 1973), and attracts the attention of the individual (Margulies, 1970). Different colors are assigned differently according to product categories (Marquardt, 1979). Hot and cold colors have different emotional effects in terms of perceived quality and positioning (Belizzi et al., 1983).

Emotions brought on visually are stored hierarchically in the consumer's memory. The memory works like a chain reaction, beginning with a visual image of the product's attributes, which leads to a sequence of links with the consumer's concept of self and his perceptions of the product's benefits. Put simply, products are bought for what they mean to the consumer (Peter & Olson, 1987; Olson, 1988).

Products either imply a cognitive treatment of information (a thinking process) and/or an emotional treatment of information (a feeling process). Motivations for purchasing a "thinking" product are utilitarian and cognitive (Clayes et al., 1995). Products that provoke a "feeling" are expressive of emotional value. The information processing is either logical, rational, and sequential, or holistic and synthetic. On the one hand, the consumer is focused on performance, cost, and tangible attributes, and, on the other, he is concerned with the valorization of self, the subjective value, and the intangible attributes. Knowledge of the product is the most important aspect for a "thinking" product, while self-knowledge prevails in a "feeling" product.

Moreover, what makes a product perfect (what is product "rightness")? Designers insist on design principles such as the unity of the shape. Adrian Forty suggests that systems of values and beliefs and designer creations have a constant impact on one another. Implicitly, designers determine the way to live (Forty, 1986). But a good product is not always the winner of a design award or an archetype of its category. It can be a product that a certain population likes, an everyday product. The right products reflect previous childhood experiences and are customized to fit consumers' personalities they are, in other words, "right for me" (Durgee et al., 1995).

Design as Message: Semiotics

According to the critic Baudrillard, postmodern society is characterized by "hyper-reality" (1983). That is, our reality is created by publicity, design, and marketing; we live in a society of spectacle (Debord, 1983). The distinction between the sign and its meaning no longer has bearing; both the product and its image play a role. When an object is no longer specified by its function, it is qualified by its "subject." Objects, then, become systems for signifying social practices (Barthes, 1970).

Postmodernism views marketing as a cultural process that erases the distinction between art and commerce. Fashion is a metaphor for the culture of consumption. Products themselves remain the same, but their mental representations are periodically varied or renewed. The consumer becomes a consumer of culture, and culture becomes a marketable product (Firat & Venkatesh, 1993).

Marketing and design have contributed extensively to this glorification of signs, or identities, as a process by which individuals define themselves. Design creates forms and connects them to existing forms or alters those forms that already exist. In doing this, it modifies the structure of the system of significance and links the new object to the collective cultural "habitus."

The consumer is the producer, not just the receiver, of the end product. Postmodern consumerism is no longer dictated by needs, but exists within a system of objects. Consumerism, then, creates the consumer. The consumer no longer tries to satisfy his needs but seeks to produce symbols (Firat & Venkatesh, 1995). People have the power to freely combine significations, and make their own associations and metaphors. Design is the semiotics of seduction (Lebahar, 1994).

For Pierre Bourdieu (1984), distinction provides a framework for the symbolic processes in consumption. Consumption takes place through social structures. In this sense, social class is key in the formation of taste. Bourdieu argues that what distinguishes people is the notion of difference—which resonates with the Derridean idea that distinction through symbolic differentiation is what underlies any cultural system.

Semiotics appreciates the physical, or formal, aspects of artifacts as forms of communication without excluding their functionality (Eco 1988; Goodsell, 1977). Objects tell us how to use them; they serve their symbolic representations and construct the symbolic environment in which we live (Langrish et al., 1996).

JEAN BAUDRILLARD, 1981

"An object is not an object of consumption unless it is released from its psychic determinations as a symbol, from its functional determinations as an instrument, from its commercial determinations as a product; and is thus liberated as a sign to be captured by the formal logic of fashion, i.e., by the logic of differentiation."

Fashion is a part of design that is ripe for semiotic analysis because of the subtleties of unconscious mechanisms that are at work behind it (Mick, 1986).

For Saussure, structural semiotics is based on the notion that there is only significance in difference.

Table 5.1. Design and Consumer Behavior

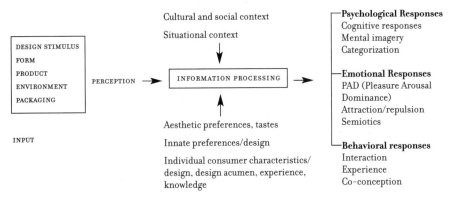

Source: Adapted from Peter Bloch, *Journal of Marketing,* Vol. 59, July 1995.

For Peirce, semiotics is the process of communication by any type of sign, a sign being anything that stands for something (its object) to somebody (the interpreter) by some means (its context). Peirce speaks of triadic relations, while Saussure talks of dyadic relations. Charles Morris's work on the science of signs treats these three dimensions on the operational level.

1. The syntactic dimension, or the sign itself: the dimensions of the object as it appears and can be described by the structure of its constitutive components (architecture, technology).
2. The pragmatic dimension, or the interpretation of the sign: the logic of the object adapted to action (its function, use).
3. The semantic dimension, or the sign-object relationship: the dimension of the object viewed in terms of "sense building," or meaning on two levels, the denotative or rational signification of the object, and the connotative, i.e., the image (the symbol, brand image).

This representation of a form as a triangle, or triadic sign, is the most helpful conceptual tool for teaching the non-designer about the nature of the design process. Designers conceive of signs that all have three dimensions: a structure, a function, and a symbol. The design process is, by definition, the link between the departments of a company that represent these dimensions: technology (structure), marketing (function), and corporate communications (symbol).

Peirce's semiotics develops a typology of the consumer's interaction with a design using tools of lexical analysis:

1. The intellectual implication: the measure of the degree of stimulation, curiosity, or potential to develop knowledge and expertise.
2. The emotional implication: the measure of the degree by which the product reinforces the ego and the idea of the self.

3. The social implication: the measure of the degree by which the product represents an affinity for a particular group—political, social, or religious (Paul, 2000).

Any sign or form satisfies a hierarchy of three logics:

1. The logic of the object: the sense of the object in itself. Is it beautiful, accessible, coherent?
2. The logic of the user: the sense of his or her relationship to the object. Why is the user buying it? What are his or her needs?
3. The logic of use: the sense of the user's relationship to others: What is the object doing in its context?

French semiotics (Hetzel & Marion, 1995) has contributed operational tools such as:

- The narrative diagram (*schéma narratif*), used, for example, in the study of a logo
- The semiotic square (*carré sémiotique*), used, for example, to provide a model of interpretation of user needs in hypermarkets (Floch, 1989)

Studies have analyzed in depth the impact of package design on consumer behavior (Dano, 1996) and established a "virtual" semiotic typology of consumers. Research reveals the correlation between the value systems of consumers and their attitudes toward and comprehension of packaging functions.

Design as Relation: The Sociology of Objects

Products are tools of communication that "put the consumer on stage" and help him exist as a social object (Solomon, 1983). The design-form becomes a stimuli for behavior. The social symbolism found in the form is the principal reason for buying the product. A design will be considered important if it projects an aspect of the consumer's self-image that is important to him.

The picture is not that of the isolated consumer confronting a design, but of the consumer in interaction with other consumers in a sociospatial environment (Everett et al., 1994). Some researchers propose a link between customer satisfaction and the quality of the customer's interaction with the design in an environment (Goodwin et al., 1992; Harris et al., 1994).

The "sense of community" is an integral part of what a firm has to offer and has a direct impact on consumers (Goodwin, 1994). There is a certain communal integration ritual when one encounters a service: These rituals of integration are social mechanisms that generate a common feeling or social implication for the customer (Siehl et al., 1990; Belk & Bryce, 1993).

Researcher Jo Bitner demonstrated the importance of the impact of the physical environment on the nature of social interaction and proposed to add to the "7 P model" in marketing a new variable, the "physical evidences" that measure consumer satisfaction in the meeting of a service (1990).

The concept of "relational value" in Bernard Cova's sociological model hypothesizes that, in the postmodern era, the global value of a service or product results as much from its social value as from its functional and symbolic values. The "tie," in other words, is more important than the goods (1994).

The aestheticization of everyday life became the mark of postmodern society, and transformed the "*Homo economicus*" into the "*Homo aestheticus,*" according to Luc Ferry (1990). Aesthetics is understood as shared emotion. The product becomes a "cult object." Aesthetics transforms a new product into a societal innovation, which is the process by which a new signification is introduced into the social system. It acts as a social tie grouping the postmodern tribes together. Consequently, there has been a reemergence of the "artist-entrepreneur," an entrepreneur who innovates by vocation rather than necessity and has a societal approach to marketing (Cova & Svanfeldt, 1993).

Consequently, "co-conception," a new way of developing the design process, emerged, making the design process more public so that everyone who is affected by design decisions can foresee what decisions can be made and, therefore, influence those decisions (Mitchell, 1993). It is necessary to externalize the design process in order to brainstorm and fully explore the complexity of the conception process (Jones, 1992). Also called "experience building," it implies a more collaborative approach to the design process (Jones, 1992).

Design is redefined in terms of the user's experience and not by the geometric criteria of form. At the center of the design process is the *experience* of the design. Intangible design is the design of the experience itself.

Examples:
Sharp uses the expression "humanware design" rather than "hardware" or "software."
Apple studies the psychological principles that sustain people's interactions with design: The criterion for success is "zero learning" (Mitchell, 1996).

Design in Context: The Situational and Cultural Perception
The laws of gestalt explain that the perception of a shape depends on the differentiation between the form and its background. Perception evolves, for example, according to the form's brightness. Any research in aesthetics should take into account these laws. Consumers' aesthetic preferences are influenced by situational factors. A situation can define itself as a set of descriptive and objective elements (Belk, 1974, 1975) or as the psychological feelings of the consumer (Lutz & Kakkar, 1975).

The consumer's mood also has an impact on his or her evaluation of a product. A consumer in a good mood will value the shopping experience more positively (Bost, 1987; Gröppel, 1992). Aesthetic preferences vary according to the consumer's socio-demographic and cultural context, as well (Holbrook, 1986). Decisions relative to product positioning, aesthetics, and packaging are highly cultural (Dubois, 1987). Cultural differences exist in design: a certain color, shape, or material will be valued more by one culture and less by another. The culture provides a consensus on visual styles, and also affects tastes concerning design on the basis of semiotic considerations: designers expect consumers to prefer products that are desirable in a certain culture (Solomon, 1983; McCracken, 1986).

THE AESTHETIC PREFERENCES OF THE CONSUMER

CLASSIC MARKETING STUDIES CONSIDER AESTHETICS a product attribute and introduce it in consumer preference scales and multi-criteria models. For example, the consumer is asked to appreciate and rate successively the attributes of a car—price, fuel consumption, durability, aesthetics, comfort, performance, and customer service.

But design-form or aesthetics is not an added, separate attribute. We know aesthetics is a result of the design and it is correlated with other attributes. For example, fuel consumption is linked to the aerodynamics of the design; the external appearance of the vehicle is linked to the internal architecture of the motor, etc.

Studying aesthetic preferences is an emerging trend in marketing research. In a postmodern society aesthetic sensitivity exists for all products. Specialists in consumer research analyze how the aesthetic variable is perceived globally. In 1981, Holbrook spoke of the "aesthetic imperative" and challenged researchers to change the focus of their studies to encompass the aesthetic attributes rather than only functional ones. Although techniques exist to measure aesthetic attributes, there is little research on the aesthetic aspects of consumption (Eckmann, 1994). It is necessary to develop this domain of investigation in the lineage of Holbrook's work, and thus create a bridge between researchers and designers (Simonson, 1997).

The form or aesthetics of a product can contribute to its success in different ways (Bloch, 1995). In saturated markets, an unusual product shape can be a means of winning the attention of the consumer (Garber, 1995). A distinctive design can render competition immediately obsolete (Goodrich, 1994; Hollins & Pugh, 1990). The quality of a design drawing is also important: if badly manufactured, the shape imagined by the designer can be undermined. Finally, certain designs are eternal and give pleasure to consumers for decades after they are first introduced (Pye, 1978; Jones, 1991).

Consumer research offers scientific methods that permit the judgment of "good design" (the one that is bought) and a context in which to observe the customer's behavior that isn't biased by subtleties of artistic appreciation. The progress of this research depends on the willingness of researchers to adopt a more practical and pragmatic view of aesthetics. To limit aesthetics to artistic objects is far too restrictive.

An aesthetic response is produced from the interaction between the appearance of an object and the person who perceives it. It offers the possibility of appreciating all products in an aesthetic sense. In the same way, the distinction between the functional product and the aesthetic product is difficult to determine, since all objects have an aesthetic side. The person who perceives the object gives the object its aesthetic sense (Veryzer, 1995).

Aesthetic Preferences and Design Principles

The perception of the aesthetic function depends on various factors: emotional (subjective sensations), cognitive (aesthetic sensations linked to what one knows, to a personal interpretation of knowledge), and physiological (the aesthetic perception depends on the quality of our sensations, the physiological steps of perception, and personal psychic conditions) (Solomon, 1988; Quarante, 1994).

Aesthetic preferences are linked to personality variables. We see product forms every day that affect the quality of our lives (Lawson, 1983). The perception and usage of beautiful products can provide sensory pleasure and stimulation.

Aesthetic preferences result from the principle of the perfect form. The aesthetic message is induced by the harmony of various factors: proportion, consistency, rhythm, modularity, order, and disorder. Often, the natural or organic shape will be preferred (Berkowitz, 1987).

Design principles have an influence on consumer preferences and act as a conceptualization of the aesthetic response. The form of an object is based in design principles, such as the principle of "unity." The aesthetic response is more favorable to objects that are consistent with this design principle. An experiment conducted on three types of products (microwave ovens, sun lotion, or radios) validates this hypothesis: Thirty percent of the interviewees used words in relation to design principles to justify their preferences—for example, "balance" or "symmetry." Design principles offer a basis by which to understand how the aesthetic response operates. Aesthetic preferences are influenced by the ways in which the form is consistent with principles of proportion and unity (Veryzer & Hutchinson, 1998). This suggests that in the future, the impact of other design principles like symmetry and contrast will be validated (Veryzer, 1993).

A product form represents a certain number of chosen elements united as a whole by a design team to produce a particular sensory effect (Lewaski, 1988; Hollins & Pugh, 1990). Designers make choices about the size, scale, rhythm, proportion, materials, color, surface, ornamentation, and texture, mixing these elements to achieve a certain level of unity (Davis, 1987).

For example, miniaturization is an ideal form that is well anchored in the Japanese tradition. (Design Policy, 1982).

Forms can be classified according to design principles first according to three characteristics of the form (based on research conducted on logos):

1. Its elaborate character (the depth and complexity of the design)
2. Its natural character (organic, round, close to daily life)
3. Its symmetrical character (Simonson, 1997)

Another model in fashion describes forms according to two variables (preference and the variable of the garment itself, or the form) and draws a typology of clothes and the interaction between different types of clothes (Holbrook, 1986). Hence, the aesthetic response also has social significance: a colleague who demonstrates harmony in his or her clothes will be judged as more competent.

Aesthetic Segmentation of the Consumer

The idea of consumer segmentation according to aesthetic preference has been developed but is complicated by the question of whether there is a special class of aesthetic objects, such as those found in art or nature. This position encourages the idea that good design is arbitrary and limited to specific sectors, and that aesthetic objects can only be present in fashion or consumer goods, and not in the industrial context.

Most business-to-business marketing literature ignores the importance of appearance as a competitive factor, as if the industrial buyer had no aesthetic sense. However, product appearance plays a limited but vital role in the selection of industrial products. Appealing aesthetics will have a positive impact on the evaluation of the product and will be added to considerations of price and performance. Industrial design can act as a weapon in industrial competition (Yamamoto et al., 1994).

Research, therefore, tends to classify forms and segment consumers according to aesthetic criteria.

For example, bottles of perfume employ the descriptive language of the user: round, square, triangular bottles drawn from the basic family of forms—the sphere, cube, and pyramid and their subdivisions. This descriptive classification is useful for the designer in describing the object in comparison with its possible competitors (Llorente (DR), 1993).

Consumers prefer products that are representative of their category: products that are more familiar, therefore, will be better loved and valued. Forms can be segmented according to their impact on visual recognition and emotion, or one can search for a positive emotional impact without thinking about the quality of the visual recognition (based on research conducted on logos, Henderson & Cote, 1998). Modifying the unity of a form affects the categorization process (Veryzer & Hutchinson, 1998).

Aesthetics helps market segmentation and the discovery of market niches and minority consumer targets, such as:

- Consumers whose preferences are for the originality of a design (Sewall, 1978).
- High-tech products have an intimidating character, which has an impact on the consumer's self-confidence. Hence, a segmentation and market niche of consumers who prefer products with simplified functionalities in contrast to the performance-oriented positioning of the high-tech market (Feldmann, 1995).

In her thesis, Leila Damak confronts the bodily parameters of the consumer (the real body, perceived and lived) to the "corporal" component of package design, examining whether consumers prefer products that have shapes similar to the way they perceive their own bodies. The tendency to choose similar shapes is true for women who are satisfied with their physical appearance. On the contrary, women who are less satisfied with their bodily appearance tend to choose shapes that are different from their own. Women tend to project their physical image onto their responses to product forms more than men. Damak concludes with the concept of the "corporality" of product design (Damak, 1996).

In his thesis, Stéphane Magne measures the consumer's aesthetic attitude toward the design form with a variable he calls the Personal Aesthetic Sensitiveness (PAS), based on a Jungian interpretative frame. First, he defines the elements of a design-form: the morphological, the verbal, iconic elements, and the rhetorical process, and the interactions between these elements. Interactions between the components must be integrated in any explanatory model of the aesthetic order.

Magne then develops a typology of how consumers react to the design-form, using book covers as examples for experimentation. The quantitative results reveal four aesthetic types:

1. The formal, color type; those who prefer abstract, colorful forms
2. The skeptical sensory type; those who perceive aesthetics in a contextual and indecisive way
3. The expressive type (either sober or exuberant); those who prefer to express themselves to the exterior environment with provocative forms
4. The aesthetic type; those who search for meaningful forms, prefer good design, and reject ugliness.

The PAS concept can be applied to market segmentation, as well as marketing research on consumer behavior.

Aesthetic Preferences:
Design Experience and Personality

Design knowledge requires education, motivation, and frequent encounters with beautiful artifacts and environments. Consequently, it is important to know the level of design knowledge in your consumer targets and to educate the consumers by highlighting the shape through publicity and point-of-sale exposure (Osborne, 1986).

Some aesthetic preferences are either innate or acquired early in life (for example, the human preference for order and symmetry in forms). Research has been trying to comprehend these innate preferences, such as those for organic forms in design. A number of researchers believe that the aesthetic sense is something some individuals are born with. These people make sensory connections faster, prefer more sophisticated design, and favor visual over verbal information (Childers et al., 1985; Bamossy et al., 1983).

Aesthetic judgments differ according to:

    ✿ The intrinsic/extrinsic motivation of the consumer. More aesthetic experience is associated with intrinsic motivation. A consumer who sees a product as a means of doing something, which is an extrinsic judgment, will have more appreciation for utilitarian aesthetics (Holbrook, 1986).

- Personal characteristics like age or sex influence product interest and the way visual information is treated (Eckman & Wagner, 1994).
- The visual versus the verbal personality. The beliefs by which visual and verbal consumers judge the aesthetics of objects differ (Holbrook, 1986). "Visualizers" have a holistic sensitivity and a preference for organic models. "Verbalizers" have an atomistic sensitivity and are attentive to isolated details. Visualizers are more attentive to the interaction of components of the form than verbalizers.
- The duration of the design observation time. Information processing is holistic at first. A longer observation time is needed for consumers to give utilitarian reasons for their preferences (Creusen & Schoormans, 1998).
- Subjective attributes, such as color or shape, influence the perception of the weight, volume, and efficiency of certain products (Pinson (DR), 1992, 1986). (Gestalt psychologists perceive products as a whole rather than atomistically [Ellis, 1950; Katz, 1950]).

Too much formal similarity generates boredom; novelty and some complexity are necessary to provoke attention. Therefore, preferences veer toward product forms that have a small degree of irregularity and disorder. The pleasure is somewhere between boredom and confusion (Berlyne, 1974; Gombrich, 1979).

In conclusion, one can measure the impact of design on a consumer's behavior, which is in opposition to how many marketers view design's role in a company as a result of:

- Arrogance ("I know what good design is")
- Contempt ("Considering the position of design in the company, what is the use of design tools?")
- Fear (of the beautiful and/or the diversity of opinions on design)
- Ignorance (designers are not educated in the importance of evaluating design) (Paul, 2000)

Aesthetic research helps marketers understand the relationship between aesthetics and their products in designing their marketing policy.

ROBERT VERYZER, 2000

"Although designers have always had a user focus, there is a need to better formulate and more clearly articulate this emphasis. Design-related work done in disciplines such as consumer research can help to enrich our understanding of design and ultimately improve design practice. . . .

"Although some design research will necessarily touch on things that designers already 'know' or have an intuitive sense about, there is still a need to formulate and validate this information. As long as aspects of the design endeavor remain vague and imprecise, design as a discipline will continue to struggle for full recognition in the corporate domain."

Design Differentiation through Branding

THE LAUNCH OF A BRAND is one of the most efficient ways to suffuse design in a company. If the brand is well developed and persuasive, it instills loyalty and commands a premium among consumers. Design is crucial to achieving coherence: it brings together the diverse elements of performance, product and service messages, marketing and support communications, employee behavior and appearance, and the spaces that represent a company and its activities—both digital and physical.

Differentiation through brand development and positioning goes beyond graphic identity. The launch of a brand is the first reason given by managers for design integration in a company (Borja de Mozota, 2000). The design profession has grown side by side with brand development, particularly within the field of package design.

ANNE ASENSIO

Executive director, Brand Character, General Motors
(Interview by Jean Léon Bouchenoire, April 2, 2002)

"The Brand Character Centers had been operating for eight years under the support of G. W. Wayne, Vice President of Design at GM, when he recruited me in 2000.

"We are trying to look at *brand management from a design perspective* rather than a purely marketing perspective. It is exciting to be intellectually inspired and to define form vocabulary. I see brands as living organisms, and what I like about the concept of brand character is that it's closer to the French view of brands as growing, changing entities. . . . Brands don't just engage your rational side, they also engage your emotions and your body.

"Pontiac is associated with the color red. But Pontiac is far more than red. It involves a promise of sportiness and performance. It's extroverted and boldly American. But that doesn't necessarily imply a particular color like red.

"When it comes to brand management the marketing people will tell you they own the brand, the advertising people think they own the brand, and designers stake their claim too. But like quality the brand is everyone's business—it also needs organization, guidelines, passion, and people who manage brand character. Designers can play a bigger role as brand integrators."

Design and Brand Promise

THE FUNCTIONS OF A BRAND ARE:

1. To create value for consumers by informing them about the product's attributes.

2. To create value for the company by differentiating the product and making tangible the intangible.

BRAND DEFINITION

With all due respect to the American Marketing Association, a brand is more than "a name, term, sign, symbol, or design or combination of them intended to identify the goods and services of one seller or group of sellers and to differentiate them from the competition." A brand is the sum of all the characteristics—tangible and intangible—that make the offer unique. A brand is a set of perceptions that are driven both by communications and experiences. It is a distinctive sign, a symbol, and a source of added value.

Brand as a Sign and Graphic Design

A sign added to a product identifies the product's origin and protects the consumer and the producer against products that are identical. A brand is therefore an intangible semiotic reality that exists only when embodied in a product or service. A product has physical components. A brand represents the products and services it guarantees, as well as the functional and emotional associations that are built within a period of time in the minds of the consumers through the diverse channels of product appearance, packaging, and advertising slogans.

The brand gives a product a network of meaning, a story, and an imaginative universe—an identity that is continuous in time and space. Identity is:

1. The sum of all of the characteristics, tangible and intangible, that make the offer unique
2. The elements of brand identification (e.g., name, symbol, and color) by which an offer can be identified

A brand can be the name that distinguishes an object. Giving a name to a product allows it to go from the no-name to the named, just as a name identifies a person.

Example: Helena Rubinstein created a new name, "Aromatherapy," for her spa products.

Brand identity is the outward manifestation of the essence of a corporate, product, service brand, or brand environment. Concepts like brand personality and brand-customer relationships are essential elements in a brand identity system.

Brand as Added Value

A brand is a means of injecting value into products in order to differentiate them from the competition. Therefore, in a relational perspective, brand status is determined by the way in which the company and its customer base appropriate the brand. Saying a brand has value means three things:

1. Brand value is the result of interaction: a brand has positioning, promise, and network functions.

2. A brand is a source of value that differs according to those who interact with it: consumers, producers, and distributors.
3. Brand value is a building over time, a sedimentation process, which evolves and changes: the brand has a mission to build customer fidelity and evoke a favorable response from the public.

A product brand is:

1. The gestalt of the brand, including its emotional and cultural associations, as well as its physical features.
2. The graphic system of identification, as applied to a single product or service or a family of products and services.

The links between design and brand are not limited to graphic design, logo, and sign. Design penetrates all of the assets that make brand value: mission, promise, positioning, expression, notoriety, and quality. There is graphic design in the brand name and symbol, product design in product performance, package design in promotion display, and environmental design in the retail setting. Logos such as Nike, Ralph Lauren, and Starbucks offer a brand essence, or vision. In the global marketplace, visual symbols have greater potential than words.

All the nonverbal elements of a brand—appearance, color, touch, odor, finish, and sound—can be "designed." A brand has multisensory design identities.

Example: The Microsoft Museum, a branded environment used as a means of storytelling about the history of the company, its culture, and products. The design team established a tactile and visual lexicon with which to address the materials, finishes, colour palette, textures, and typography.

The consulting firm Enterprise IG defines four attributes shared by thirty great corporate brands (Allen, 2000):

1. A clear understanding of its purpose and what it stands for, which remains over time.

Figure 5.2. What Is a Brand?

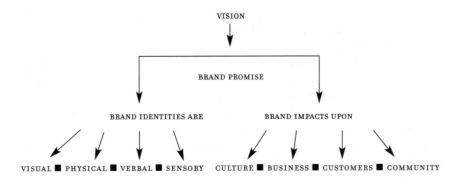

VISION

BRAND PROMISE

BRAND IDENTITIES ARE   BRAND IMPACTS UPON

VISUAL ■ PHYSICAL ■ VERBAL ■ SENSORY   CULTURE ■ BUSINESS ■ CUSTOMERS ■ COMMUNITY

2. A clear vision about how the firm wants to be perceived by the outside world. They manage their brand attributes and shape their corporate personalities to support their core ideas. The values of the brand have been internalized. Employees understand what behavior and action is needed to deliver the brand promise.
3. A strong brand theme that underpins everything it does.
4. A clear visual identity, strong and well-managed.

Example: The British Petroleum slogan, "The brand is your people."

POSITIONING THE BRAND

BRAND POSITIONING IS THE SPECIFIC NICHE the brand defines itself as occupying in the competitive environment. Positioning differentiates brand attributes, user benefits, and target segments. A positioning statement should address three basic questions:

1. Definition: How does the company define its business?
2. Differentiation: What makes the brand special?
3. Deliverable: What benefit does the brand deliver to its customers?

According to the brand positioning brief, the designer adopts a graphic sign and color, which become the central elements of the brand: either a symbol (such as Nike), a logotype (a unique typographical name treatment, like FedEx), or a combination of both (such as AT&T). Coca-Cola, IBM, and Mercedes-Benz are good examples of successful identity programs that have withstood the test of time. Graphic design is the first asset in brand notoriety. The modern brand does not belong to the universe of commerce anymore, but, rather, to the realm of communication. Logos are designed specifically to bridge the gap between corporations and people, and these connected brand designs help to define and communicate the desired persona of the company.

Examples: Ralph Lauren's perception of the American look broke open the doors of exclusivity by giving permission to buy the private lifestyle of the upper-middle class.

Nike, Gap, the Body Shop, and Virgin Atlantic broke the rules by creating a counter-culture that focused on *people*. Their corporate symbols reflect the companies' innovative cultures. The digital generation of Amazon.com and Yahoo! mirrors the quirky spirit of the Internet generation: speed and a willingness to change are their essence.

Marc Gobé of the Desgrippes Gobé group developed the concept of "emotional branding." There are unemotional brands, such as Compaq, and emotional brands, such as Apple. Corporate identity programs evolved from an approach purely based on visibility and impact to one based on emotional contact with consumers, founded on interaction and dialogue (a people-driven economy)—in other words, from impact to contact. Any graphic identity can be positioned in a matrix of two axes: graphic expression and emotional meaning (Gobé, 2001).

The symbol creates an emotional tie with the consumer because it is easier to memorize pictures (symbols) than words (names).

Example: The Le Coq Pathé identity rested on its logo, which featured a stylized rooster on a yellow background with the company name. Landor contributed to a revitalized award-winning Pathé identity.

Design or Advertising: Which Comes First?

Advertising and corporate communications are both used by companies to build and sustain brand image. In marketing, brand management is often synonymous with communication strategy. Interest has grown recently in the integration of communications due to budget pressures. Most companies prefer one or two agencies to provide advice instead of four or five. They want a single strategy that works across the board, and many companies already naturally integrate communications and successfully communicate from the inside out.

Example: The essence of BMW permeates everything the company does.

Brand or Product: Which Comes First?

Product multiplication, market saturation, and media pollution weaken the efficiency of brand messages and brands that do not have strong or differentiated product attributes. Timing is crucial for brands, and, therefore, the importance of product design is also critical. Jean-Noël Kapferer exhorts firms to rediscover "the physical dimension" (*"le sens du matériel"*), without which the brand is nothing, and to give product managers strong responsibility or designate a brand concept champion (Kapferer et al., 1989).

Core purpose	Brand attributes	Brand theme	Living the brand internally	Living the brand externally	Visual identity	Product identity
The spirit of refreshment.	Refreshing Exciting Social	"Always Coca-Cola"	Brand induction for all new employees.	Universal awareness and availability.	Logo Coca-Cola	Glass bottle
Only the original will do. Bringing people together.	Red		Statements of commitments to distributors.	Strong defense of trademark. Sponsorship only of exciting ventures. Ads always show people enjoying themselves.		

Table 5.3. Describing a Brand: Coca-Cola (Enterprise IG™)

Product innovation is more lucrative than image innovation. Unfortunately, marketers are not trained to appreciate the value of technological innovations. The brand that does not maintain its added value is sure to become fragile. When a brand is nothing more than publicity, it is a false brand. Branding is creating difference. It is, therefore, necessary to continually communicate on the nature of this difference and maintain it when innovating to heighten product performance, quality, and user satisfaction. The hidden face of the brand is the production, research and development, innovation, and risk taking. The brand pulls the market upward by consistently trying to exceed its performance and create a more effective product (Keller, 1999).

BRAND EQUITY

BRAND EQUITY IS THE VALUE OF THE BRAND TO ITS OWNERS, in a holistic sense, as a corporate asset. It consists of the marketing effects that are uniquely attributable to the brand. Brand equity is made of the brand assets (or liabilities) linked to a brand's name and symbol, which add to (or subtract from) a product or service (Aaker & Joachimstahler, 2001).

Brand equity is studied in market research for financially based motivation, asset valuation of the balance sheet for merger, or acquisition, or from a strategy-based standpoint in order to improve marketing productivity. Customer-based equity occurs when consumers are familiar with the brand and hold favorable, strong, or unique brand associations in their memory (Keller, 1993). Customer brand equity is based on customers' knowledge of the brand.

SCOTT ELIAS

CEO, Elias Arts Sound Design Agency, 1999

"Brand experts have traditionally focused on the consumer promise and emphasize brand delivery. However, brand touch points, because they convey brand experiences, are in a very real sense the brand. . . .

"When customers feel that the brand experience matches their expectations, they become *emotional stakeholders*. Emotional stakeholders are the brand's most significant resource and equity stream.

"At Elias Arts we developed the Sound Identity System, which is the result of an extensive process to articulate the sonic form of the brand's essence, its sound identity."

The importance of knowledge and memory to consumer decision making has been well documented. Most widely accepted conceptualizations of memory structure involve some type of associative model formulation. The associative network memory model views semantic memory or knowledge as consisting of a set of nodes and links. Nodes are stored information connected by links that vary in strength. A spreading activation system process from node to node determines the extent of retrieval in memory.

The relevant dimensions that distinguish brand knowledge and affect consumer response are:

- Brand awareness: in terms of brand recall and recognition
- Brand image: the favorability, strength, and uniqueness of brand associations in the consumer's memory

These assets provide a conceptual framework for marketers and designers to develop brand strategy and research (Figure 5.4):

- Brand awareness: people like what is familiar, and are prepared to ascribe all sorts of good attitudes to items that are familiar to them.
- Brand associations: anything that connects the customer to the brand: user imagery, product attributes, use situations, brand personality, and symbols. Much of brand management involves determining what associations to develop, then creating programs that link the associations to the brand.
- Brand loyalty: the heart of brand value. The goal is to strengthen the size and intensity of each loyalty segment. Core brand values are the values customers and other people outside the company associate with the brand.

Brand associations are:

- Attributes: The descriptive features that describe a product or service
- Benefits: The personal value consumers attach to the product or service; what consumers think the product can do for them in terms of its functional, experiential, and symbolic benefits
- Attitudes: Consumers' overall evaluation of a brand, the basis for consumer behavior

Marketing models view attitude as a multiplicative function of:

- The salient beliefs a consumer has about the product or service; the extent to which consumers think the brand has certain attributes or benefits
- The evaluative judgments of these beliefs: Is it good or bad that the brand has these attributes or benefits?

Preferred brand values are the values that customers say are the most important attributes in a given category. For a brand to be most preferred in a category, its associations or attributes must equal or closely resemble the attributes determined by the marketplace to be the most preferred. Brand management equates core brand values with preferred brand values. Building brand equity can be done through the initial choice of brand identities and the leverage of brand associations,

Figure 5.4. The Framework of Brand Knowledge and Customer Based Brand Equity

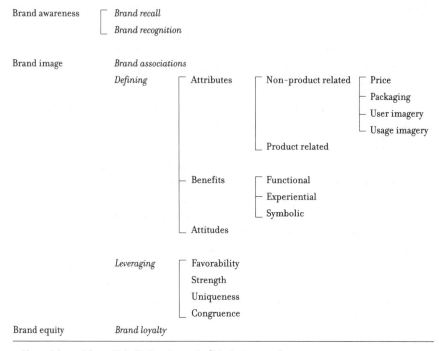

Note: Adapted from K. L. Keller, *Journal of Marketing*, 1993.

hence, the importance for design research to measure brand knowledge, which depends upon:

- Recall: the correct identification of the brand given the product category
- Recognition: the correct discrimination of the brand
- Types of brand associations: free association tasks, projective techniques, and depth interviews
- Favorability: ratings of the evaluations of associations
- Strength: ratings of the beliefs in associations

It is also important to examine the relationships among brand associations, in terms of:

- Uniqueness. Compare the characteristics of associations with competitors; ask consumers what they consider to be the unique aspects of the brand.
- Congruence. Compare patterns of associations across consumers (indirect measure); ask consumers what their conditional expectations of the associations are (direct measure).

* Leverage. Compare characteristics of secondary associations with those of a primary brand association (indirect measure); ask consumers directly what inferences they would make about the brand based on the primary brand association (direct measure).

CHOOSING A BRAND ARCHITECTURE

FROM A SEMIOTIC POINT OF VIEW, A BRAND IS A SIGN, a product named, and an entire universe of meaning. Branding an offer introduces two questions: What is the relationship between the product and the name, and, is the relationship exclusive or not? What is the visibility of the company behind its brands? Some companies, such as IBM, play with that transparency. Brand architecture defines the communications relationships between the company, the operating units, and their brands, products, and services. Ultimately, the architecture creates a system much like a road map, which helps consumers and key constituents navigate easily among brands and make the right choices.

As branding systems evolve to address more complex corporate needs, it is important for companies not to lose sight of the fundamental aim of branding—to guide customer choice and build lasting relationships with consumers. Traditionally, brand architecture is comprised of two major tiers:

1. The parent brand. Companies that develop the corporate brand as an umbrella for their overall products and services. (AT&T and American Express are examples of strong parent brands.)
2. The product brand. Companies that primarily support their product and service brands. This is the route taken most consistently by consumer goods companies, such as Procter & Gamble.

However, there is no difference between what you sell and who you are. A brand is a promise, and you have to keep promises. So, the frontier between corporate and product branding is now unclear. Some companies are setting their architecture between the parent and the product/service brands. They focus on fewer brands and provide a platform for a new brand, which allows the parent brand to expand through endorsement.

Example: IBM created "e-business" as a global brand. It serves as an umbrella for all of IBM's business lines with the online economy. Recent studies by IBM have shown that the new brand has already begun to give the company conceptual ownership of "e-business" worldwide.

In the near future, we will see more brands that are less rooted in product and more conceptual in nature, and we will see a more synergistic relationship between the tiers of brands.

Example: Lippincott & Marguilies, a New York design agency, uses three basic models in its brand architecture.

In order to build brand architecture and initiate a "brand stewardship process," engage the executive leadership in articulating a vision and perspective on key marketplace relationships (Speak, 1998). The relationships are:

- One brand/multiple brands: family brand
- Regional/global brand: "Think globally, act locally"
- Manufacturer brand/distributor brand

    The visibility of manufacturer brands decreases because of the trivialization introduced by distributor brands that use graphic codes similar to those of market brand leaders. Distributor brands (for example, chains such as K-mart and Wal-Mart) are brands. The competition they introduce tends to eliminate manufacturer brands that do not have specific brand positioning and disturb consumers who wonder about the real profit of a brand.

- Brand extension/brand concentration

    Design participates in the definition of brand territory as knowledge representation. Categorization helps to understand the phenomenon of information transfer for brand extension.

Brand Dynamics

Branding is dynamic. There is no room for motionless brands. A brand manages itself in the long run with imagination and creativity.

Example: The luxury market, where brands are now shrewdly tailoring their offers to reflect aspects of what might be called "the new sobriety," such as BMW promoting its "certified pre-owned" vehicle programs, which recondition used cars and offer the same aspiration appeal; or the Louis Vuitton luxury design brand promoting "junior" items at Neiman Marcus department stores.

Successful brands are those that possess the talent to continually reproduce while conjugating the hereditary phenomenon (the brand know-how) and validating the necessity of innovation (new ideas that come from outside the brand universe) in order to avoid inbred impoverishment (Caron, 1996).

JOHN RECKER AND JERRY KATHMAN

(Interview by Libby Perszyk Kathman, 2001)

"As brand building practitioners our role is to develop and manage valuable brand building equity. Therefore the manipulation of visual equity is a key component of effective, strategic design. Equity represents both rational and emotional triggers of trust. Visual and verbal components that are leveraged over time become touchstones for a brand."

Design is used to create brand identity, extend the brand's range of impact, and to optimize brand value while communicating to the consumer the nature and profits of the brand dynamics (Meyers, 1994). Design benefits when less foreseeable consumption patterns are anticipated and brand consistency is reinforced (Semprini, 1992).

Example: Target developed a compelling value proposition and viewed designers like Michael Graves' collection and Philippe Starck's retail design as brands that significantly enhance the image of their brand through partnership.

Design participates in brand valorization by making it live on different supports: packaging, product, advertisement, and, in the long run, different markets. Brand resources include credibility, legitimacy, and affectivity. For design management, this means consistency in aesthetics and shape, permanence of graphic and symbolic codes, and the creation of new emotions. Companies that take advantage of the promise-delivery equation realize the crucial role that design plays in the integration of product and brand experiences.

Brand as a Person

People relate to brands in exactly the same way they relate to people. In people's minds, a brand is a person just as surely as a person is a brand. People have names, and so do brands. People belong to families, and so do brands. People project certain styles and images, and so do brands. People experience life cycles, and so do brands. This is a fruitful metaphor. People are born. Brands are created.

MARIE-CLAUDE PEYRACHE, 2000

France Telecom

"Our brand driver is about relationships. We needed to select a symbol that would connote relationships as our main brand driver. That's why we chose the ampersand (&). It means 'you and me.' It means France Telecom and its customers.

"The integration of digital relationships with other customer constructs as experience architecture allows us to design personalized customer interactions."

Typography is about personality. Form is content. Many enduring corporate identities have been built solely on typography.

Example: Microsoft used the services of famous designer and typesetter David Carson.

Corporate branding promotes interaction, connection, and synergy in order to define a personality. It has changed from algebra to geometry, from 2-D to 3-D (Gobé, 2001). Conceptualizing a brand through personalization has become a very powerful way to build brand identity. If the identity of your brand is not well defined, you will have visibility but no personality (Gobé, 2001). Good brands manage customer "touch points" in the hope that they will be appropriated.

DESIGN AND MARKETING RESEARCH

FACING THE CHANGES FROM MASS MARKETING to a marketing of niches, research in marketing adopts a diversity of approaches and research topics. Market research is also asking fundamental questions about the role of marketing research in society; rational marketing models, for instance, are in crisis in modern-day society (Bergadaa & Nyeck, 1999; Marion, 1999).

Design follows marketing evolution from classic marketing based on existing products and markets toward a strategic and relational vision of marketing that encompasses new products, potential new markets, and new customer relationships. Design contributes to a strategic marketing decision process because it insists on the uncertainty of the problem or the pertinence of the need: Is the problem to create a new need or to find ways for the firm to defend its competitive position?

Critics of present marketing research methods call for setting up methods oriented toward society at large and not toward specific market segments. Marketing practices are changing toward:

- A relational definition of needs and more importance given to the different participants in the exchange
- A consumer constructed by marketing, which invents the relationship
- Various critics of the concept of market segments, or a scientific statute of marketing

Designers often criticize the methods of market research—and, probably, with good reason. These methods are often extrapolations of the past, but can one foresee the future in a postmodern economy? The methods are centered on the "conscious need," but our consumers have become beings of unconscious desires rather than needs. This might lead us to conclude that market research is pointless, because people consume *unconscious desires*, and market research can only track rational, *conscious statements of need*. A conceptual idea is always the consequence of thorough research on environmental trends and individual behaviors. What is changing is the need to investigate the field of consumers' needs in two directions:

1. Macro-design research on societal and cultural mutations. For an object to become a sign of recognition or a social code, it has to attain a maximum competitive advantage over its competitor substitutes on the market.
2. Micro-design research or sociological study aimed at the consumer "body," or "ethno-design."

Design theories can be used as a framework for further marketing research (see Table 5.5).

The rise of individual needs encourages the emergence of a "demand for design" that is varied: demand for products designed by star designers; for products or retail spaces signed by design firms; for individually designed identity differences; for "no-design" as a criticism of hyperconsumption.

Human needs are limited, whereas the field of desires is without limit. Urban life is a powerful means of creating needs and signs. Needs increase vertically not by appetite but by competition. The need of need is a human constant. One might believe that the need creates the thing (marketing logic), whereas it really is the thing that creates the need (new marketing logic, or proactive design logic: competition through strategic creation).

Design methods used in the creative process become useful to the optimization of marketing research in three directions: the diffusion of the fashion marketing model, common research methods, and the emergence of tools that measure perception.

DESIGN THEORY	KEY "FORM" CONCEPTS	RESEARCH ISSUES
AESTHETICS	Form as a resultant Form as unity	Product differentiation Coherence
PERCEPTION	Design = to link seeing with making	Experiential model of consumption Perceived value of the product
GESTALT THEORY	The form cannot be dissociated from its space A good form is a form with maximum unity A form is a whole A form is more than the sum of its parts	A firm's efficiency is more than the sum of its departments (Chandler)
SYSTEMS THEORY	A form is a coherent, complex, and open system A form is interfacing its environment	A firm is a system of forms
SEMIOTICS	A form is a sign at three dimensions: syntactic (structure), pragmatic (function), symbolic (sense) Reality is created	The interpretative dimension of marketing Brand value
SOCIOLOGY OF OBJECTS	An object is a coordination system Symmetric importance of the object and the user The object as social mediator	Societal value of the company offer Interaction between object and subject in creating the offer

Table 5.5. Design Theories Applied to Marketing Research

Diffusion of the Fashion Marketing Model

The specificities of fashion marketing—the rarity of the production and the intimacy of destination—have developed an intuitive marketing, in which success is generated by a target segment recognizing the designer's genius, entailing the cult of her name and the culture of her "house." For luxury goods, marketing, as fashion, develops a homogeneous concept (product, presentation, price) whose objective is its coherence with the new market targets (Allères, 1990). This marketing rests on a rational analysis of each of the emergent criteria of the new concept, and on the aggregation of each of these criteria, while taking into account their hierarchy in the final concept. Depending on the brand, the place given to creativity will vary.

The fashion designer-entrepreneur ignores market research, tests, and marketing techniques if faced with erratic consumer behavior. The designer imposes herself through the originality and strength of her style and creates a need. Some fashion companies become virtual; they center themselves around the necessity of flexibility and creativity to develop a short circuit, keep inside design, branding, and marketing, and externalize production. Fashion tends to become the postmodern consumption model with the emergence of the artist-entrepreneur, or "design director," enabling the company in its new role as a vector of culture.

Design Research and Marketing Research

Design enriches the field of marketing research by:

- Giving a new way to segment a market according to consumer perceptive and aesthetic preferences (Sewall, 1978).
- Enriching consumer behavior research (see section 1): A design-form is perceived as a marketing input that can be measured in its different dimensions—cognitive, emotional, and behavioral—and can play a role as a segmentation tool (Hansen and Deutscher, 1978; Lindquist, 1974).
- Providing models for analyzing product attributes according to design attributes.

Bob Veryzer developed a complete checklist of selected references for these design properties that can help in defining new product policy (Veryzer, 2000). Customer experience-based descriptions are grouped according to the more general dimensions—operative, comprehensive, constructive, and decidable (Table 5.6).

Classic marketing methods can be enriched by certain design issues, such as:

- The relation between sociology and the aesthetic
- The mechanisms of appropriation of the object in the consumer's life
- The value-signs in new social groups
- Studies of consumer tastes and design experience

Since all firms in an economic sector apply the same marketing methods, to succeed the enterprise must transgress the rules and introduce creative design thinking

Operative	Comprehensive	Constructive	Decidable
Performance	Understandability	Parsimony	Attractiveness
Utility	Identity	Adaptability (flexibility,	Appropriateness
Innovativeness	Discovery	modularity)	Value
Quality		Maintainability	
Durability		Recyclability	
Conformity		Manufacturability	
Proficiency		Economy	
Suitability			
Universality			
Safety			

Table 5.6. Checklist of Design Properties (adapted from Veryzer, 2000)

at all levels of marketing decision making. Marketers become "marketing stylists," renewing the tie between industry and culture. There is no separation between material culture and culture itself.

Neo-marketing research methods look like the design process. It is the marketing of trends with a macro-sociological character ("trendology") that valorizes the role of the experts and social strivers, and requires a perceptual immersion in the environment.

For Andrea Branzi, researcher for the Domus Academy, the new industrial strategy is based on the immediate cultural identity of a product that selects its user, promoting itself to a given social group by becoming a known point of reference. The Domus Academy developed market analysis that combines trend scanning, real-time corrective test systems, and the launch of beta-products. Design scanning is a sociological analysis of the connections between fashions and social or ideological phenomena by studying the expression of personality in the participators.

Designers bring to marketing research their talent of observation. Ethnographic analysis is the observation, in situ, of the user without his or her knowing. This technique gives a more individualized knowledge of the consumer's behavior. Micro-marketing targets the individual. Design develops tools for consumer behavior research that are based on observation (assisted by video, particularly in interface design) with the help of specialists in ergonomics, ethnology, and psychosociology.

Neo-marketing research encourages dialogue between the different poles of creativity, R&D, marketing, and new product development. There is a double process of integration between marketing and design: upstream in the concept phase, downstream in the action phase. Research tends to finance itself with the business made from the first stream of customers. These new professional practices privilege market launch feedback that is in phase with the creative design process.

The Emergence of Tools for Measuring Perception

"Good design" implies having the user in mind (Buchanan, in Morello, 1995). In a project team, the designer is the guarantor of the consumer-user and the idea passing from a material to a conceptual space. Perception measures are, therefore, useful to the designer in the creative process and help to write a qualitative design brief. Perception can be measured on two different levels: psychometric and sensory. Perceptive judgment can be evaluated from a perceptual mapping or from a cultural and situational context (Bassereau (DR), 1994). Tools like the "semantic differential" help determine the sensory profile.

The objective of all sensory evaluation is to measure the response to the stimulus identified by psychosociological measures. The perceptive response takes into account several stimuli identified in a list of variables used to describe a phenomenon. The semantic space permits an approach to the sensory space by the determination of the describers. The sensory profile of the product is thus suitable to a mathematical approach. One can develop a methodology to quantify perception. From a sampling of component shapes, an evaluation matrix of each attribute is constructed by consumers, who manipulate choices of attributes and express their preferences on a scale model (Swift, 1997).

"Sensory metrology" is the scientific future of the semantic differential and a way of measuring design quality and craftsmanship (Bassereau et al., 1997). The apprehension of an object must be global, and touch is important in the influx of competition. Therefore, it is important to create a tactile palette in communications and design (Chéné et al. (DR), 1994).

New methods are developed that allow for a verbal and quantitative description of the immaterial aspects of an object as sensed by the user. A quantified description of the various attributes of the object is drawn from the user's description of her wants in her own words, and her own point of view, from which a graphic representation is produced. One way to represent a user's description of the various attributes of an object is to draw it with a cluster of dots, each dot representing a word in the user's description.

This model can be used for design and become a tool for facilitating the dialogue between the designer and the manufacturer. The lexical analysis clarifies the perception the consumer has of a product or problem and establishes a comprehensive picture as a reference (Credoc, 1992).

This method of market research is useful for developing new concepts in "experiential marketing": an evolution of concepts of aesthetics seen as the consumer's multisensory experience, or "marketing aesthetics" (for instance, creating the scent along with the shape)—the marketing of the *complete experience* within the creative design process (Schmitt, 1997, 1999).

One last type of research aims to identify the users' different acceptances of the shape, function, and value of an innovation and the implications this has for the design. Solving recurrent problems, such as the nature of the relationship between form and function, can be done using a semantic analysis of the three approaches of design:

1. Industrial and commercial design, in which the form supports the readability and use of the product.

2. Cultural or anthropological design, in which the form represents a way of seeing things, an ideological choice, or a vision of society: The function is aesthetic and communicational, and the value is plural or prospective.
3. Methodological design, which tries to articulate the two previous approaches: The form materializes the underlying cultural value of the product, a differentiating value.

Design has as an objective the mixture of these different approaches, and new product development can serve as a foundation for new managerial methods (Floch, 1993).

In summary, the future of design in marketing research is vast, as marketing develops more toward a customer relationship model (CRM), in which design plays an important role in various macro- and nano-relationships, such as:

- The service encounter
- The relationship to the customer
- The close versus the distant relationship
- The relationship to the dissatisfied customer
- The e-relationship
- The noncommercial or green relationship
- The knowledge alliance relationship
- The internal customer and internal marketing relationships
- The relationship to external providers of marketing services
- The owner or financial relationship

CONCLUSION

- Design creates a differentiation of the form, which has an impact on consumer behavior.
- The design-form encompasses cognition, emotion, message, and the social relationship with the consumer.
- The consumer has aesthetic preferences that come from design principles but vary according to the context and his or her experience with design.
- Design creates differentiation through brand identity development, building brand equity and brand architecture.

Design brings new methods to marketing research that combine design theories and attributes, fashion marketing models, observation techniques, and sensory evaluation.

CHAPTER 6

DESIGN AND INNOVATION: COORDINATION THROUGH DESIGN

D esign is a management tool that creates differentiation in the internal capabilities of the company. Design is no longer seen as the output of design-form, but as a creative and management process that can be integrated into other organization processes, such as idea management, innovation management, and research and development management, and that modifies the traditional structure of process management in a company.

Design relates to key innovation management issues and new product development (NPD) success, in phase with important factors that are critical to innovation success: competitive advantage, the understanding of user needs, and the synergy between innovation and the company's technological strengths (Table 6.1).

But a good product is not enough for innovation success: further studies emphasize the importance of innovation management in innovation performance. Here, design creates value because it participates in the improvement of the NPD process quality, the definition of product strategy, and the quality of new product teams (Table 6.2).

---

1. **A product differential advantage.** A unique, superior product in the eyes of the customer, a high performance-cost ratio, and economic advantages to the customer.
2. **An understanding of user needs, wants, and preferences and a strong market orientation,** with marketing inputs playing an important role in shaping the concept and design of the product.
3. **A strong launch effort** selling promotion and distribution.
4. **Technological strengths and synergy.** A good fit between the product technology and the technical resources and skills of the company.
5. **Marketing synergy.** A good fit between the marketing, sales force, and distribution needs of the products and the company's marketing resources and skills.
6. **An attractive market** for the new product.
7. **Top management** support and commitment.

Table 6.1. Key Factors for New Product Success: Related to Design Input (adapted from Cooper & Kleinschmidt, 1986)

Successful innovation requires the improvement of products and organizational processes. Design is value-creating in both areas. Innovation is a collective and interactive process that is close to the reality of the design process, since it mixes internal and external factors. Design is valued both for its superior product quality and its superior NPD process (Borja de Mozota, 1985, 1990b).

This chapter develops successively these two critical paths for design in terms of innovation value:

1. Creating a better product: the conceptual dimension of design innovation, radical innovation, and design.
2. Improving the innovation process—coordinating through design on three levels: marketing time, project team innovation, and innovation as a learning process.

The major cornerstones of NPD performance	Other important factors

1. High-quality NPD process
  ✿ Emphasis on up-front homework
  ✿ Tough "Go" or "Kill" decision points
  ✿ Focus on quality of execution in project activities
  ✿ A complete and thorough process without hasty corner-cutting
  ✿ A flexible process
	1. High-quality new product teams
	  ✿ Use of a cross-functional team
	  ✿ Team leader dedicated to a specific project
	  ✿ Team communicates and interacts well with frequent update meetings
	  ✿ Decisions made by outsiders handled quickly and efficiently

2. Defined new product strategy for the business unit
  ✿ Objectives for the new product effort (sales, profits)
  ✿ NPD role for achieving business goals communicated to all
  ✿ Clearly defined strategic product/market arenas
  ✿ A long-term thrust and focus for NPD
	2. Senior management commitment
	  ✿ Commitment to risk taking
	  ✿ Clear messages about the importance of NPD
	
	3. Innovative climate and culture
	  ✿ Encouraging entrepreneurship
	  ✿ Providing support (rewards, autonomy, acceptance of failures)
	  ✿ Fostering submission of new product ideas

3. Adequate resources of people and money
  ✿ R&D budgets to achieve the stated objectives
  ✿ Necessary people in place and release time given for specific new product projects
	4. Senior management accountability
	  ✿ NPD performance part of personal performance objectives
	  ✿ Senior management compensation and bonus scheme tied to NPD performance
	  ✿ Performance results of NPD program actually measured

Table 6.2. Key Factors for Innovation Process Management (adapted from Cooper & Kleinschmidt, 1996)

The Conceptual Dimension of Design Innovation

"INNOVATE TO SURVIVE" IS OUR WORLD'S MOTTO. Design is innovation that can add value, giving a company a profitable edge in the quest to influence consumer preferences (Carpenter & Nakamoto, 1990). An innovative design process can help create a superior product through:

1. Its conscious and prospective research of environment opportunities. The designer is an innovator who goes out, watches, inquires, and listens to the world that surrounds him, which means the first value of design is the development of ideas that then become concepts.

   The sociocultural sources of design ideas are highly original and valued in terms of innovation. A thorough environment scan combines visual stimuli, directional keywords, colors and fabrics, and a preview of the main design trends in prints and patterns with the evolution of transversal sociocultural trends. From this dual sociocultural and design prospective information gathering, a cross-fertilization of ideas flows.

   Example: The publication by the international styling agency, Peclers Paris, of their new prospective tool-book, Futur(s), a visionary trend publication that aims to better understand today's consumer attitudes and respond to upcoming trends.

2. Its user-oriented philosophy: High-performance products and services need technological sophistication and innovation of use. This means a market-oriented NPD process and internalized customer information.

TOM KELLEY

IDEO, 1999

"Designers are experts in using the power of observation. Observation has the power to inspire and inform. In my experience the best source of expertise for innovation-oriented observations is the design community."

Design innovation is dynamic. Design management has to program a continued flow of new products, both radical and incremental (Landry, 1987). Design innovation is just like any other innovation—either autonomous or strategy-oriented, conceptual or perceptual, analytic or holistic.

Design and Idea Management

IMAGINATION IS THE NEW FUEL OF THE COMPANY. Ideas are the basis of innovation. An idea becomes an innovation when it is integrated with success strategies. In a context where the role of science in innovation tends to decrease, a new power is given to individuals with unconventional profiles (Steiner, 1995), such as designers. Design can generate ideas at every stage of the innovation process. Design fosters this generative approach of ideas and imagination.

Design means accepting chaos. The deviance generated by new ideas protects against conservatism, while the process of exploring new design ideas is protected from its own excess by sound design management.

GERARD VERGNEAU

Design director, Thomson Multimedia, 2001

"The design strategy at Thomson is a global business strategy. Several options are opened that find their common essence in a prospective commission. First materialized as 'dream products,' the designs are destined to enrich the 'collection line.'"

Design management requires a capacity to manage the autonomy and imagination of the collaborators. Each individual can be placed under the traits of creative individuals according to Kirton Adaptation Invention (KAI):

- An adaptable individual who produces a quantity of ideas, but in a formalized environment
- An inventive individual who deconstructs and reconstructs his environment

Both creative profiles are necessary for a successful design idea path, because imagination is both creative and integrative.

An idea is not a fact, like "Eureka!" It is a process that begins with the existence of either a problem or a resource to be exploited.

TOM KELLEY

IDEO, 2001

"A good idea is a lot of ideas."

The idea process is both:

1. An idea-building process: a convergence of a problem and a resource, establishing a focal point that identifies the sources and forges the way
2. An idea-formalizing process: the formalization of the idea in order to make it understandable to others and set up an idea processing system

When a designer explains her idea, she describes precisely the result of a long-lasting convergence and formalization process.

Creativity is an individual approach that works in a discontinuous and instantaneous process, whereas innovation is a collective and continuous process. The design process uses various design methods to develop creativity, from traditional brainstorming to creative studio outings and rapid prototyping.

TOM KELLEY

IDEO, 2001

"Prototyping doesn't solve straightforward problems. When you start drawing or making things you open up new possibilities of discovery. Jeff Bezos's Amazon.com story would make a great movie about how rapid prototyping can give you a business edge.

"Models often surprisingly make it easier to change your mind and accept new ideas. Give your management team a report and it is likely they won't be able to make a crisp decision. But a prototype is a spokesperson for a particular point of view, crystallizing the group's feedback. At IDEO a good prototype is worth a thousand pictures. Good prototypes don't just communicate, they persuade. Take the example of Apple Duo Dock in the '90s and its VCR metaphor. Prototype with energy and enthusiasm and you have a good chance of hitting upon the very feature or product that resonates with the customer."

In order to foster design ideas, design management decisions are issued from idea management methods:

- The implication of the individuals in the profit derived by their creativity
- Flexible information systems adaptable to outside information flows
- Managers' bonuses linked to the creativity of their teams
- Organizing new product idea banks
- Setting idea scenario systems

A structure favorable to idea flows is flexible, organic, decentralized, and network-oriented. Generating ideas is particularly critical for radical innovations. Recommendations for stimulating idea generation are to:

- Create and sustain strategic momentum for radical innovation.
- Proactively implement organizational mechanisms for getting radical innovation out of the laboratory and into commercialization projects.
- Develop a "receiving" capacity for radical ideas so creative people have a place to go with their ideas (Leifer et al., 2000).

Idea screening is best managed collectively by an idea screening group. This is a "gentle screen" and amounts to submitting the project to a handful of must-meet and should-meet criteria. These criteria often deal with strategic alignment, project feasibility, the magnitude of opportunity and market attractiveness, competitive advantage, and synergy with business resources.

Innovation intervenes in a social context and is produced by the interaction between a creative company and its creative people (Henry, 1991). The "ideal" company of the future is one in which people are at ease with both systems of creativity and respect for strategic norms.

THE CONCEPTUAL DIMENSION OF DESIGN INNOVATION

A DESIGN NPD POLICY selects segments or niches with high potential, develops new product concepts adapted to changing needs, diversifies product portfolios, and defines the lasting competitive advantages of each business unit.

Design has a conceptual dimension that has the advantage of uniting all the innovators around a common objective focused on the client. Innovation defined by its physical attributes and performances is not needed in future markets. What is needed are ideas transformed into concepts or unique user experiences.

This conceptual dimension does not only show visions of the future, such as "concept cars." It includes the wide range of possible NPD scenarios.

Example: The story of the car model Twingo at Renault. In 1986–87, this advanced design department worked on a project for an attractive car that would not compete with another Renault and would have a strong, specific style with a transformable interior (known as the "W60 Project"). The project was relaunched in the fall of 1988 under a new CEO, when marketing research confirmed that the new concept was a unique automotive offer. But by the end of 1988, debates about the exterior style of the car were far from closed. The results of marketing tests were conflicting: The design was either disliked or adored. Patrick Le Quement, design director, remembers this long and solitary time. After a week of reflection, he sent a now famous note to his president asking the president to help him in the launch decision and declaring: "I prefer instinctive style to extinctive marketing." (Midler, 1993).

Design innovation leans on user-oriented strategic marketing. What designers look for is "market-in," or the introduction of user satisfaction into all areas of innovation. Design changes in nature. It is a process that is at the same time a source of ideas and a source of organizational change, shifting the value chain by infusing it with a certain market orientation.

Concept-Oriented Innovation

A product concept is the intellectual representation of an artifact created by the mind. The mind imagines a metaphor that represents customer benefits and helps make the collaborative work of the innovators cohesive.

The design process integrates the concept:

- Upstream with prospective marketing, which defines the concept (the abstract promise)
- Downstream with operational marketing, which makes this concept live in the mind of the consumer (the product or brand image)

```
┌─────────────────────────────┐
│     New product strategy     │
│              ↓               │
│       Idea generation        │
│              ↓               │
│        Idea screening        │
│              ↓               │
│     Concept development      │
│              ↓               │
│        Concept testing       │
└─────────────────────────────┘
```

Table 6.3. The Early Stages of NPD

Example: Thomson Multimedia's "Seeing is believing." The product design team saw itself as responsible for experiences and interactions between the customer and the product, whether visual, tactile, or interactive.

This conceptual approach to innovation, which favors the creation of a product concept, is not limited to the world of fashion or entertainment sectors, like leisure, sports, and food. It is valid for the identity-building of all products and organizations. "Total design" in a creative process insists on product specifications according to the market and the importance of the upstream and conceptual phases of the process, as well as information coming from different sources (Jenkins et al., 1997). The key to the success of innovation management results from the fact that all of the NPD process is consumer-oriented. It implies that all of the customer's different spokespersons—for marketing, design, commercial, and quality—must agree. All of these partners are interpreting the customer's latent needs. Thus, information on these needs and uses must be integrated into all areas of production: processes, equipment, and employee procedures. Production management is modified to accommodate a "market-in" business setting.

Example: The innovation model in the automobile industry is an integrated process-product innovation in which the artifact is a combination of diverse inputs from engineers and designers to suppliers and buyers.

Design establishes an innovative way for a company to view the consumer. It generates an interaction between the subject and object. If a concept is a palpable vision of the product experience, it will, consequently, reorganize the innovation launch into a simulation of the experience of product consumption. Innovation leads to continued information sharing between consumer and company. Fashioned from and nurtured by this information, design can become a living experience.

Concept as Company Representation

Companies that succeed differentiate themselves through the integrity of their products. Every product reflects the company and the process of development that created it. Enterprises that develop products with integrity are themselves coherent and integrated. They differentiate themselves by a "seamless" model of organization and management. The manner in which the staff works, the way decisions are made, and the way suppliers are integrated into the company's efforts are all coherent and relate to its strategy.

Innovation should generate processes that infuse a strong product concept into all design details. This entails designating certain product managers with high responsibilities, or naming a "concept champion" or project coordinator who has top decision power. The key to product integrity lies in leadership, in the necessity of finding "heavy-duty" product managers who act as guardians of the product concept. A company cannot change everyone on its staff, but it can train new leaders and give power to people who are in harmony with these new directions, such as the designers (Clark & Fujimoto, 1991).

An integrity-oriented innovation implies that:

- Innovation management is based on the matrix of project and function management and team project management in order to generate the coherence of product and process.
- Innovation management is based on a matrix of both physical and informational flux in order to solve the problem of coherence between internal and external integrity.

The NPD process depends as much on the information flux as on the material, physical flux. From beginning to end—when the product is in the consumer's hand—a product is nothing more than information. The client consumes the product experience, not the physical product.

This internal-external process is the most important task in launching a new product. It requires imaginative tools. Design managers organize tools in order to ensure this integrity.

1. There must be a process in place that will ensure that current market information is passed on to those who are in charge of innovation projects.
2. There is consistency between formal and informal information.

The process of concept generation entails a reorganization of innovation processes where the informational and physical production systems are intertwined. It requires a high level of integration between the internal and external and between the customer, concept, product, and suppliers.

TAKAHIRO FUJIMOTO, 1991

"Another feature evident in corporations that exploit the 'designer-as-integrator' strategy is an orientation to customer satisfaction in the form of total product integrity."

Internal integrity refers to the consistency between the structures and functions of the product itself. External integrity refers to the match between the product and user. A company must address this dual focus: product integrity and organizational structure. The complement to internal and external product integrity is internal and external organizational integrity. For design managers, this means both the design of a competitive object and the design of a competitive process for developing objects.

Concept creation is proactive and grows out of an intuitive and imaginative market vision. NPD implies a continuous development of innovations through early and intensive communication between the different units of concept generation, product planning, engineering, production, and suppliers. Cycles of problem solving overlap, and problems are solved quickly at every stage to respond to continuously changing data. Critical assets such as tools and prototypes are generated rapidly (Clark & Fujimoto, 1990).

The product becomes an extract of the company. The way it is designed reflects upon the idea the company has of itself. The product is, then, the image of the way the company represents itself to the market. To structure the offer is to structure the company.

Example: Kanebo, a Japanese textile firm, divides its marketing department in two: one that handles the "pull" or demand marketing, directed by an executive with a marketing background, and one that handles the "push" marketing, directed by an engineer in research and development. Each department has multidisciplinary teams that include designers, illustrating how a company can integrate the contradictory logics of technology and marketing.

Outside of the classic company models of "technology driven" or "market driven" is another company type that is "interaction driven." This type of company questions society, defines a universal want, and proposes an offer that "revolutionizes" the market. Design is used to inject intelligence into the company offer: It is centered on the interaction between the subject and object. From the earliest phase of the design process on, the role innovation will play in the social imagination is envisioned.

In sum, the offer is seen as training through making: by making products, the company learns how to learn (Hetzel, 1994).

Concept Generation Methods and Testing

The concept generation method is a five-step base from which designers can develop and refine their problem-solving strategies (Ulrich & Eppinger, 2000).

1. Clarify the problem.

   * Understand the problem
   * Deconstruct the problem
   * Focus on critical subproblems

2. Search externally.

   * Find leading potential users of proposed product

- Search for experts on the problem
- Research patents already dealing with the problem
- Read literature on the problem
- Benchmark on similar problems

3. Search internally.

- Individual
- Group

4. Explore systematically.

- Classification tree
- Combination table

5. Reflect on the solutions and the process.

- Constructive feedback

Finally, the concept should be selected and tested. Concept selection is the process of evaluating concepts with respect to customer needs and other criteria, comparing the relative strengths and weaknesses of the concepts, and selecting one or more concepts for further investigation.

Successful design is facilitated by structured concept selection, often performed using two methods. Both methods follow a six-step process: prepare the list of concepts, rate them, rank them, combine and improve them, select one or more, and reflect on the results and the process.

- "Concept screening" uses a reference concept to evaluate concept variants against selection criteria and a comparison system to narrow the range of concepts under consideration.
- "Concept scoring" uses different reference points for each criterion.

DESIGN AS INTEGRATOR

IT IS NECESSARY TO MAKE A DELIBERATE EFFORT in order to integrate consumers in new product development, and to better follow the market it is necessary to anticipate it. During the design cycle, the designer integrates customer requirement information gathered by management, the design principles' requirements, and customer requirement information gathered locally by designers into a new design model (Bailetti & Litva, 1995).

The key factor in superior innovation is to take into account customer requirements in all company functions. This entails the diffusion of market information to all areas and efficient interfunctional coordination (Hayes, 1990). Design is valued because, through its outputs (sketches, roughs, mock-ups, and prototypes), it concretizes customer information and facilitates the participation of all company levels in the creation of a market-oriented culture.

The adaptation of the product to its environment also remains a dominant key factor in innovation success. This adaptation determines how the product will do in the market, which points to the fact that there is an "ecological theory" of innovation. The innovation must provoke the customer's enthusiasm, so the mentality of the design manager must shift from a farmer's to a hunter's mentality.

The user-centered design innovation process develops a process-oriented management. The logic of the quality moves from product quality toward the quality of the company. A healthy design innovation policy will do its best to:

- Implement a clear market-oriented strategy
- Intertwine competencies and processes in order to improve customer knowledge
- Focalize the customer-supplier chain on the added value brought to the final customer
- Establish the customer-supplier relationship
- Focus on causes and prevention of risks in management decisions
- Develop the continuous improvement of transversal processes such as user satisfaction
- Consider the final customer as the judge

Process-oriented management gives the customer the power to be the unique judge of the benefits he or she receives and the level of perceived quality. Indifferent to the technical sophistication of the product, users often discern its value through design features (Moody [DP], 1982).

One reinvents the marketing function around two types of positions:

1. Experts on marketing methods
2. Integrators who are responsible for piloting company activities and identifying new potential segments.

Designers, then, are either specialists or integrators.

Innovation success, especially incremental innovation, stems from the integration of all tools and routines. Design managers should develop a design process that:

- Builds on routines that act as "integrator tools"—that is, decision-making routines that help keep everyone and everything integrated—constantly improving upon them, since these routines are a recognizable competitive advantage (Bessant & Caffyn, 1997).
- Enriches innovation tools in order to transform them into a dynamic, continuous, iterative, and informative process (Hughes & Chafin, 1996).

Design and R&D Management: Radical Innovation

No one can evade technology. The new substantive theory contends that technology has become not only necessary, but has also become inconspicuous, if not invisible. Technology management now has a more systemic and holistic orientation

(Badawy, 1996). It applies to all activities and technical processes, administrative and interpersonal. Its systemic and holistic nature calls for a designer's expertise.

Design management is part of R&D management because any design project involves technological diagnoses and decision making (Cooper et al., 1995). The management of technology looks at technological resources and their applications from all sides. Design develops new applications for existing technologies.

There are four types of technology that will be predominant in society by 2025: information technology, genetics, material technology, and environmental and energy technology (Coates, 1997). Obviously, design has no relation to the emergence of these technologies but has a lot to do with the societal acceptance of them. Too often, technological innovations are launched because they are available rather than needed.

DESIGN AND THE TECHNOLOGICAL POSITIONING OF THE COMPANY

DESIGN INNOVATION VARIES according to the company's technological positioning in its sector and its technological strategy.

Design and Technological Strategy

The relationship between technology and strategy explains the nature of design innovation:

- If strategy capitalizes on technology with no direct interaction between the two, design strategy is directed toward the social acceptance of technology.
- If strategy cultivates technology, the implemented strategy nourishes the future capacities of the company with R&D investment and design is devoted to R&D return on investment.
- If strategy emerges from technology, technology is the source of design strategy.

According to the company's technological strategy, the focus of design innovation will differ in:

- Technological leadership: design strategy will focus on creativity
- Follower policy: design strategy will focus on the users' needs
- "Me-too" manufacturing: design will focus on the capacity to produce (Holt, 1991).

A company approaches R&D management in two different ways:

1. The defense of its technological advancement (retention)
2. The sharing of its technological knowledge (diffusion), while hoping to impose a standard

The diffusion policy implies permanent capability of creative destruction and calls for design expertise.

Design and Life Cycle Technology

Design innovation depends on the life cycle of the technology in the industry (Walsh, 1995) and the company's balanced portfolio of technologies. Design ideas for differentiating technology will be different if the focus is on incremental or radical innovation.

According to Arthur D. Little, a well-known strategy consulting firm, there are four technologies in an industry:

1. The basic technology necessary for a company to exist in the industry
2. Key technology that has a competitive impact and stems from differentiation possibilities
3. Emerging technology in the experimental phase that has a strong differentiation potential
4. "Embryo" technology in the research phase that has uncertain but promising differentiation potential

A company can choose continuity in R&D policy or look for radical change. Technology in an industry follows a dynamic of alternative phases of radical and incremental innovation and phases in the evolution of products versus processes.

Phase one: Product innovations are frequent and process innovations less frequent.

Phase two: Innovation rhythm diminishes. Products evolve toward a "dominant design," but process innovation accelerates.

Phase three: Product and process are strongly interdependent. Increasing process efficiency rigidifies product innovation.

DESIGN AND TECHNOLOGY DIFFUSION

MANAGEMENT RECOGNIZES THE IMPORTANCE OF DESIGN for the technological evolution of the transfer of technology from one industry to another and the diffusion of technology (Hargadon, 1997, 1998).

Designers as "Knowledge Brokers"

Research conducted at IDEO, a leading design agency, revealed that design can play a significant role in the transfer of technology and that the designer often plays the role of "technology broker." A technology broker depends on his or her network and the company memory in the process of cross-pollination. Past technology is useful information for future designs. Research from thirty projects with technical solutions incorporated from other industries developed a model for design contribution:

> As technological access. The deficit in information exchange between industries made IDEO designers discover technical solutions that were potentially valid but had been "invisible" because they had been developed in other industries. Industries tend to look only within their own fields for innovations.

- As a learning process. The designers bring these technical solutions to the company memory for potential use in future projects.
- As idea storage. These potential technical solutions remain in memory until other design projects come along and can benefit from them.
- As idea extraction. Designers working on new products extract technical solutions from the company memory and appropriate forms to fit new combinations they create.
- As results. Designers create design solutions that are new combinations of existing solutions.

This has implications in IDEO strategic management of the design agency. IDEO recommends, in its methodological guide, that its designers create opportunities in order to expand the IDEO network and their knowledge of the industry. The recruiting of new designers also takes into account the role of technology broker.

Designers as Technology Infusers

In our postmodern world, social strengths determine technological and organizational change (Sweeney, 1996). Designers can help in avoiding the determinisms of the past where technical and organizational innovations were the only issue. The most widely distributed technological knowledge, and, therefore, the most accessible to consumers, is contained in the object itself (Boisot et al., 1995). The product is a system, a matrix of components that combines functions and technologies used into one unit; it puts all the agents of the company together (Maisseu, 1995). The implementation of new technology is a training process. For Schumpeter, technology is a knowledge set contained in objects, documents, or the minds of certain individuals.

JOHN MAEDA, 2002

"The Aesthetics and Computation Group was founded at the MIT Media Laboratory in 1996 as an experimental research studio dedicated to synthesizing a closer dialogue between design and technology. It performs research in developing paradigms for deconstructing digital tools and environments. The Design By Numbers project demonstrates a system for teaching basic computer science concepts to a primarily visual audience. . . . Only by regaining control of technology can design and art establish a safe and relevant future for humanity."

Designers are valuable because they can help train others in technological strategies. And by helping to implement new technology, they favor organizational change (Levin, 1997). According to Rogers (1995) and the innovation diffusion model, consumers adopt different strategies when faced with a new technology, as either early adopters or rejecters. Innovation in design makes it less likely people will assume that new technology is always beneficial.

Toward a "Dominant Design"

Any innovation has a dual economic and managerial impact on the company: It improves the competitiveness of the company's products and transforms its capacities (Afuah, 1998). Innovation transforms capacities, and this change can be either conservative (by reinforcing existing capacities or happening incrementally) or destabilizing (radically transforming the company, and even destroying its capacities). The importance of innovation in the competitive game depends on its "transilience," i.e., its capacity to modify and redefine the resources, competencies, and know-how of the company (Abernathy & Clark, 1988).

Authors Abernathy and Clark classify innovation according to its effect on competition:

- Structural innovation creates new market relations but requires new knowledge. Often the consequence of a technological rupture, it is the best barrier against imitation.
- Revolutionary innovation reinforces the links between the company and its markets by technologically offering new solutions to satisfy existing needs.
- Niche-oriented innovation relies on existing technologies but creates new market relations.
- Routine innovation is the most frequent form and improves the performance of existing products.

One can classify design innovation according to the new knowledge it generates:

1. Knowledge about product components
2. Structural knowledge about the links between product components

The more radical an innovation is, the more the company will want to turn to outside experts and technology facilitators, such as designers, in order to manage innovation.

The integration of a new technology into an industry is a dynamic process of constructing a "dominant design." A dominant design is one which the major components and underlying concepts do not vary substantially from one model to another. This process follows two phases:

1. Technological and market uncertainty, during which various designs are tested and competition is based on product attributes
2. "Dominant design emergence," during which emphasis is placed on process innovation

The more complex the innovation, the more important the role nontechnical factors (such as commercial ones) play in the innovation success and the higher the risk of seeing the new design fail.

Hence the importance for the designer to instill customer-oriented technology management. Rather than understanding design, design the understanding.

> "An innovation's design is *robust* when its arrangement of concrete details are immediately effective in locating the novel product or process within the familiar world. . . . Prospective innovators must carefully choose designs that couch some features in the familiar, present others as new, and keep others hidden from view."

Designers work toward the acceptance of technology by the customers, but customers are likely to have paradoxical responses to innovations in technology. These responses are likely to provoke conflict and ambivalence, and stimulate anxiety and stress. They arouse strong negative emotions that trigger an assortment of coping strategies for customers: avoidance or confrontation (Mick, 1998).

DESIGN AND MODULAR STRUCTURE

THE TOYOTA PRODUCTION MODEL, or "lean production" model, for example, constitutes the reference model for the automobile industry, in which design has acquired a specific role. In order to maintain cost reduction, companies have discovered that volume is not the only potential source of economizing. There exist other ways to economize in the design of the nonvisible parts of the vehicle.

The emerging model of flexible production was at first an answer to changes in consumer demand, but the flexibility of production is more and more a modification of interrelational structures between companies and product architecture.

A new organizational structure has emerged: the "modular" production structure. Numerous industries have shifted the modularity of the production process toward the design phase (Baldwin & Clark, 1997). A few examples include:

- In the automobile industry, different parts are manufactured in different places, then collected on an assembly line.
- In the computer industry, a company like Dell has shifted its base to a modular structure.

A modular structure is one in which each functional element of the product is implemented by exactly one physical element and in which there are well-defined interactions between the elements. Such a structure allows a design change to be made in terms of one element without requiring a change to other elements for the product to function correctly (Ulrich & Eppinger, 2000).

The adoption of this new modular design model increases the rate of innovation in a market by developing new market segmentation. Modularity develops innovation, but also increases the degree of uncertainty in the design process, which is a challenge for design. It diminishes design, production, and distribution costs, generates a wide variety of products, develops "technologically rich" products, and puts products more quickly on the market (Sanchez, 2000).

In the classic system, creation revolves around product attributes defined by market research. In the modular system, the product structure is conceived as a means of leveraging product and process variations. These changes modify the types of knowledge from a "know-how" (practical understanding of how the system works) to a "know-why" (theoretical understanding of why the system functions). The tie between these two types of knowledge permits the innovation of a "know-what."

A modular structure requires another type of design management: If interface specifications are a component, there will be less need for teams or experts, since designers can take care of interfaces. The role of the design manager will be to encourage the articulation of new knowledge and to codify its architecture.

For marketing, modularity permits the management of change by allowing common elements to be used within a certain range of products. The coordination of market segmentation with modular product structures and processes increases the potential for market segmentation. Modularity changes the objective of creation. Rather than conceiving products, design conceives *platforms* (Sanchez, 1999).

RADICAL INNOVATION:
A NEW MODEL FOR DESIGN MANAGEMENT

IT IS DIFFICULT FOR A WELL-ESTABLISHED COMPANY to generate radical innovation, which often makes the success of new entrants in an industry. The routine inertia tends to limit managers' visions of what is technologically possible (Ehrnberg & Jacobsson, 1996). Design plays a different role according to the type of innovation:

- For a new concept or radical innovation, design gives higher priority to the training of the consumer and the staff.
- For a static product or incremental innovation, design focuses on brand reputation and after-sales service (Hollins & Stuart, 1990).

Radical innovations change the criteria consumers use in evaluating a product and may generate resistance to the new product. Aesthetics can either reduce or increase the acceptance of a product (Veryzer, 1998) and its purchase potential (Looschilder et al., 1995).

The involvement of industrial design (ID) expertise in new product development suggests a very different picture of ID's role. An IDSA report in 1999 indicates that many industrial groups enter the NPD process very early and play an important role in the initial product planning. Most research and development managers, however, underestimate the importance of ID in the success of these new products. For them, ID plays a limited role in the early stages of the design process.

One of the most important aspects of the development process for these discontinuous projects is the role the prototype plays. Most often in new product development, design activities precede the development of a prototype. For discontinuous products, prototypes that demonstrate technical feasibility play a key role in gaining formal recognition and support. This early emphasis on prototype building and focus on technical challenges results in delaying ID activities until later in the process. ID comes in basically when one is starting to talk about "embodiments." The prototype sent to ID is sent as a "proof of concept," but has zero "ease of use."

ID, therefore, ends up designing a brand new system. In contrast to R&D managers, design managers point out the importance of the role played by ID in valid customer research for radical innovation. Given the challenges of discontinuous NPD and the reality that many critical user interfaces may be determined during the development phase when the product is in the hands of R&D managers, there is a need to better integrate ID considerations into the process earlier on. One way to accomplish this in a high-uncertainty environment is to focus early in the design process on benefit- and consumption-pattern discontinuities (Veryzer, 2000a).

Radical or discontinuous products involve new management models because of the uncertainty throughout the course of their development. *Radical Innovation* (Leifer et al., 2000) relates research conducted on discontinuous products launched by a wide range of different companies (Air Products, Analog Devices, DuPont, General Electric, General Motors, IBM, Nortel Networks, Otis Elevator, Polaroid, and Texas Instruments). The book describes the differences between the two management models and gives design management a new path for future improvement (Table 6.4). In order to enhance their capacity for radical innovation, these companies use methods that are appropriate for design managers:

- For reducing organizational and resource uncertainty by establishing a radical innovation hub, benchmarking, and radical innovation project advisory boards
- For developing radical innovation competency: radical innovation transition teams, and internal venture capital companies (Leifer et al., 2000)

The experience of design managers can be useful for managers facing increasing uncertainty. The role of design is not so much the problem resolution as the interpretation of the new situation (Lester et al., 1998). The interpretative manager, or design manager, considers ambiguity and improvisation to be part of innovation (Wheelwright, 1992).

IMPROVING THE NPD PROCESS THROUGH DESIGN

THE SUCCESS OF COMPETITIVE COMPANIES resides in the close links they have been able to establish between marketing and R&D in both a permanent and flexible way. The integration of functions during the innovation process and, in particular, the R&D/marketing interface is fundamental to solving complex projects (Johne & Snelson, 1998). It is, therefore, important to develop a climate in the company that fosters interfunctional cooperation (Griffing & Hauser, 1996).

	INCREMENTAL	RADICAL
PROJECT TIMELINE	*Short term: months to two years*	*Long term: ten years or more*
TRAJECTORY	*Linear and continuous path*	*Path with multiple discontinuities and gaps to bridge*
IDEA GENERATION	*Front end*	*Sporadically throughout the life cycle*
PROCESS	*Formal approved*	*Formal for funding but treated with disdain by participants*
BUSINESS MODEL	*Complete and detailed at the beginning*	*Business model evolves through discovery-based techniques as uncertainty is reduced*
PLAYERS	*Cross-functional team*	*Cross-functional individuals who come and go in a network that grows around the project*
ORGANIZATIONAL STRUCTURE	*Cross-functional team in a business unit*	*Starts in R&D in an incubating organization, then changes into a goal-driven project organization*
RESOURCES AND COMPETENCIES	*All the competencies required and subject to standard resource allocation*	*Creativity and skill in resource and competency acquisition*
OPERATING UNIT INVOLVEMENT	*Involved from the beginning*	*Informal*

Table 6.4. Comparing Incremental and Radical Innovation Management (Leifer et al., 2000, p. 19)

Coordinating NPD through Design

Cooperation and communication between R&D and marketing functions increase chances of success (Griffin & Hauser, 1996). As we explained earlier, the design process is, in essence, a cross-functional process, integrating constraints from both R&D and marketing. In innovation management, it has the consequence of developing a cross-functional team management of innovation. This coordinating value of design has been well documented. A recent study demonstrates design increasing cross-functional integration in high-tech companies (Rioche, 2002). The research conducted on 185 French high-tech companies shows:

- ❧ A direct correlation between the existence of a design function in a given company and the importance given to design in the company
- ❧ In companies where design is given high importance, it is perceived as a factor favoring transfunctional collaborations
- ❧ A direct correlation between the importance given to design management and being quality certified

Obstacles to communication and cooperation are numerous:

- Personality and cultural barriers, in terms of intolerance of ambiguity, problems of language, organizational barriers, and physical barriers.
- Loosely defined roles, lack of communication, lack of multidisciplinary teams.
- A deficit in design management, leading to slow responses from designers, marketing misunderstanding the design process, low mutual respect between marketing and design, and production not being well integrated with design (Cooper et al., 1994).

Design helps to overcome integration barriers by creating transversal teams, increasing communications, encouraging learning from other disciplines, and fostering a common culture.

Design is interdependent on both R&D and marketing. There are fewer conflicts if integration entails more group interaction. Interaction is influenced by the perception of dependence in order to achieve the tasks. The more a function believes it depends on another function, the more important interaction is, causing resources to flow across functional borders.

DOROTHY LEONARD BARTON, 1991

"Physical representation of the product under development spans the language boundaries between disciplines. First, such models represent the emerging product in a relatively neutral language. Second, such models serve as integrating mechanisms communicating a consistent message of product/process meaning to the team and unifying it."

To succeed, design management needs to:

- Promote integration as its objective, keep creativity flowing, and encourage networking
- Use the communicated information and transactions through functions and process coordination to solve conflicts

To this end, visualization and rapid prototyping are the most valued tools, but other decisions are also important: relocation, staff changes, the casualness of the social system, the organizational structure, rewards, a formalized integrative decision-making process, etc.

THE LOGICS OF INNOVATION AND DESIGN

DESIGN INPUT ON IMPROVING THE NPD PROCESS is measured by three variables: reducing time to market, networking innovation, and improving the learning process (Table 6.5).

THE IMPACT OF DESIGN PROCESS ON INNOVATION

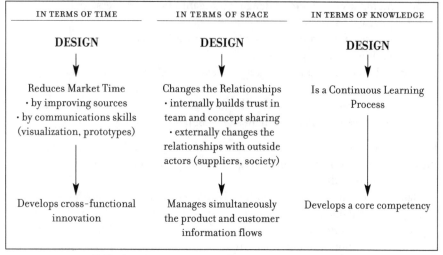

IN TERMS OF TIME	IN TERMS OF SPACE	IN TERMS OF KNOWLEDGE
DESIGN ↓	**DESIGN** ↓	**DESIGN** ↓
Reduces Market Time • by improving sources • by communications skills (visualization, prototypes) ↓	Changes the Relationships • internally builds trust in team and concept sharing • externally changes the relationships with outside actors (suppliers, society) ↓	Is a Continuous Learning Process ↓
Develops cross-functional innovation	Manages simultaneously the product and customer information flows	Develops a core competency

Table 6.5. Improving the NPD Process through Design

ROBERT HAYES, 1988

"Four themes shape the behavior of the truly superior manufacturing company:

❧ Management makes the difference
❧ A holistic perspective is essential
❧ Customer value and competitive advantage should be relentlessly pursued
❧ Continual learning and improvement is the objective"

The impact of the design process on the logics of innovation can be organized under three headings: time, space, and learning.

Design and the NPD Stage/Gate Process

The design process is a stage process similar to the classic NPD process model: the Stage-Gate process, with which it mixes easily (Table 6.6). This model breaks the new product project into discrete and identifiable stages. Each stage:

❧ Consists of a set of parallel activities undertaken by people from different functional areas
❧ Is designed to gather information needed to advance the project to the new gate, or decision point
❧ Is cross-functional: no stage is owned by a functional area or department

The process is, at the same time, a dual managerial and consumer process, a sub-process of managerial decisions, and consumer response measurement.

PHASES/GATES	STAGE-GATE™ (COOPER)	TEAM KEY ACTIVITIES	DESIGN IN NPD (ULRICH & EPPINGER)
BEGIN STEP 1 STOP OR GO ON TO:	Ideation	Initial screening	Exploration · Consider product plat- form and architecture · Assess new technolo- gies and needs
STEP 2 STOP OR GO ON TO:	Preliminary investigation	Market assessment Technical assessment Business assessment	Concept development · Investigate feasibility of product concepts · Develop industrial design concepts · Build and test experi- mental prototypes
STEP 3 STOP OR GO ON TO:	Detailed investigation (ends with business case)	Market research · User needs and wants studies · Value in use studies Competitive analysis Concept testing Detailed technical assessment Manufacturing appraisals Detailed financial analysis	System level design · Generate alternative architectures · Define major sub- systems and interfaces · Refine industrial design
STEP 4 STOP OR GO ON TO:	Development (money gate)	Product development	Detail design · Define part geometry · Choose materials · Assign tolerances · Complete ID documentation
STEP 5 STOP OR GO ON TO:	Testing and validation	In-house product testing Customer test of products Market test	Testing · Reliability test · Life testing · Performance testing · Regulatory approvals · Implement design changes
STEP 6	Market launch	Trial production Precommercialization Business analysis Production start-up Market launch	Production ramp-up · Evaluate early production output

Table 6.6. The Stage-Gate™ Process (adapted from Cooper, 1998)

The design process can shorten the length of the NPD process through its source-finding and communication activities, which include:

    ❁ Seeking out external sources, and finding and networking with new specialized suppliers

* Organizing peer review groups to assess prototypes or visual outputs in order to better define product strategy

Reducing design time must be a priority for the design function. Process speed is a new norm of company efficiency: Since demand is not foreseeable, it is a waste of time and resources to spend the company's creative efforts on abstract market research. What is necessary is to proceed as in a poker game: to put the product on the market and "pay to see."

Design influences half the total development time. The leverage effect can be high if the design group changes its ways of operating. For example, at BMW, though the company has always prided itself in its handcraftsmanship, this question was asked: To what extent should new design technology drive design? The result was the redesign of the development process using digital design expertise. Different design tasks could now be carried out simultaneously, so "virtual cars" could be tested at the same time as ongoing activities. Pruning was now unnecessary, since physical prototyping could be done digitally, and any remaining design changes could be completed more quickly.

The sequential innovation model is completed by simultaneous engineering and design activities developed in parallel to improve the holistic approach and overlap tasks. In order to make concept building more feasible, designers work alongside production engineers, and alongside communications and advertising. This keeps the engineers from appropriating the concept of concurrent engineering and dissociating NPD from strategy.

The success of simultaneous engineering stems from methodologies in Japan (Barkan, 1991). This holistic approach is a direct result of the design process and consistent with the instability of any creative process. In this approach, teams organize themselves to work alone, and at different points, they intersect with other teams to transfer knowledge (Takeuchi & Nonaka, 1986).

The process looks like a rugby match, in which the ball passes from one to the other in the middle of the scrum while it moves in block on the land. This "rugby" approach between engineering, sales, marketing, and design functions is used in companies like Fuji, Xerox, and Honda, where design management principles aim at the coordination and promotion of innovation. This raises the status of design and gives it a human-centered design philosophy, as in Sony, Ricoh, and Sharp (Cooper & Press, 1997).

The difference between "total design" and simultaneous engineering is based in interfunctional communication. In this new approach, the design process becomes a circle in which the designer or design manager remains the champion of the product (Hollins, 1995). Design should reinforce innovation, viewing it in a problem-solving perspective, which can be achieved by:

* Effective project-to-project knowledge transfer; using "post-mortem" records of past projects as a resource
* Rapid problem solving; using advanced technologies and computer simulation to allow for faster problem-solving cycles

Example: At Toyota, a systematic effort to front-load the development process has shifted problem identification to earlier stages of product development (Thomke & Fujimoto, 2000).

STEPHAN THOMKE AND TAKAHIRO FUJIMOTO, 2000

"We started our discussion by describing product development as a bundle of problem solving cycles. We introduce the concept of front-loading problem solving which we define as a strategy that seeks to increase development performance by shifting the identification and solving of design problems to earlier phases of a product development process."

Innovation Design as a "Space" System

The link between enhanced innovation performance and more efficient group coherence signals the need for design managers with a high level of responsibility (Holland, 1995) in creating both an internal and external innovation "space." In this way, innovation is viewed as a social scheme. Design creates an internal space or team for innovation. It helps management decompartmentalize functions and implement project management.

Example: The Renault Twingo is a good example of design's role in the modification of the organizational structure (Le Quement, 1994). The Twingo project closed the gap separating two generations of project organization: that used before 1988 and the newer organization consisting of project managers in senior management. In the spring of 1990, a new organization was implemented that consisted of a "functional group" with the objective of forcing interprofessional communication and improving the mastering of the program, according to the three criteria that constitute "the golden triangle of project control: quality, costs, deadlines." The car was divided into approximately thirty subsystems and project groups. The project director formalized contracts with the different professions in order to seal engagements and consolidate them: "We want involved actors, not consultants" (Midler, 1993).

Around the project director, a team is constituted of project chiefs that represent all the specialists who will be working on the project, including those in design. The project director, however, is independent of functions or professions. He or she coordinates the efforts of all participants. Instead of being built upon a power hierarchy, the team is built upon a network structure. Cooperation and mutual power delegation replaces relationships based on rivalry and authority.

In the modern approach to project management, the project leader is a person of influence who is unconnected to operational hierarchy. The project director must understand the "big picture," the multiple project risks, and create a team spirit between the visible team and the invisible "virtual" team of project partners. A good project director is a catalyst who must:

- Explore new combinations and information acquisition that reduces uncertainty

❦ Make decisions that help the innovation affirm itself progressively,
by reducing alternative options

The design manager organizes working methods in the design department in order to set up an integrated model of innovation management in the company as a whole. This model means managing together, in design management, *the process of communication* and *the process of production.* The objective is to develop concept sharing and mutual confidence at every stage or loop in the project cycle. This integrative conceptual involvement requires multidisciplinary competencies. Education predestines both designers and architects to this role (Lebahar, 1994). There is an evolution from a very controlled, linear model of innovation, with tasks that require little expertise, toward a new model, where the major tasks are team-work, competency-building, interchangeability of tasks, and the capacity to self-govern. Finally, the most important issue is to build trust (Rhodes et al., 1995).

The common space grows out of the combined expertise of the various people involved in the NPD process, and their search for consensus and compromise when the process encounters incompatible constraints. Design teams and centers develop organic structures that share information and center around the customer rather than the function (Olson et al., 1995). One way to enhance the interdependence and sharing of diverse project participants is to have them all work together in the same physical space and on "intermediary objects."

For example, at IDEO, building teams and trust is essential. The company co-locates people who will need to interact, creating "hot studio" passion by recruiting crazy characters, budgeting in t-shirts as "metaphors in motion," and building communities to foster innovation. Intermediate objects, such as models provided by computer assisted design (CAD), help in the development of a cooperative dynamic. This means that interface is now less and less a question of understanding the other expertise and more and more a question of confrontation about a common "work in progress." Integral NPD development is rooted in both an intertwined physical/informational system and in high internal/external integration, like integrated supplier linkage. Intensive, early, and ongoing communication with a number of first-tier parts suppliers effectively speeds the procurement of prototype parts and improves product integration.

DR. ROBIN ROY, 1996

"The trend toward organizing design, development, and manufacture via supply chains and buyer-supplier relationships poses major challenges for design management. For companies such as service operators or equipment end-users (like airline companies) the supplier designs fully devolved designs, which can be an effective option. This approach is not suited to manufacturing organizations further down the supply chain whose main function is the design and development of product components; for these a mix of in-house design and partnerships with key suppliers is the best combination."

The question is the extended "space" given to the innovation project: spreading the group outside the company to supplier design teams, or the extent to which the company outputs its design work to outside designers. External design allows external arbitrations between different functions, reduces the power of technology in decision making, and reinforces creativity in the innovation process. Optimizing the "space" of innovation becomes a managerial issue concerning the efficiency of innovation. It means applying the concepts developed by the "transaction cost theory" (Williamson, 1999) to design outsourcing practices, with outside designers seen as long-term partners, not short-term interim subcontractors. For example, an issue like the specificity of assets generated by design projects entails making explicit contract terms with external design partners.

The *externalization of design in product innovation* is a new fundamental direction for design management. It is certainly one of the most interesting topics in building a competitive advantage through design management.

MICHAEL PIORE AND RICHARD LESTER

Massachusetts Institute of Technology, 2001

"It may be that innovative activity is becoming increasingly dependent upon these 'public' conversational communities and less upon the 'private' spaces with large firms."

Finally, design acts as an interface between the consumer, the society at large, and the company, and its value is to widen the external space of innovation. Design is integrated into this system by which agents coming from different departments of the company and outside persons actively collaborate toward a common objective. Innovation space is less and less limited to the company and more and more open to interactions between the "form" and society. These interactions transform the innovation all through the NPD process. The idea transforms itself progressively through a series of experimentations that confront it with society at large.

This new model, the "sociological model of innovation" (Ackrich, Callon, & Latour, 1988), insists on the various changes and discontinuities in the innovation development through the interactions between the NPD team, its outputs (roughs, ideas, prototypes), and the various social communities. Though in the literature both models (linear and sociological) reject each other, in fact, their opposition is artificial. The "whirl," or sociological, model is more adaptable to radical innovation, and the linear model is more appropriate for incremental innovation.

The view points are complementary: The manager will be interested in setting up an NPD process that serves the customer and works with the structure of the company. The sociological model is interested in looking into the mechanisms that make the market and society accept the innovation. But this sociological model of "conversational communities" has the great advantage of insisting on the necessity of integrating external professionals into the NPD process in order to simultaneously build the market and innovation. The value of designers for the managers is they frequently and intuitively ask for external expertise in design decisions, such as testing design options with expert consumers.

Innovation process improvement might encourage developing strong relationships with MBA programs and design schools (though that might be difficult because there are very few university campuses that provide both; in the United States, there are only two: Carnegie Mellon and Michigan State) and spreading the pioneering programs at MIT and Rhode Island School of Design in cross-functional product development into business schools.

Design and the Learning Process of Innovation

Innovation is a competitive advantage if innovations are introduced at a steady rhythm. In such a context, the ability to rapidly transform scientific development into innovation is a fundamental necessity. The dynamic of core-competency building in the company is that of building new knowledge capacities, both of individuals and the company.

It is obvious that designers build new knowledge. It is their everyday "bread and butter." Design is a continuous process; it is, therefore, reasonable to keep design teams together in one place long after the product launch (Whitney, 1988) and to develop methods to infuse design knowledge into the company. In order to operate successfully, one has to internalize knowledge. In a competition driven by innovation, a company must be able to assimilate the new information produced by the professionals on its development team (Nonaka & Konno, 1998).

What is important is the notion of continuous cultural change (Ingram & Heppenstall, 1996). Although managers routinely review their product development processes to ensure that each is achieving its objectives, they seldom review the development process itself to improve upon its shortcomings. Any design project that only produces an excellent product on time and within budget has only obtained half of the total possible benefit. Process reviews are beneficial to produce data that support process change. The objective is to continuously learn how to do the job better, faster, or more effectively. Companies that do well view learning and improving their development processes as an integral part of business activity (Smith, 1996).

The key design management issues are:

1. The organization of project reporting methods; the selection of a professional whose mission is to spread learning; and the organization of the collective dimension of knowledge through design.
2. The redefinition of the hierarchy of competence centered around the function of learning and production of knowledge.
3. The linking of projects to an overall objective of design competency, so that the knowledge gained in any one process can be used in future design development.

CONCLUSION

✿ Innovation's key success factors can be attained through design innovation, creating a better product, and improving the quality of the NPD process.

✿ Innovation's key success factors can be attained through design innovation, creating a better product and improving the quality of the NPD process.

✿ Design develops a conceptual dimension of idea generation, concept development, and the concept as integrator.

✿ Design management is an NPD development process centered on the consumer.

✿ Design plays a role in the management of the technology; the designer is a "knowledge broker," and design becomes "modular."

✿ Radical innovation requires a different NPD process.

✿ Design management develops coordination through design process:

- Communication through visualization.
- Using a formal stage-gate process for design decision making alongside concurrent engineering.
- A strong project team leader is preferred to create trust and confidence sharing.
- Innovation space is created through internal and external professional networks like suppliers and practitioner communities.
- Design innovation is a continual learning process.

CHAPTER 7

DESIGN AND STRATEGY:
TRANSFORMATION THROUGH DESIGN

T
o manage design at a strategic level is to manage the contribution of design to the strategy formulation process: to define the responsibility and leadership assigned to design and its contribution to the organizational culture, search for opportunities for design innovations, and multiply demonstrations of identity through design. This third level of design management establishes links between design, corporate communications, and top management.

INTRODUCTION:
THE TWO MODELS OF DESIGN STRATEGIC POSITIONING

THERE ARE TWO MODELS OF DESIGN strategic positioning: the "innate" and the "acquired."

The "Innate" Model

This model grows out of organizations that consider design a core competency from the start of the company. Design is part of the founder's entrepreneurial scheme. Examples of this "innate" strategic role of design include all companies that have been founded by a designer-entrepreneur in fashion, textiles, distribution, or furniture, such as Marimekko, Habitat, Ikea, Herman Miller, Cassina, and Castelli, as well as Alessi, Braun, Olivetti, and Apple in other sectors. All of these companies have in common a global design strategy with a design spirit that penetrates all organization processes—the entire value chain, from product to communications.

ALBERTO ALESSI, 1998

"Alessi was founded in 1921 by Giovanni, my grandfather, a real stickler for quality who won acclaim for quality workmanship and perfect-finish coffee pots and trays. Design as we know it now made its first appearance with my father Carlo, trained as an industrial designer. He joined the company when he was still very young and dedicated himself to design from the start.

"Uncle Ettore joined my father in 1945. I affectionately refer to him as our 'mega-technical director.' As head of the technical department in 1955 he opened Alessi up to collaboration with external designers.

"Officially my career at Alessi began in July 1970, the day after I graduated in law. With a truly utopian view of 'multiplied art,' I developed my own brand of cultural theoretic manifesto, championing a new commercial civilization offering the consuming masses veritable artistic items at low prices. Franco Sargiani and Eija Helander are the first designers I brought to Alessi. Ettore Sottsass came in 1972 at Sargiani's invitation. It was with him that I began talking over the 'high' topics of design, the role of industry in society. In 1978 he came up with our condiment set, one of our best designs that comes close to industry standards. He recommended Richard Sapper. 'He is the Tizio lamp guy, the guy that has never done a bad design.' Sapper has designed some items which have become historic not just in design terms but for Alessi's economic fortunes, like the 'whistle' kettle (1982).

"Then we worked with Achille Castiglioni, Alessandro Mendini, Aldo Rossi, Michael Graves, Philippe Starck, Stefano Giovannoni, and Guido Venturini.... The Alessi Museum opened in 1998 to reinforce our 'meta' project outlook and production policy."

The "Experience" Model

The model of "acquired" design or of design learned by experience, as in Sony or Philips, shows a progressive valorization of design in the company. For Sony, this valorization is linked to the personality of one of the founders, Akio Morita, and followed the launch of the Walkman in the 1980s, created by a project team called the PP Design Center (Product, Presentation, Proposal, Promotion), which regrouped more than 130 designers. Since 1984, this design center has been organized according to consumer logic and not by product categories.

Strategic Design at Philips

Although Philips cannot be considered a design leader, design is part of its strategic policy. In the postwar period, the changing pattern of the company was reflected in the organization of the design function headed by Louis Kalff, director of the product division. Little evidence exists regarding the early internal structure, but the product group had draftsmen and used outside consultants, including Raymond Loewy, who collaborated on the Philips electric razor.

In 1953, the Artistic Propaganda department (at Philips, the precursor of the design department) was split into two product sections. Its head was Rein Veersema, an architect trained at Delft University. He set out to develop design competency in such areas as ergonomics and pricing, so that designers could reinforce their case. In 1961, he developed his idea of industrial design as the "unification of both aesthetic and scientific refinement." One of the most important aspects of his work was "the creation of a Philips family feature."

Knut Yran from Norway was appointed director of design in 1966. A man of powerful convictions who believed completely in the value of design, he introduced many initiatives that profoundly changed the role and nature of design at Philips. By 1969, he had completed an organizational structure for the Concern Industrial Design Center (CIDC) with established control over the designers and a method of systematic planning: the "design track." He defined a new house style for Philips based on a manual launched in 1973, and supervised the dissemination of information on design theory and practice through the journal *Design Signals*.

In the late 1980s, Robert Blaich was appointed managing director of CIDC. In order to make design a permanent factor in Philips's future competitive advantage, he proposed a strategy with four major elements: design policy, design management, improved professional design standards, and equal partnership of design in NPD. He was emphatic that the design function be a structure and policy consonant with the structure and policy of the company. He addressed fundamental problems such as the unwritten imperative that different products must be designed for different countries and the lack of communication between product sections. By 1982, a new organizational structure was implemented: It simplified the function of support services and administration and created new design manager posts for each major product sector, with a brief to achieve tighter cooperation within their product division.

In 1985, CIDC changed to CID, Corporate Industrial Design, reflecting a desire to come up with worldwide design solutions. By 1984, the design policy committee had prepared a definitive statement of design policy emphasizing the equality of design in the interdisciplinary teams of the product development process. An ongoing program of professional development embracing all staff and activities within CID was set up. Its intent was to stimulate fresh thinking and invite visitors to inject new ideas from outside the company, using workshops as concept generators. Other initiatives included recruiting the best talents from design schools, developing expertise in new CAD techniques, applying ergonomics, and organizing a communications department in order to sell the necessity of design to the company.

These examples show how the design community views the strategic value of design. Some authors explain, in detail, strategic design management decisions that are used to implement a design strategy, but do not explain the links between design and the company strategy formulation process. They tend to let us think a design strategy can be built as a satellite disconnected from the company's overall strategic thinking, which is an error.

In order to better qualify the strategic, transforming value of design, we first need to understand what makes a decision strategic, and what strategy is. This chapter introduces the various models of strategic thinking and develops the models that are pertinent to strategic design: the political and cognitive approaches to strategy, as well as the economic and competitive approaches. Therefore, this chapter concentrates on strategy formulation and ideation, leaving to chapter 11 strategy implementation and practical decisions.

A FRAMEWORK FOR A STRATEGIC MANAGEMENT OF DESIGN

How Businesses Formulate Their Strategies

Henry Mintzberg investigated the origins of strategy, paying particular attention to exploring the relationship between plans and intentions, and how the companies actualized their plans. Comparing intended strategy with realized strategy allowed him to distinguish "deliberate strategies"—realized as intended—from "emergent strategies"—patterns or consistencies realized despite or in the absence of intentions.

The first question for strategic design is whether there is or is not an intentional character or strategic intent. Strategy formulation comes from the will of managers, cultural or political processes, or external pressures. Designers are used to a *deliberate* strategy process, which results in a manager issuing a design brief for a new logo or space. They are less familiar with the *emergent* strategy process, though it is probably the most interesting aspect of strategic design management: it inserts design opinions and ideas into the collective process of strategy consensus-building through the company's different social and power coalitions. This social and progressive pattern of strategy formulation is the most useful for long-term design infusion in the company. Rather than relying on the rational model of strategic planning, design management should explore the "fuzzy" model of emerging strategy as a social consensus process.

What is Strategy?
Competitive strategy is about being different. It means deliberately choosing a different set of activities to deliver a unique mix of value.

The "Competition" Porter Model of Strategy
Strategy comes from an analysis of the company's competitive context. A company chooses a unique position in its industry according to the balance of the forces in its market: the rivalry among the competitors, the external threats of new entrants and potential substitute products, and the market power of its suppliers and customers.

According to the competitive context, alternative strategic formulation emerges from strategic analysis methods and planning, such as:

* Volume strategy; cost leadership
* Specialization strategy; niche strategy differentiation, such as variety-based, needs-based (serving most of the needs of a particular set of customers), and access-based positioning (customer geography or scale)

MICHAEL PORTER, 1998

"Strategy is making tradeoffs in competing. The essence of strategy is choosing what not to do. Positioning choices determine not only which activities a company will perform and how it will configure individual activities but also how activities relate to one another. While operational effectiveness is about achieving excellence in individual activities and functions, strategy is about combining activities."

Simply identifying the sources of competitive advantage is not enough. The company must build its position and organize the value chain in order to develop a real

Table 7.1. The Strategy Process

advantage over competitors. Competitive advantage grows out of the entire value chain. Fit is important because discrete activities affect one another. There are three types of fit:

1. The first-order fit is the simple consistency between each activity (function) and the overall strategy.
2. The second-order fit occurs when activities are reinforced.
3. The third-order fit goes beyond to optimization of effort (such as the coordination and information exchange across activities to eliminate redundancy).

"Strategy" creates a fit among a company's activities. The success of strategy and strategic design depends on doing many things well and integrating them. The whole matters more than any individual part. Strategic fit is fundamental not only for competitive advantage but also for the sustainability of that advantage.

Other Models of Strategy Formulation

Beyond the Porter integrator paradigm, the domain of strategy has been amended by theories developed from social science: economy, sociology, and politics.

Theoretical models for strategy formulation based on competitive advantage apply to design management. But other models based on the company's capacity to construct its outside environment (Resource-Based View and Knowledge Management) or on the cognitive approach of representation of the company environment are also pertinent for design management and go beyond the Porter competitive advantage.

These different approaches to strategy provide a balanced structural framework for strategic design management.

STRATEGY IDEATION

STRATEGY IDEATION ARTICULATES both the logic of analysis (positivist) and the logic of design (constructivist):

- Constructivist logic: conception, invention, pattern creation, staging, and sense-making. Which strategic and organizational dynamics can be used to invent and create?
- Positivist logic: analysis and calculation, designation of possible/impossible futures, and action and implementation. How can we explain and predict evolutions?

Strategy cannot be based strictly on the logic of analysis. Strategy is also a global conception, a homogeneous figure, a significance that concentrates on a flow of actions and representations. Analysis discriminates and describes the characteristics of the strategic dynamics. Strategic creation and design institutes the specificity of a company and aims at challenging contingent futures.

Design Vision as Strategy Ideation

Strategy can create radically new competitive conditions. Deviance is at the heart of this process, and explains how the mechanisms of the reference framework in the industry change. Deviance is at the origin of vision.

The manager's vision breaks away from routine and proposes a radically different way of contemplating future reality, and questions the conditions that are considered normal in the industry. Vision deconstructs what is "normal" in order to propose an atypical design. Strategic vision is close to the divergent design process. Vision induces a dissonance, a gap between traditional thinking and the constraints imposed.

LEE GREEN

Director of corporate identity and design
IBM Corporation, 2001

(Lee Green has held this position since 1993, when Lou Gerstner became CEO of IBM. He is responsible for IBM's worldwide product industrial design, identity programs, graphics, packaging, and Internet design. Mr. Green has played a pivotal role in recent branding and design initiatives, including the launch of IBM's new e-business identity program and the redesign of IBM's desktop, mobile, and server products. He also leads the corporation's efforts in the area of "advanced concept design.)

"When Lou Gerstner arrived at IBM we presented a visual audit to him that demonstrated how IBM was being 'collectively' viewed by our customers. This audit included a representation of how we were presenting IBM in the marketplace, via our logos, advertising, naming, product design, exhibits, publications, etc. The key here being the collective, aggregate-level view. What we found was that because design decisions were being made transactionally, or execution by execution, the result was a fractured presentation of the IBM brand. Customers told us that this fractured visual presentation also sent the signal that IBM was not operating cohesively. That one IBM group did not work with the other IBM group.

"Mr. Gerstner recognized this immediately, and recognized that the same operational problems existed across IBM. As a result, there was a strategic shift in philosophy that emphasized the importance of rebuilding a strong, integrated, single IBM brand and leveraging IBM's collective strengths. Design has played a significant role in that revitalization effort, with a focus on all of IBM's visual expressions. The Corporate Design function has once again become proactive, and influential in setting design strategy, and stimulating business strategy.

"IBM's first and most important design principle emphasizes the need to begin any design initiative by *understanding both customer intent and customer aspiration*. This process involves the synthesis of user context and technology context. This leads to scenario modeling to allow targeted focus on a specific type of user and specific tasks.

"The second principle deals with our *design image*, or *visual language*. Here the focus remains on pure geometry, simplicity, elegance, and emotional appeal. Sometimes this manifests in 'whimsical' form. Often the result is a design impression that signals strength, reliability, and coherence. Regardless of style or personality, IBM's design decisions are always intended to reflect authenticity, via purposeful form.

"The last principle has to do with *vision*. Thinking in big shifts. Filtering all the knowledge about how people want to work, along with all that is possible, given emerging technologies. And, creating visions of the future. The automobile industry refers to this as 'concept car' design, or advanced design. It's this process, and applied principles, that has led to design solutions like IBM's Wearable Computer. Or, concepts like the e-newspaper that imagine a new world of functioning through specific e-business-enabled devices."

- -

The design process is a combination of analysis (like strategic planning) and synthesis. It creates a virtual world of mental experiments. Analysis discovers the laws that govern today's reality, and the designer invents a different future. The design process is adductive—it uses the logic of conjecture. "Adduction" suggests that something *might* be.

Example: The Guggenheim Museum at Bilbao by Frank Gehry was an unfolding process of creating new forms of architecture that, nonetheless, speak to the man in the street and revitalize an entire geographical region.

Design is concerned with fit, and so is strategy. The metaphor of design offers a window into a deeper understanding of the strategy-making process for design managers (Liedtka, 2000). Mintzberg's "design school" criticizes this design metaphor because it believes the design process is primarily one of reflection—of cognition rather than action—that devalues the role of organizational members other than the CEO or architect (Mintzberg, 1990).

Aesthetics and Company Vision

Design is at ease when confronted with a strategy formulation process that aims toward a future to create rather than an environment to serve, and favors improvisation (Berton et al., 1999; Crossan, 1998). Patrick Hetzel developed a model of an interaction-driven company that is pertinent for design strategic management. The "interaction-driven" enterprise is oriented siimultaneously around the object and the subject, and its offer is built by the interaction between the subject and the object. The company asks society and proposes an offer that satisfies universal needs; design innovates by injecting interaction intelligence, as well as an element of surprise, into the offer.

Aesthetics can become a dimension of valorization for the company with the mission to disseminate beauty in society. This mission reveals the company's vision of the world that it has built internally. Aesthetics governs the complexity produced by the company and the consumer (Hetzel, 1993).

The ability to produce beauty can be seen as a sign of power used by the strategic nexus. Aesthetics is a sort of "donation" that authenticates the interaction between the company and the customer. Aesthetics goes back to the cultural project. To bring beauty into the world through art and design is to pull the individual out of nature, making him a cultural being. In this context, design management can be a source of competitive advantage by helping the strategic nexus in three complementary directions:

1. The product creation and rhetoric
2. The creation of a strategic intent and its logic of change
3. The creation of an "ethics of aesthetics" (Hetzel, 1993)

New company models have appeared, like Benetton, which focus on aesthetics and creation. For example, Nike is a virtual and international company made up of a coordinated network of multiple interdependent companies. In terms of its design process, the 4,000 products are designed at the same time by an internal team of about twenty designers—who are hired only for four or five seasons, in order to ensure the renewal of ideas—and 200 independent freelance designers. This allows for maximal creativity, relying on ultrarapid reactivity and prototyping (Fréry, 2000).

One can also transform the company vision by federating it around a universal value, such as ecological and environmental concern (Reinhardt, 1998). The designer must contribute to develop a world in which humans not only live but develop their cultural and spiritual possibilities—an ecology of the artificial (Manzini, 1995). He applies to the artificial environment the models of interpretation that ecology developed for the natural environment. An ecological analysis of the artificial environment develops a new ethics in the process of "making."

One passes from the idea of "making for producing" to the idea of "making for reproducing." The quality of our existence is directly connected to the quality of our care for the reality of our world. Knowledge of craftsmanship is essential for the future: we will need to rediscover the personal care a craftsman takes in creating a specific object . It is a re-creation (Fry, 1995). Ecology integrates the environmental factor into product design, parallels the flux of material and energy necessary for the complete life cycle of the product in NPD, and advocates for an eco-design (Mueller, 1995).

The Rhetoric of Strategic Design

The strategy process implies finding words for describing and explaining the vision. Strategy as language simultaneously provokes the formation of mental images of the reality, of what is possible or not possible, and of what is potential and desirable. Progressively, the opinions of the strategic nexus will be crystallized into a few words.

Is graphic design just a change of logo? Or is it the design of change? Graphic signs serve as projections of the future for a company. They are associated with the future of human society. They also tend to assert the power of company leadership by giving it a sign it can master. Graphic design is directly linked to the power of influence in an organization. The designer's work superimposes itself on top management's interpretive work.

RICHARD LESTER AND MICHAEL PIORE, 1998

"In an uncertain environment, conversation becomes more important than closure. For Levi's jeans, the notion of a conversation with the consumer is more than just a metaphor. The conversation is extended into the company itself through meetings at which the designers discuss. Levi's is an effective listener but it is by no means just a listener. Rather, it strives to be an active participant in the conversation."

Interpretive managers constantly question the boundaries of their company's core competency and, sometimes, deliberately stray across those boundaries. They bring together individuals within and outside the company who might have something to say to one another. They arrange who should talk to whom. Managers have a very developed analytical apparatus but lack a way of keeping things moving forward without closure. Visionary managers will see that the ambiguity in this lack of closure need not lead to paralysis, but could, instead, provide the opportunity for continuing conversation.

THE COGNITIVE APPROACH TO STRATEGIC DESIGN

FOR PORTER, THE ENVIRONMENT IS TRANSPARENT AND EASY TO ANALYZE. On the contrary, the cognitive approach of strategy develops the idea that a company has access to its environment through a selection of representations or mental images of its environment, and that the environment is itself constituted of entities carrying representations of the company.

The relationship between a company and its environment means:

- Enactment. The concept of "blindness." There is a gap between the image and the reality of the company's relationship to its environment. Lack of awareness of reality can lead to errors in decision making.
- Identity. The process of "sense making" (Weick, 1995) has its roots in social identity. There is no representation independent of an identity, no look on the environment that is not also a look at who is looking—a reflexive look.

✒ Inter-creation. The reciprocal construction of the company by its environment and of the environment by the company; the existence of collective cognitive representations in the industry, and strategy groups in the sector.

This cognitive approach to strategy explains the importance of identity for strategic design. The company identity rests on a set of representations. These representations are mental images associated internally and externally with a company. The images are received communication that balances the present identity (the reality of the company), the dreamed identity (the strategic intent), and the acceptable identity (the interaction with the environment).

Symbolic identity can bring a company together. It expresses itself through the visual identity (logotypes, shapes, and color) and the organizational visual identity (signage and environmental design). Corporate identity appears as the set of visual elements through which the public recognizes the company and differentiates it from others.

Designing a Graphic Identity

THE DESIGN OF A VISUAL IDENTITY PROGRAM requires the definition of strategic objectives and explicit company values, or a mission statement.

WOLFF OLINS, 1989

"Every organization is unique and the identity must spring from the organization's own roots, its personality, its strengths and weaknesses. This is true of the modern corporation as it has been of any other institution, from the Christian church to the nation-state."

Verbal and Visual Identity Models

Corporate identity is defined differently by visual conceptualizers (i.e., design schools) and verbal conceptualizers (i.e., business schools). There is a lack of managerial content in most corporate identity management literature from visual schools. Consequently, authors from the verbal schools dominate in the field of corporate identity management (Balmer, 2001).

The variables of corporate identity management are as follows (see Table 7.2):

✒ Corporate personality: The company philosophy, values, and mission
✒ Corporate strategy: Top management's vision, the products and services produced, the organizational structure, and the corporate identity structure
✒ Corporate identity: The behavior of management and employees, style of communications, and use of symbols

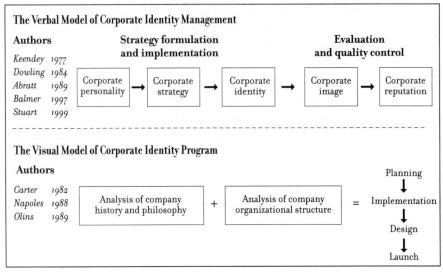

Table 7.2. Verbal versus Visual Corporate Identity Models
(adapted from Rufaidah, 2002)

* Corporate image
* Corporate reputation

The different distribution of these variables is explained in the texts of thirty-eight authors who come from both visual and verbal environments. Both models agree on the importance of the variables of symbolism and communication. Other common variables are products and services, behavior, and corporate image. But variables such as philosophy, values, mission, top management vision, organizational structure, and corporate identity structure, which always appear in verbal models, are rare in visual models. Authors from the design world have a limited view of identity as either corporate personality or corporate strategy (Rufaidah, 2002).

Identity in management is analyzed through three questions:

1. Is there a real specificity of the company that makes it different from its competitors?
2. If this specificity exists, how can different individuals contribute to the creation of a collective identity?
3. What is the relationship between individual personality and collective identity?

Identity is a set of features that shows the unique character of a company, and allows its members to identify themselves within it and outside people to recognize it. The factors that determine the specificity of a company are:

* The political factors or characteristics of power and strategy formulation

* The structural factors or organizational structure, systems, and procedures of management (performance, incentives, human resource management, system of control, organizational symbolism, organizational speech, office-space design)
* The symbolic production, or induced symbolism (myths, history, rituals, taboos, organizational culture) and systems of action or strategic games of coalitions, the informal social structure, the ideology and symbols instituted, and time and space planning
* The organizational imagery or psychic representations the individual has of the company (the corporate image, professional image and qualities, and the mapping of power)

For a company today, the possibility of possessing a coherent and specific identity is greater than in the past, but what remains complex is the problem of integrating individual behaviors. Design management must participate in the management of both graphic and architectural identity in the building of a collective identity—an organizational identity that is either focused on an activity, on a style or behavior, or on the leader.

Time gives a global coherence to a company's symbolism and helps facilitate the sense-making process of a symbol. It is history that makes a symbol credible incrementally over time. An employee can read the history of a company and find the common thread that links the present to the past, and points to the company's potential futures.

DESIGN, IDENTITY, AND CULTURE

COMPANY CULTURE IS THE VISIBLE DEMONSTRATION OF ITS IDENTITY. Culture is a set of representations, symbols, values, and beliefs shared by the human group that constitutes the institution. Culture allows the different members to recognize themselves in the institution through tangible elements, such as day-to-day management practices, behaviors, and symbols.

So, the links between design, identity, and culture are to be found in the visual symbols (graphic and spatial), but also in the psychological climate that is developed by the way these signs are perceived. Symbols are subjective proofs of an organizational climate to be added to objective proofs. Under certain conditions, visual symbols in companies can serve as efficient management tools. Symbolism expresses a company's underlying character, ideology, and value system (Dandridge, 1983). This underlying character is revealed by:

1. Histories and myths that a company concocts deliberately or invents unconsciously
2. The different types of ceremonies or rituals a company uses, such as training programs, parties, marketing seminars, and coffee breaks
3. The company logo: the externalized, concrete sign a company chooses to communicate its distinctive character to an external environment and itself

4. The emotional and political daily life, as revealed by anecdotes and jokes that inevitably circulate in a company

This list expresses the profound significances inherent in all human organizations and cultures. Symbols can be:

- Verbal: Myths, legends, histories, names, rumors, or jokes
- Action: Parties, rituals of passage, meals, breaks, or starts to the day
- Material symbols: Status symbols, company products, badges, flags, or logos

According to the Goodsell typology, symbols are symbols of authority, empathy, or reward.

Symbols have different functions:

- They are descriptive, providing an expression of the company.
- They control the energy of the company, recruiting new members, facilitating the reexperience of a sensation (commemorative medal), and decreasing tension (ritual).
- They help maintain the existing system, giving sense, providing consistency, order, and stability, and managing individual or organizational change (Dandridge, 1983).

Symbols are physical artifacts that exist in an organizational context and connote an organizational sense that will be different from the same signs seen in another context (Ornstein, 1986).

The work environment is composed of three elements: the physical structure, the physical stimuli, and the symbolic artifacts. The physical structure of a workspace or environment influences interactions, relationships, and behaviors. The layout of the space, furniture, and chairs all affect the character of this interaction.

The symbolic artifacts are aspects of the physical environment that individually or collectively guide the interpretation of the social space. Environmental design gives indications of the type of work, a person's status, efficiency, and aesthetic preferences. These aesthetic impressions can be important in their impact on staff recruitment and behavior (Davis, 1984).

Creating and Implementing a Corporate Identity

A company chooses a graphic visual style and identity architecture according to its strategy and structure:

- A monolithic identity, when the company uses one name and visual style throughout
- An endorsed identity, when a company has a group of activities or companies it endorses with the group name and identity
- A branded identity, when the company operates through a series of brands that may be unrelated either to each other or to the company

Design (graphic and environmental) is situated between identity and image. Identity, or personality, is "what one is," design is "what one wants to be," and image is "what one appears to be." Design creates signs and symbols that reflect the personality or company identity. Design does not create the company image. An image is perceived.

A graphic sign is a typographical character (a logotype) and/or a symbol and color. It is not always necessary to choose between typography and symbol. Some letters have a symbolic architectural language. Words are pictures. Logotypes with symbols are more easily memorized. Symbols are either abstract or figurative. Abstract symbols are shapes, such as a circle, square, rectangle, triangle, or other shapes less easily perceived, such as a lozenge, oval, hexagon, or parallelogram. The choice of an abstract sign is often preferred, and, most often, a circle or a square is preferred. But, at the same time, they are less differentiating and do not convey the specific roots and culture of the company.

A figurative symbol is either "associative," which describes the product or activity, or "allusive," which describes the product and the activity indirectly. There are several types of descriptive symbols: the pilot product of the company; a tool from the activity; graphics of an animal (Ferrari); graphics of a vegetable (Apple); graphics of earth elements, such as a shell, stars, or snow crystals; and graphics with objects (Diligence Hermes).

The quality of a logotype is measured according to two criteria: 1) the intrinsic quality of the visual shape—its balance, accent, and the relationship between the form and its background, and 2) the extrinsic quality, or its functional quality—how well it makes visible the company identity, history, profession, and distinctive character to its markets, as well as its potential for a diversification of uses.

In a "good logo," a balance must be struck between differentiation, for specificity, and the necessity of categorization within a given industry.

A visual identity system regroups the visual components of a business in a distinctive, coherent, and economic way. The difference between a visual identity system and a graphic resides in the number and complexity of supports the graphic uses, and in the decision to create a coherent and unique message and impose graphic norms on a unifying corporate identity.

The Design of a Company's Spatial Identity

ANOTHER COMPONENT OF IDENTITY is the design of the company's spaces and buildings. Any company needs two types of spaces: 1) workspaces—offices, headquarters, and factories, and 2) commercial spaces—exhibition stands, boutiques, and retail agencies. Architecture is the permanent media of the company. An original architecture has an impact in terms of corporate image and profitability.

Example: The Danish firm Novo, specializing in diabetes care, considers workspace design to be strategic and a concern of human resources. If the staff finds its workspace attractive, the space will, hopefully, stimulate its creativity.

Interior design has an impact on company performance. Business structures are witnessing major changes in terms of the flexibility of workspaces and teams. All businesses need a workspace. In seeking out a workspace, businesses often try to minimize costs. Environmental design means going beyond only taking into consideration economic efficiency. Interior design helps rationalize a company's production and technical systems, and communicate a better image. Bringing together a team in the same space encourages casual communication, socialization, and procedural fluidity.

Example: Technocentre at Guyancourt (France). Renault uses the same location for its design and R&D departments.

The exterior and interior architecture are permanent messages of corporate communications and the coherence of its communication to both external and internal constituencies. They become the visible demonstration of a company culture and its management systems. The quality of architecture is measured by:

- The quality of the form itself. The exterior shape stages technology and plays a managerial role in terms of energy savings and communications space. Buildings developed now are intelligent; they control themselves and have flexible, integrated information systems. Office furniture is more ergonomic and systemic (for stocking, lighting, and computing).
- The quality of its integration into its environment. Numerous recent architectural creations are the result of an original dialogue between the building's shape and its environment.
- The quality of its relationship with the company's activity and personality, such as office spaces that are functional and modular.

A company selects the configuration of its interior space in order to express a certain management style, identity, and innovation culture. A space now does not have to choose between being open or partitioned. The office "landscape" has evolved toward an open space with improved acoustic insulation. The two approaches become complementary. The choice of the best space configuration is made according to the activity, such as designing an open-plan office when the activity requires a good deal of interaction. The designer's role is to transcribe the philosophy of the company, to make its organizational structure visible through the partition of space and differentiation of office furniture.

DEANNE BECKWITH

Herman Miller, 2000

"Herman Miller is a western Michigan–based international firm in the manufacture and sale of furniture systems, products, and related services. Herman Miller has celebrated the importance of design throughout its seventy-five-year history. Many of Herman Miller's designs are in the permanent collections of museums.

"Founder D.J. De Pree instilled his unwavering trust in the value of design with his father-in-law Herman Miller. In the 1960s Herman Miller introduced the open-plan office furniture system.

"Design permeates this organization in a way that makes its presence known and expected, from the placement of tools on a shelf in the factory to the selection of the color and shape of flowers in building landscapes. Herman Miller receives worldwide attention for its corporate culture and progressive management style."

Retail Design Identity

Retail design is not very different, but its growing importance in service industries justifies developing some of its specificities. The objective is a compromise between standardization of commercial space for cost-effective reasons and building a strong and unique identity. The store sign is, therefore, at once global, integrative, and sense-building.

Retail design must convey the marketing policy to the target audiences and seduce these consumers so they want to enter the store or commercial center. Consequently, the development of the following elements must be taken into consideration:

- An original outside architecture and the relationship between the exterior (the shop window) and interior design.
- The shop sign is an essential element of visualization that usually works within strict urban constraints, like periphery (totems visible from far away).
- The door or porch is the element that has certainly inspired designers the most. Foremost, it illustrates the need for a total customer experience. The boutique entrance must be an invitation to the pleasure of shopping. The imperative of visibility makes a sign a real work of art that is seen all over town.

The quality of a retail space is measured by the coherence between the outside envelope and the interior decoration. We have already discussed how much of an impact the quality of store design has on the consumer's behavior. To build a retail-space identity, the designer looks for different levels of coherence: between space planning and market positioning, the graphic system and interior design, and between the outside envelope and the interior display.

Design is managed differently according to different retailers:

- Externalized and coordinated by top management for specialized distributors
- Integrated or "mixed" and decentralized in marketing for general distributors

Decisions are made on size criteria, different design decisions, and the nature of the store offer. If the offer is specialized, the concept is easily defined and can be externalized, whereas a general distributor needs continuous control and redefinition of its positioning and differentiation.

The design function has an instrumental value in the expression of the positioning, consistency of signage, differentiation factors, and store identity. Recent concept stores occupy a niche, and design makes tangible their conceptual positioning so it represents the entrepreneur's sensibility.

Design and Corporate Communications

Corporate communications relates to corporate culture and strategy in terms of such tools as the mission statement, which helps creativity and includes:

- A history of the company to create a feeling of membership
- Values that guide the company's actions
- A collective challenge that gives meaning to the activity of each individual employee
- Game rules of everyday management as a basis for common "law"

The mission statement symbolizes the expression of what the company's collectivity hopes for its future through value sharing, not the will of top management.

Corporate communications considers design to be one of the professional techniques it can use in sponsorship, press relations, and public relations. It supports design input in order to change a packaging or product presentation, and speaks of "global communication," encompassing communications design, field communication, direct communication, and communication media. Communications design includes all of the design disciplines. The necessity of global communication stems from the risk of dispersion of communications efforts. The company must make sure its messages are understood and memorized, and the crucial task lies in supervising the messages.

But if design communicates, it is also a process and not just a form. The interface between corporate communications and design is systemic, which means it is verbal, formal, and visual. The objective is to look for coherence between the verbal, graphic, or architectural signs, whether for a product brochure, an annual report, an exhibition stand, or an event, and between external and internal communications policies.

THE ECONOMIC APPROACH
TO STRATEGIC DESIGN

DESIGN CAN BUILD A COMPANY'S COMPETITIVE ADVANTAGE externally by developing a unique offer and position in a market, and internally by developing a strong core competency.

TOM PETERS, 1989

"A narrow interpretation of design ignores the strategic value of design in the corporation. Design is only secondary about pretty objects and primarily about a whole approach to doing business, serving customers, and providing value."

Design as a Competitive Advantage

Design participates in strategy formulation and ideation because strategy is produced by a creative tension between the available resources in the company and its long-term aspirations. Strategy is about finding resources for the business units. Business units within industries differ a great deal more from one to another than industries differ from each other. Competition directs resources toward those uses that offer the highest returns, and design input and differentiation are important to strategizing where the highest returns might be.

Can strategic design be helped by strategic planning, and is strategic planning still in use? Mintzberg predicted the fall of strategic planning; however, it is still in use, though in a changed form. Design managers can implement strategic planning because it is more decentralized and involves less sophisticated methods, so it is not reserved for experts anymore. In order to suggest the strategic direction for competitive advantage, design managers can use various strategic planning tools that have been developed, such as:

- The competition analysis matrix (BCG, McKinsey, and ADL; see chapter 11)
- The SWOT analysis of strengths and weaknesses, scenarios, and benchmarking

These tools support the procedure to propose, argue, and negotiate resource allocation, positioning, and fit.

Strategic planning is compelling for strategic design management because of its systemic reconstruction of the mental patterns of the company, its focus on "sense making" and strategic intent, and its generation of scenarios and assumptions. Today, the keywords of strategic design management are *knowledge, conversation, interaction,* and *network.*

Design as Internal Competitive Advantage

There are other theories based on competitive advantage, but they differ in the definition of this advantage. Porter's traditional approach has been changed from:

- Strategy as fit to strategy as stretch
- Resource allocation to resource leverage
- A portfolio of business to a portfolio of competencies
- Competition as confrontation to competition as collaboration

These theories and their relation to strategic design will be briefly presented: the resource-based view (RBV) and knowledge management (KM), the management of change, and the Transaction Cost Theory (TCT) (Table 7.2).

Design as a Resource

The resource-based view (RBV) of the company studies the phenomena of resource accumulation and the various degrees of resource duplication that result (Amit & Shoemaker, 1993; Wernerfelt, 1984). It considers as a resource everything a company can mobilize to generate a competitive advantage.

Design as Knowledge

The knowledge management view (KM) concentrates on knowledge as a resource for the company's success. It studies learning processes such as the sharing and transfer of knowledge. The capacity to "produce" knowledge is seen as what differentiates the company in the market. A company becomes a means to create a social identity and a collective learning process (Kogut & Zander, 1996).

Nonaka distinguishes explicit or declarative knowledge from tacit or procedural knowledge (Nonaka, 1991). Design knowledge is tacit. Tacit knowledge cannot be codified. It is transmitted by imitation and experience. Design brings knowledge to the different stages of NPD in terms of process change, creativity, and teamwork dynamics. When strategic, design knowledge is often "hidden" because it is infused into the norms and the company culture. Design is in the domain of the tacit, intuitive, and continuous process of change (Kristensen, 1995).

For the company, it is essential to pass from tacit to explicit knowledge in order to diffuse knowledge in the company (Nonaka & Takeuchi, 1995).

Nonimitative resources are not codified, but in order to create value, they have to be codified and, therefore, become imitative.

Design does not consider knowledge a transfer of information (knowledge as substance); it has a new vision of knowledge as a building process of collaborative "sense making" (knowledge as a tool). The objective is, then, to learn while doing (cognitive learning), to provide a context for conversations and for the social construction of knowledge.

CHRIS ARGYRIS, 1999

"Learning is defined as occurring in two conditions:

"First, learning occurs when an organization achieves what it intended; that is, there is a match between its design for action and the outcome.

"Second, learning occurs when a mismatch between intentions and outcomes is identified and it is corrected; that is, a mismatch is turned into a match....

"Single-loop learning occurs when matches are created or when mismatches are corrected by changing actions. Double-loop learning occurs when mismatches are corrected by first examining and altering the governing variables and then the actions."

Design management oversees a learning process that regenerates the settings for the action, regenerating both the products and the company, if done well (Urban & Hauser, 1980). If knowledge is not considered as information but, rather, as conception, it is managed in a proactive way so that it is used and reused, not stored away.

Learning organizations believe in learning and individual creativity. They are, therefore, hospitable to design. The structure of these learning organizations is decentralized and adaptable through networks of alliances (Xerox, 1990). Leaders favor actions that generate learning and mobilize multiple knowledge sources as well as a coherent vision (Leonard & Barton, 1995). Design management has to learn to see the underlying variables that influence long-term behavior and actions and apply them to product ideas, technology, and management know-how (Jonas, 1997).

Design is in itself new knowledge for the company, as well as a builder of knowledge:

- By increasing the knowledge value of other assets such as marketing and production and catalyzing imagination and motivation (Leonard & Sensiper, 1998).
- By constructing relationships with the customer to form a competitive advantage as an act of cognition and creation (Von Krogh, 1998).

Design knowledge is strategic if:

- It is difficult to replicate, which implies that design protects its input in product creation (Teece, 1998) and quantifies its intangible assets (Bukowitz & Petrash, 1997).
- It helps the circulation of knowledge in the company by having a leveraging effect on other knowledge or by transforming tacit knowledge into social capital (Zack, 1999; Madahvan & Grover, 1998).
- It makes the company's knowledge visible; this could happen by systematically using graphic design in every management decision (different data presentation highlights differences in problem-solving processes) (Tabachneck & Simon, 1997) or by developing prototypes (Oxman, 1998).

Design as a Core Competency

The competence-based view (CBV) introduces a dynamic perspective. It considers resources imitative and the efficiency of the company dependent on its competencies. In the long run, the efficiency of a company stems from its capacity to build strategic competencies that will generate tomorrow's products (Hamel & Pralahad, 1990, 1993). This approach is similar to design because it insists on innovation, learning, and research. The strategic intent induces systematic and constant research of new competitive advantages and generates a dynamic of *encircling* rather than competitive *confrontation*.

In the future, competition will be different. Companies must develop tools to change the industry and develop new visions. The transformation of the industry is unavoidable, and design management has to anticipate this transformation. Resources become capacities when they are combined, integrated, and coordinated in the context of an activity. Resources are not intrinsically strategic; they become strategic when they are embedded in strategic processes, such as those that modify the integration of the company into its environment and give lasting competitive advantage (Tarondeau, 1998).

Design has several characteristics of core competency:

- ❧ It gives access to a wide variety of markets
- ❧ It contributes significantly to the benefits perceived by the final consumer
- ❧ It is difficult for competitors to imitate

The capacity to resort to design, manage and integrate design expertise, and combine the resource with the other functions becomes a core competency for the company (Jevnaker, 1998).

Design can become a core competency if its imagination is not developed in an ivory tower. Ideas arrive when thoughts meet. Just as the designer must encroach on others' work, in the same way, others must stimulate the designers in a disciplined form of anarchy.

Design as a Source of Organizational Change

The study of change and development is a great theme in the social sciences. A longitudinal comparative case study, like the "procedural analysis" conducted by Andrew Pettigrew at Warwick University, is needed to explain the "what," "why," and "how" of the links between context, processes, and outcomes in design management: for example, why a design pilot project creates networks and how design creates change in organizational frames (Senge, 1999).

Cultural change articulates itself around three fundamental elements: those causing the change, the action of the change, and the context of the action. The introduction of a cultural change in a company concerns the political and structural factors of identity, but the psychological dimension of the change is also essential. Even if all of the elements—strategy, structure, and systems, such as the graphic system—change, the participators can retain their habits and attachments.

For the collaborators, all change is felt like a loss. So, the company has to make sure the change is perceived as necessary and not imposed, to encourage training while ensuring continuity, and to treat the problem of the resistance to change in order to make sure the new reality is accepted.

Leadership plays a central role in all cultural change and in the creation of a positive culture. Leaders' actions, and their new visions, entail a new cultural model of appropriation of their ideas. Graphic symbols are in direct contact with processes of influence, negotiation, and the power game.

Example: The 1992 graphic sign for RATP (the Paris Metro) under a new CEO symbolizes a more human-oriented philosophy, represented graphically by a human profile following the Seine's geographical curves.

Graphic design strikes a subtle balance between two poles: of conformity and originality and innovation. The logic of change articulates itself around two fundamental axes: continuity and rupture.

Design introduces an applied vision to this paradoxical relationship. Graphic innovation is the visual output of change, and its success depends on the phenomenon of synergy between the project and its context. Designers are accepted if, as innovators, they make something new that is not "frightening." Graphic design is a paradox: a guarantee of continuity and a vector of change, it must reconcile pertinence and impertinence.

Graphic signs are the visual tokens of the relationship a company has with change. Change has no concrete effect without the capacity to direct, influence, or achieve it. Graphic signs are objects and subjects of change. Graphic communication contributes to negotiating change (Quinton, 1997).

Design managers object to change imposed by top management and recommend a process of appropriation by the social group. According to the sociology of organizations, change is, first, the transformation of a system of action. In order to have change, three elements must be modified: the nature of the social relations, the model of regulation, and the nature of social control.

Change is the discovery and acquisition of new capacities, but social constructions can be obstacles to this training process. Change is a rupture from past constructs. The only means to solve this paradox is to consider change at both the system and employee level. The involvement of employees in the creative process is fundamental for appropriation, project coherence, and cultural continuity (Dormer, 1990). In order to implement change, a company must provide an environment that links people with processes (Herbruck & Umbach, 1997). The emotional dimension of change is also to be taken into account in the definition of a new visual identity.

DESIGN AS INTERORGANIZATIONAL COOPERATION

THE INTENSE DEBATE ABOUT THE BOUNDARIES OF THE COMPANY and the arrival of hybrid crosses between the logic of the market (or externalization) and the logic of hierarchy (or internalization) places the problem of design externalization in a new perspective—that of *cooperation.*

Most often, when design is externalized—except in the automobile industry, where codesign exists—it is subcontracted between the company and the external designer, which creates a relationship of domination.

PROBLEM	DESIGN MADE WITHOUT INTERORGANIZATIONAL COOPERATION	DESIGN MADE WITH INTERORGANIZATIONAL COOPERATION	MAKING DESIGN TOGETHER	DESIGN MADE ALONE
THEORY	*TCT*			*TCT*
SOLUTION	*Subcontract*	*Strategic externalization*	*R&D consortium Network strategy*	*Internalization*

Table 7.3. **Design and Interorganizational Cooperation**

Example: The textile industry in Northern France. The design initiative in the textile sector is shifting from manufacturers to distributors, specialized chains, and brand-name designers. The new division of labor takes advantage of both vertical integration (low costs and lean retailing management) and disintegration (the ability to innovate by subcontractors and outsourcing of risks) (Vervaeke, 2002).

But the issue of "outsourcing" design is now more about building competitive advantage through interorganizational cooperation. Interorganizational cooperation is a formal or informal agreement established for a duration of time, implying an interaction between two or more independent companies that combine or put in common assets and resources with an objective of efficiency. Interorganizational cooperation has two aspects: resource allocation and the production of knowledge and know-how.

The Theory of Cost Transaction (TCT) explains that, in conditions of bounded rationality, asymmetry of information, and opportunism of external players, a hierarchy integrating design is superior to reaching a balance through the market. Hierarchies economize on transaction costs when there is uncertainty, frequent or sequential transactions, or transaction-specific investments (Williamson, 1975).

Also, if the transaction is externalized, the transfer is costly. The difference between a subcontract and externalization is in the transfer of assets to the provider—the transfer of personnel and equipment. Generally, externalization implies the dismantling of internal services, so the reintegration is often considered impossible.

The contract between the company and the design firm outlines a cession of assets and the expectancy of future realizations. Because of transfer costs, the uncertainty of results, and the risk of opportunism in the transaction, long-term relationships must be researched.

Interorganizational cooperation is also about producing knowledge. Cost issues and "opportunism" do not account for all of the problems. Strategic design must decide the way the company wants "to make design": alone, or in collaboration with others (Table 7.4).

Externalization or "outsourcing" entrusts to an external provider an activity previously realized internally. Already widely used in value chain support activities such as maintenance and information systems, it is now developing in more critical activities: "strategic externalization."

Reducing costs is not always the principal criterion. Outsourcing is motivated by the objective to increase the performance of the design function and to avoid the difficulties of accumulation of resources and competencies. This objective can be defeated by an increase in transaction costs.

Long-term relationships with outside partners are not always a source of opportunism; they can also build trust. The relationship between a company and a design provider over the long run has many merits:

- It cuts research costs, negotiation, control, insurance, and conflict settlement.

* It favors the mutual exchange of information and increases the "predictability" of mutual behavior.

Design managers within the company will, nevertheless, need analytical instruments in order to control the opportunism of the design provider, such as instruments that analyze the provider's performance, quality, and implementation.

The strategic externalization of design builds knowledge, trust, and networking, as in an R&D consortium. It is characterized by reciprocity, mutual support, and pooled resources, and is best suited to the reliable and efficient transfer of information. Cooperation in "how to make" design can build a unique competitive advantage for a company.

CONCLUSION

* A design strategy is either *innate* or *experience-based.*
* Strategy formulation is either *deliberate* or *emergent.*
* The three stages of strategy are formulation, ideation, and implementation.
* Strategy stems from competitive advantage, positioning, and fit.
* Competitive advantage is either market- or resource-based.
* Design vision is a vector for strategy ideation.
* Rhetoric and interpretive management are essential for strategy design.
* Representation and identity are part of the cognitive approach to strategic design.
* A company identity is visual, spatial, and verbal.
* Design competition is a resource, a source of knowledge, and a generator of core competency.
* Design helps in organizational change.
* Design helps in interorganizational cooperation.

PART III

DESIGN MANAGEMENT

in

PRACTICE

CHAPTER 8

THE DESIGN FIRM

NOTHER ASPECT OF DESIGN MANAGEMENT is management of the design firm. Since there are books written for designers on the "how-to" aspects of business (how to organize their marketing, write their contracts, and protect their designs), this book does not go into these areas. Nor does it cover the basic general methods of management that apply just as much to design firms as to any other kind of company. The objective here is to focus on the management tools specific to a design firm and the methods that give a design firm a competitive edge.

The goal here is twofold: 1) to help design firms understand what strategies are available to them, what core competencies are necessary, and what makes a firm's reputation; and 2) to give managers the knowledge needed to select the right design firm. Because integrating design has a great impact on company performance, the selection of the design firm is a key issue for managers.

THE DESIGN FIRM STRATEGY

DESIGN FIRMS ARE CREATED BY DESIGNERS (see chapter 2, on design history). Consequently, the approaches of design firms are based upon their founders' backgrounds, philosophies, and business strategies.

What Is a Design Firm For?

Both design firms and freelance designers tend to choose their business strategies according to their own area of design expertise and the markets they have experience in. The design firms often have difficulty running differentiated strategies from their competitors. In each design discipline, they run similar policies.

However, strategy is about differentiation, and a design firm—like any other business—differentiates itself by performing the job with core competencies it has built over time, not with the basic techniques intrinsic to its trade. Successful design firms differentiate themselves by specializing, globalizing, or creating specific tools for managing design projects, keeping a high level of management excellence, and expertly building a reputation (Table 8.2).

What is the demand for design? Companies need either purely "technical" design services or consulting on their design strategy. Companies rarely have inhouse design expertise, so they subcontract the projects to outside design consultants. But when the design projects border on management issues in terms of the company's identity and marketing issues such as branding, the demand for design changes in nature. The company needs designers who have expertise in brand management and in strategy formulation. Even so, the company can choose between:

* In-house design capabilities
* External design capabilities—those that lie outside the company
* A mixture of in-house and external design capabilities

Over the past ten years, the subcontracting of design has grown substantially. At the same time, design firms must compete with the creation of in-house design departments. The reasons for acquiring design services on a subcontracting or "outsourcing" basis, rather than purely via the company's own employees, are:

* The lack of financial resources to hire staff designers with a wide range of professional skills
* A matter of the company's strategy and transaction costs

There has been a trend toward outsourcing design at a conceptual or idea-management level, where the design firm creates the entire concept.

Example: FITCH developed a new concept for steak houses in the Midwest after it found that there was a shift in public interest in fine dining, and that it no longer pertained only to large metropolitan areas.

What is the strategic positioning of a design firm? Here are some examples:

* A brand management firm, which works with many design firms, especially graphic and package design firms.
* A concept development firm. For example, P'reference, a design firm in France, developed specific concepts, such as the "Adieu au Franc" (a large chocolate French coin that was introduced before the launch of the euro) and the *"Bol d'air"* (a cup of air captured in the last minute of the century before the change of the millennium), or the concepts of tea- or coffee-flavored water (*eau de thé* and *eau de café*). These concepts were not developed by clients of the firm, but are the firm's conceptual creations.
* An engineering-oriented firm which R&D expertise in engineering and prototyping.
* A user-interface design firm which in high-quality ergonomic and behavioral creativity.
* A design specialist, or a firm that solves design briefs. This is often the case in package design and consumer goods, where marketing product managers are responsible for the design brief.
* A specialist in technical implementation skills. A fundamental resource in retail design, where there is often a chain of identical stores to be designed quickly and efficiently and updated regularly.

The strategic positioning of a firm will also determine at which decision level the design firm will enter the company. The work will be different if it has access to the corporate decision level—often the case in corporate identity—where the firm will then be able to develop a whole scheme that is not only visual but also behavioral in order to pilot change inside the company. Output will also differ if the firm has access to the marketing decision level, where the marketing manager position is always changing hands or is often resistant to major design changes.

The positioning of the design firm is often the result of the personality of the designers that founded the firm and desire to either specialize or not in a design discipline.

The Importance of the Design "Founders"

A DESIGNER-ENTREPRENEUR USUALLY STARTS HIS DESIGN FIRM as a freelance design consultant. He brings to the firm a leadership style and strategic positioning based on his philosophy of design, his preference for a specific design expertise, and his opinions about the design process (this is particularly true for "design stars"). For a manager, the history of the foundation of the firm is often a sign of its core competencies.

ALAN SIEGEL

Chairman and CEO, Siegelgale

"Basically we produce a visual product, and on a regular basis we are working with visual artists. What excites me is strong visual images and communicating ideas."

There are two different types of designer-entrepreneurs:

1. A designer who chooses to be herself. She works only for companies that share her own interests, whether they are product design, fashion design, or luxury packaging, and she greatly impacts the firm with her personal design talent.
2. A designer who chooses to be a partner. This partnership often makes a strategic choice on the "way to design." Partnerships vary, and can explain many differences in the philosophies of design consultancies.

   ❧ A team of an engineer and a designer will fit perfectly into highly technical, sophisticated industrial and medical markets.
   ❧ A team of a designer and a specialist of qualitative marketing will work best in consumer goods packaging.
   ❧ A team of a designer and a specialist in strategic planning from an advertising firm will import "good" management methods and brand management expertise, and will have the competency to develop leadership in design.

Can a design firm survive after the departure of its founder? More than in any business, the issue of the company's survival after its founder has moved on is crucial. The answer has often been to develop the design firm as a brand: to transform the name of the founder into the brand values of the design firm.

Example: Carré Noir, part of Publicis Consultants, Paris. The spirit of the founder, and, particularly, of Gérard Caron, a well-known design theorist who had a wonderful talent for selling design in simple terms to companies, is still transmitted through Béatrice Mariotti, who has been at the firm since 1983. Since 2000, Carré Noir has become part of Publicis Consultants, and its strategy is defined in brand terms. Carré Noir helps its clients define their "off-line" and "online" strategies and to make them visible, interactive, and competitive through the signs they send out. The design firm has five areas of expertise: languages and strategic branding, corporate branding, package branding, e-design branding, and architecture. Recent creations include: Dalloyau, the adventure of the taste—chocolate with Roquefort cheese; and Hennessy Pure White, with a round bottle design that puts an end to "macho" shapes in this market.

Example: Architral, the well-known retail design firm that has acquired an international reputation under the very personalized leadership of Gérard Barrau, well known for his talent to re-qualify a market with his conceptual repositioning of brands such as FNAC, Grand Optical, Citadium, and many others all over the world. Barrau has the reputation of being the "eye" of the firm, seeing to every decision and even drawing every detail. The firm's survival has depended on partnering in March 2001 with the top brand specialist, Interbrand (Omnicom), which has the capacity to capitalize on the conceptual positioning of the firm by developing specific creative methods, and serve the international positioning of the firm.

TYPES OF DESIGN FIRMS

DESIGN FIRMS ALSO DIFFERENTIATE THEIR STRATEGIES through the types of design expertise they prefer and master. In product design, one thinks of IDEO or Frog Design, for brand design of Landor or Siegel & Gale, and for retail design, of Fitch in the U.K. Global and specialized firms or freelance designers are equally as prevalent.

SYLVIE DE FRANCE, 2002

Freelance designer for Lolita Lempicka, Issey Miyake, and Chantal Thomass

"I know this specific world well, the techniques, the industrial know-how. I feel confident and credible with the brands in this universe."

A specialized design firm will choose between product, retail, graphic/package, or Web design. Historically, design firms specialized according to design disciplines as taught in design schools. But the development of digital technology formed a convergence in design among these disciplines. This erosion of the boundaries between different types of design expertise poses new strategic challenges for specialized design firms in their strategic positioning.

Large firms are most likely to offer full design services. They diversify over the years by internal development, mergers and acquisitions, and alliances and joint ventures. Design firm leaders are most likely to be global.

GERDA GEMSER, 2001

"Many of the well-reputed design firms deliver a broad range of services. The fact that these design firms are partnering with their clients to solve larger and more complex problems makes them evolve into strategic resources. In contrast, less-known firms are reluctant to cross boundaries between industrial design and other design areas."

This trend toward full design services is also stimulated by the companies' demand to satisfy multiple needs in a single transaction. "One-stop shopping" allows clients to lower transaction costs, particularly with regard to contact and control phases. Offering a full line of design services creates economies of scale.

This strategy of diversification toward a wide range of design services permits the cross-fertilization of ideas. A diversification strategy also presents a financial interest because front-end strategic services directed toward strategic decisions, such as creating a new market and vision for brand identity, generate more compensation than strict product design services.

But there are also leading design firms in the world that specialize either in a particular design discipline or in specific market niches. The best design firms have a globalization strategy in which they actively seek to serve both clients located abroad and domestic clients operating internationally. For example, they either open a subsidiary in a foreign country (such as Design Continuum in Boston, Milan, and Korea), or establish formal cooperation agreements with foreign partners (such as Plan Créatif in France, with Crabtree Hall in Great Britain). This has some direct consequences on human resources management. These types of companies recruit designers in different countries; by operating in different continents, they will be able to transfer employees to work with the client and cross-fertilize by working across various cultures.

THE CORE COMPETENCIES OF A DESIGN FIRM

BUILDING A COMPETITIVE ADVANTAGE through internal resources is a strategic issue. Design firms have developed differences in the firm-client relationship, in creativity methods, and in specific design process tools, which are their core competencies.

THE FIRM-CLIENT RELATIONSHIP

LONG-TERM AND CLOSE CLIENT RELATIONSHIPS are preferable, since they allow the design companies to develop a deep understanding of the client business and market conditions, and, thereby, provide better design solutions. Long-term firm-client relationships facilitate the development of a certain degree of "trust and mutual respect" among the partners involved, which, in turn, facilitates information exchange (Bruce & Morris, 1994). Leading design companies know the importance of attracting and retaining clients as a competitive-edge ability. Truly customer-driven, they establish profitable long-term and close client relationships and keep a close eye on the wishes and needs of their future clients.

The firm-client relationship goes through a three-stage life cycle (Bruce & Morris, 1998). This model serves to formalize the types of decisions required at each stage by the company:

1. Compatibility: decisions that reflect the firm's ability to choose a designer based on the initial contact, the initial presentation, and the "gut feeling."
2. Familiarity: decisions that assess the compatibility, build mutual stability (social and economic), and promote loyalty and trust.
3. Competency: decisions that are associated with much more than a single design project; design becomes embedded in the norms and values of the organization.

With the trend in corporate downsizing, the importance of corporate-consultant design teams is heightened. Corporations that outsource design gain organizational flexibility and realize opportunities for a continuous flow of ideas, as well as information flow from the external environment. Through building long-term relationships, design firms gain knowledge, stability, client-oriented management skills (as in total-quality management), and process-oriented management skills (Table 8.1).

Client Benefit	Phases	Firm Benefit
• understanding the effectiveness of design input • sourcing the firm, identifying the type of design expertise • "gut feeling"	1. COMPATIBILITY	• understanding the client problem • knowledge building
• stability reduces management anxiety and uncertainty • optimizes design information in NPD and marketing	2. FAMILIARITY	• client-oriented project management • sharing organizational, information, and communication process • stability in turnover
• ensuring brand positioning remains the same by using the same consultant • integrating design into organization's values	3. COMPETENCY	• anticipating client's needs • continuous learning and creative process improvement

Table 8.1. The Design Firm-Client Relationship

The Relationship as a Knowledge Process

One of the objectives of the firm-client relationship is to build shared knowledge. The design firm will, therefore:

- Encourage its clients to join them in their studio office
- Work intensely for a certain period with the client at its office
- Delegate part of its staff to work with the client innovation team
- Work side by side upstream in the project with the advertising firm in sharing brand values

----

GIANFRANCO ZACCAI

Design Continuum

"We like it best when clients bring us problems rather than wished-for results. Corporate managers who say this: 'We think the problem is. . . . What do you think?' are a delight to work with. . . . I always want to know how willing a client is to step back and let us get directly in touch with their customers rather than just have us look at their marketing data."

Working side by side, the consultant and corporate staff help each other sort out how to approach the problem. To work effectively together requires shared knowledge and experiences that are built over time and come from a shared culture of information, managing, and optimizing the organizational processes of market and design information (Table 8.2).

The Relationship as a Cultural Shift

Since the client's selection of a design firm is based upon the design firm's ability to relate to the client, as well as on cost and creativity issues, the design firm has to shift toward a client-oriented strategy.

For most design firms, this shift toward a customer-oriented approach results in:

- reeducating project managers to be client managers and be able to develop productive relationships with clients, not just manage projects
- investing in people with divergent capabilities, a necessity as design firms position themselves as strategic pathfinding resources for their clients
- enriching their staff with financial, marketing, social research, programming, and technology specialists
- employing engineers in development teams, because technology in the design process allows them to have direct control and responsibility for the finished product

The shift also concerns design associations that take responsibility for fostering the market value of design, such as the Association of Professional Design Firms, founded in 1985 in the U.S.

The Relationship as "Good Business"

Long-term clients are a key business issue. Design firms always have a high proportion of regular clients. The percentage is often close to 50 percent, but can reach 70 percent. When she starts a design firm, the designer-owner often brings her own clients. And it is not uncommon that the design firm will still be working with these "pioneer" clients after fifteen or twenty years.

Client fidelity means stability in business and is a guarantee of good design. First, fidelity facilitates the design firm's business vision. Unlike advertising firms that have a rather precise idea of their business in advance, resulting from the middle-term contracts and budgets they sign with their clients, design firms only guess from past experience and recurrent design projects coming from faithful clients. Design consultancies don't have so many contracts signed. Only one third of their yearly turnover is foreseeable at the start of the year.

Some say this fidelity is individually based on the trust built between a small group of persons rather than a design firm and a company—that it is a "man meeting another man," a specific person who trusts another person. Therefore, the social aspect of the relationship has to be stressed.

This also happens with companies. Recurrent clients are frequent; this is true even with large companies like L'Oreal, Nestlé, Dannon, and Colgate, which, obviously, have access to information about the various existing design consultancies and can easily change partners. If they don't, it is most likely because they find added value in long-term relationships.

Second, client fidelity also has an impact in terms of the quality of the performance of the design firm. Fidelity and regularity in the relationship is a guarantee of design quality.

Hence the saying that the design firm knows more about the story of your brand than your company:

- Because a design firm has seven to eight times more clients than an advertising firm. Having so many brands on their hands gives the designers a great diversity of viewpoints, knowledge in brand experiences, and the possibility of synthesizing cross-cultural social trends.
- Because design staff stay for some years. The managers of a design firm do their best to retain their talented staff. The permanence of the workforce in a design firm is a competitive advantage. A client will feel reassured when talking to a person who has known the brand for years and, sometimes, knows more about the various steps of brand equity building than the marketing manager does, because he has stuck with the brand, whereas many marketing managers do not stay long in their companies.

The danger in having regular clients is that it can limit creativity, because often, the firm will be working on the same operational implementation projects.

Sometimes, the design firm will lose a client because the client decides to start its own design department and hires consultants from another design firm to run it.

How to Keep Your Design Firm Creative

CREATIVE SKILL IS THE CORE COMPETENCY of a design firm. All designers are creative, but how do you keep a design firm creative over time? The answers are: the diversification of skills and techniques for nurturing creativity.

The Diversification of Design Skills

Traditional design firms adopt standard skills that are "craftsmanship" skills as learned in design schools. The only new skills they will probably insist that their employees acquire are CAD computer skills, because they still think in terms of project/product strategy. Consequently, they have similar strategic positioning and can easily be replaced by one another. In contrast, market-oriented design firms require a much more diverse set of skills, and will add social science or ergonomics specialists to the design process, diversifying the cultural origin of their staff and trying to develop creative skills to communicate more effectively with the client.

LUNAR DESIGN

"The diversity of our staff, representing nationalities from all over the world, gives us a broad perspective and enables us to design for a global audience."

A workforce that is varied in terms of education and cultural background will generate more ideas, as well as more internationally relevant concepts, simply by learning from each other.

Nurturing Creative Skills

For a design firm, creative excellence is its permanent objective. The more design becomes strategic, the more the competitive edge is placed on idea generation and creativity.

Example: Landor has developed "learn and lunch" sessions, during which information about all projects is shared, a visual presentation is made of all the main ideas and decisions of a project so the project team can be challenged by other teams, and ideas and training programs are generated.

Design firms utilize various methods: staff rotation, brainstorming, information sharing, concept generation, and new talent search.

❦ Staff rotation is systematic, especially in international design firms. It is a good way to stimulate talented people by challenging them with different problems and environments. But the rotation of staff also takes place among the various departments of a design firm.

* Brainstorming is also stimulating. For example, IDEO's motto is, "Brainstorm every day."

* Information sharing on past and present projects: keeping a record of the main decision points of each project.

* Creativity seminars. For example, Design Continuum runs dialogue sessions on what makes the difference between "good design" and "great design," and goes on team outings to galleries and exhibitions, the movies, etc.

* Concept development. Often, the demand comes for public relations reasons, but it is a good way to foster a creative scenario and communicate the firm's creative skills.

* New talent search. A successful design firm will find top-quality staff and have access to talented graduates. It takes the time to select interesting profiles from among the numerous résumés it receives every day and offers internship positions. It also establishes close relationships with design schools in order to sort out the best potential students. It can be the school of the founder or simply those schools with whose educational philosophy the firm agrees, or schools where the top management of the design firm are themselves professors or board members.

HOW TO KEEP YOUR DESIGN FIRM EFFICIENT

CREATIVITY IS NOT SUFFICIENT to make the design firm more efficient. Efficiency comes from developing specific skills designed by the firm to help improve client business. They are organizational skills that strengthen NPD process management, including:

* Developing innovation management skills like prototyping and quality certification.

* Developing brand identity management with specific brand evaluation and auditing.

* Developing ideas that reduce marketing time—for example, information processing.

* Developing strategy formulation skills in order to search out new business opportunities for the client. (For example, a design firm can act as a hidden partner in order to help a client respond to complex high-technology competition.)

All design firms differ in the way they master and develop specific tools for technology innovation, rapid prototyping, user-interface expertise in product design, and brand management and evaluation, or any formal, written method that makes the design process more tangible for clients and helps build trust.

1. Being a full design service provider or niche specialist.
2. Maintaining excellent long-term client relationships and achieving customer satisfaction.
3. Entrepreneurship: being future-oriented, and ready to grab and act on opportunities.
4. Interdisciplinary and multicultural orientation.
5. Strong focus on building and sustaining an excellent image.
6. Engaging in a cycle of continuous learning by constantly evaluating service and practices.

Table 8.2. A Design Firm's Critical Success Factors (Gemser & van Zee, 2002)

IDEO CASE STUDY: PRADA

"Prada opened their first 'epicenter' store in New York City in December 2001. The epicenter is seen as a working experiment and is a space designed specifically to accommodate change, change in the store's functionality, interaction, and content. Interactive dressing rooms are a collaborative design by AMO and IDEO and the wireless handheld staff devices have been developed by IDEO.

"All merchandise has its own RFID technology tag. When scanned and detected, immediate access is provided to a database where there is a rich stream of content in the form of sketches, video clips, and color swatches; and up-to-date information on stock availability: this enables the sales associate to spend more time attending personally to a customer. An RFID tag is also part of the Prada customer card. Customer preferences are stored in the database and only the customer card provides access."

BUILDING A DESIGN FIRM REPUTATION

CRITICAL SUCCESS FACTORS FOR DESIGN FIRMS are strategy, international scope, and long-term client relationships, as well as reputation and excellence in management. The ability to build and sustain a good image and the capacity to organize continuous learning and proactive management are likely to enhance a design firm's competitive edge (Table 8.2).

A corporate reputation is built on a set of economic and noneconomic attributes ascribed to a company that are inferred from the company's past actions. A favorable reputation is a source of sustainable competitive advantage. Reputation explains differences in performance among companies. But, if reputation is an important intangible asset, it is also fragile because it is easily lost.

Design firms develop strong reputations by differentiating themselves through innovation and customer service. Success grown from a reputation of being innovative is an incentive to continuously innovate. In order to improve their corporate reputation, design firms should be on the lookout for consistent, strategic exposure in both the design and business communities.

Example: Lippincott & Marguilies was nominated in January 2002 by Global Finance Marketing as the world's best design consultant because of its professional reputation and prospective growth in the coming year.

Corporate communications for design firms directed toward reputation building implies:

- participating as speakers at major or international symposia or conferences
- publishing articles in design journals and interviews in the economic press
- holding part-time professorships or giving guest lectures at universities and top business and design schools
- participating in prestigious design contests

DESIGN AWARDS AND PEER RECOGNITION

AWARDS ARE IMPORTANT for shaping the competitive process. The design market works on a dynamic similar to that of other cultural industries.

THE FUTURE IS ORANGE

"In November 1996 Wolff Olins won the Design Business Association's prestigious Design Effectiveness Award for the Orange Corporate Identity. The brand was set to launch in April 1994. Considering the subsequent triumph it is difficult now to imagine what a tremendous risk it was at the time of this launch. Orange had gone from being an unknown business to the status of the brand of the decade. In August 2000 France Telecom acquired Orange from Vodafone."

Awards give the award winner many different types of benefits and values (Gemser & Wijnberg, 2002):

- The value of the award itself in terms of prize money, rights, and privileges.
- The value of the award as a signal to competitors. The award makes it clear that the winner belongs to a particular subgroup of competitors. The award reinforces existing governance systems, shows what kinds of competitive behavior are preferred, and is an attractive passport for the company and its design consultant to an elite group.

Design prizes are also an interesting form of protection. Winning an award may not only have a positive impact on communicating your ability to innovate and manage design. It can also help in optimizing the returns of your innovation. Winning an award prevents competitive imitation. As the design award may increase the visibility of the company and its products, it thereby enhances the chance that an imitator will be quickly discovered and cast out of the design community network. Strategies for winning awards can even be more effective than the traditional legal forms of protection, especially in countries where legal protection for design is not well organized, such as Italy.

❧ The value of the award as a signal to consumers or distributors. Winning design awards helps companies and designers increase their status and enhance their reputation in the marketplace. A company's reputation is an important determinant of demand, especially when the product quality can't be determined at the time of purchase. A reputation functions as a surrogate measure of quality and can enhance the ability to charge premium prices. In this sense, consumers tend to rely on surrogate measures of quality, such as an advertisement stating a prize awarded, or a recommendation from a knowledgeable source. When a company has won an award it has earned a kind of certification by a knowledgeable evaluator, which helps build credibility and legitimacy.

Other indirect benefits of awards are that they make it easier to recruit talented staff and to attract and retain clients. Having received awards in the past minimizes transaction costs in winning new clients and increases market barriers to potential new competitors and substitute products.

Design firms are well aware of the significance of winning awards. Most design firms quote their design awards on their Web sites. The impact of a design award on competitive success is more likely to be significant if the quality of the products of the award-winning company is difficult to evaluate prior to consumption. Also, the impact of a design award is more likely to be significant if the design award is held in high esteem, such as the IDSA awards (USA) or iF (Germany). A design award is more likely to be held in high esteem if the selection system for the award corresponds to the selection system of the industry involved.

COMMUNICATIONS STRATEGY

DESIGN FIRMS DEVELOP COMMUNICATIONS POLICIES that support and complement their managers' direct communication through conferences and interviews. By using professional expertise in corporate communications in the form of a specialist recruited to the firm, design firms can create a better press relationship and public relations policy.

Press Relationships

Building long-term relationships with some key journalists and media is crucial for image building. This policy requires:

* Regular press releases about projects sent to the professional, economic, and design press
* Relationships with the general press and TV media, especially for consumer goods innovation, in order to foster the role of the design profession in the larger public

Public Relations

The design community—consisting of designers and design-oriented firms—is a small community network that has a limited number of members organizing opportunities to help increase the frequency of relationships and decrease the amount of opportunism in future transactions. Building a reputation requires building relationships with new design community members and helping to improve relationships with present and past members. Design consultancies:

* Develop opportunities for PR events that can bring in concept development and press coverage
* Organize specific marketing events for clients like exhibitions on new consumer trends
* Participate in design events, such as Designers' Week and design exhibitions

But design is also about thinking *differently*. Rather than communicating after doing, communications is itself a design process. We know strategy can be both emergent and deliberate. Most design firms have adopted a "deliberate" communications policy, but there are other ways.

The most outstanding example of an "indirect" communication strategy is the case of the famous French designer, Philippe Starck. Celebrated in the press as a superstar, Philippe Starck's work is everywhere, and the more it is written that Philippe Starck is famous, the more famous he becomes! To reiterate that Starck is famous facilitates his celebrity—the reality is augmented by the media's discourse. How can this proclaimed notoriety be explained?

CHRISTINE BAUER, 2001

"The press around Philippe Starck illustrates that his popularity essentially resides in the fact that he is often reproached. No one knows which side he will take; he champions immateriality so that he can make products that don't exist; he manipulates us without our knowing it; he invents nothing, and ultimately lives his life saying one thing and then the exact opposite."

Philippe Starck is a strategist with no strategies—or, rather, he uses indirect strategies inspired by "Chinese" tactics (to appear where you are not expected) that are based on efficient information processing (Bauer, 2001):

- The "escape" strategy. "I am not a designer, I am a political agitator." Being where nobody expects him to be gives Starck great freedom. His design firm is named Ubik for "ubiquity."
- The "immateriality" strategy. "Tomorrow will be less." Examples: his transparent chair, La Marie; the mail-order catalogue, *Good Goods*, a success as a catalogue with no great commercial effect, a concept of "no-objects for no-consumers."
- The "upstream" strategy: using his prestige to impose ideas that actualize others' desires. Hiring Starck as a consultant is recruiting a savior. His products have sign value more than use value. (For instance, the Alessi lemon squeeze was not designed to be a lemon squeezer but a "topic of conversation.")
- The "potential" strategy: to have the capacity to discern at the "embryo state" or potential of any situation. This is why Starck so often speaks as a visionary on different issues of the times, not just as a designer.

This no-strategy communication scheme illustrates how communication is a process of differentiation and anticipation.

MANAGEMENT EXCELLENCE

EACH DESIGN FIRM HAS A VISION of its positioning strategy that entails a specific management model: either Taylor- or process-oriented. Just as in any other business activity, management excellence and success are found in design firms that adopt a client-oriented, total-quality management (Table 8.3).

An interesting study was conducted that benchmarked successful design firms and compared them with other less-successful firms in four different countries. The researchers compared work practices and organizational structures between the two groups. The results show that design firms differ in their management expertise, and that quality in management gives a design firm an edge over its competitors (Gemser & van Zee, 2002).

The results synthesized below follow McKinsey's "7 S model," the "basic management model for excellence," as a framework for presenting some of the critical success factors for design firms.

Structure

Successful firms have a flat, horizontally based organizational structure, in which self-organizing multidisciplinary project teams are responsible for executing specific projects. The workspaces of project teams are laid out in flexible ways. Unsuccessful

DESIGN FIRM MODEL	TAYLOR ORGANIZED	PROCESS ORGANIZED
ORGANIZATION FOUNDED ON	*Division of tasks and competencies`*	*Autonomy of management of a polyvalent team*
COMPETENCY	*Professional skills*	*Project skill oriented toward client needs*
ACCENT ON	*Productivity*	*Quality indicators*
ACCESS TO INFORMATION	*Minimum*	*Transparent*
DECISION	*Hierarchical control*	*Staff empowerment*

Table 8.3. Comparing the Design Firm Management Models

firms are more vertical in their structure, with teams tightly directed by the firm's managing directors.

Project teams of successful design firms operate as if they are a part of the client organization. It is not unusual to physically site the design teams within the client organization for some amount of time. Through this organizational practice of "co-production," the design firm staff members become insiders in order to speed up the NPD process. The tendency to outsource design activity stimulates coproduction and the early, continuous involvement of the design firm.

Successful design firms are owned and managed by partners with different backgrounds. They have an explicit policy to increase their number of partners. Conscious of the limitations of their competency, they work with outside specialists, develop long-term relationships with them, and focus on building up a sophisticated network of experts in design services and the "orchestration" of talent.

Systems

Successful design firms tend to tune their systems to those of their clients. By doing so, it becomes difficult and costly to put an end to the relationship. These integrated systems require a proactive investment policy in improving communications with the clients. Investments in systems that facilitate the communication process include videoconferencing and software to better plan and structure the design process. Successful design firms self-audit the quality of their products and design processes and act on the results.

Other systems involve the ability to manage transaction costs through specific contractual clauses concerning exclusivity and compensation. Traditional consultant compensation formula fees for design services place all the risk on clients and none on consultants. To move beyond this scenario, consultants must be given some type of equity position or property ownership. Property ownership is the mechanism that links consultant compensation to concrete results (Cellini & Hull, 1996).

There are seven models of consultant compensation:

1. Work-for-hire on a fixed-fee basis. A virtually complete transfer of property rights from consultant to client. The consultant gives substantial value and assumes great risk, yet abjures any hope of significant reward.
2. Work-for-hire on a contingency basis. This ties the firm compensation to some external indicator of client success.
3. Royalty-free licenses. The consultant grants royalty-free exclusive licenses in a specific field while reserving for itself all other rights.
4. Royalty-paying licenses. These are very risky for the design firm because there are many issues the design firm does not control. A good product can be ruined by wrong market positioning.
5. Stock options. The design firm takes as its remuneration stock options in the company. This has developed with the new economy start-up companies. The risk is just like any stock market investment.
6. Unilateral direct investment. The design firm invests in a product or a prototype and tries afterwards to find a partner to manufacture and market the idea.
7. Joint ventures. Just like joint ventures in an R&D network and consortium. This system is rare in the design community, but frequent for technology innovation. It has great potential for design firms.

The rise of results-based compensation systems is likely to be a main force, dividing the design profession into highly compensated business strategists on one side and tacticians on the other. Such revenues are likely to have a transforming effect on the quality and range of services offered by these firms. Successful firms will fully metamorphose from design firms specializing in management to management firms specializing in design.

Some design firms, especially in the U.S., are similar to entrepreneurships and are generally willing to work with start-up firms at a reduced hourly rate, if that can be recouped by means of royalties, option shares, or profit sharing.

This will also be true of the way design firms manage other intangible costs, such as exclusivity and confidentiality. Most clients require both in the transaction, but the extent to which the design firm accepts exclusivity or the way it is able to limit it within time and market constraints can bring competitive advantage. Confidentiality is also fundamental in these highly creative relationships. Some design firms are able to provide secured "confidential" office spaces for their clients' specific projects.

Shared Values

Designers in successful design firms are not afraid to make mistakes. They concentrate on simplifying the work process and working faster, and are solidly embedded in a continuous learning process. They are not inclined to accept their clients' briefings as givens. For them, a design brief is a document on which both parties have to agree. In the analysis phase, they critique the client's brief and work on getting the right brief instead of striving to execute the client's. Successful design firms strive to be actively involved in determining the attributes of the product at the front end of product development, or the idea search phase.

Different design philosophies value design differently, has an effect on attitudes about compensation. English and German firms require an "honest dollar for an honest per-day work," and if there is additional funding needed they will discuss it with the clients. Some other firms, including Italian firms, are more indulged in designing the "perfect product," even if it implies additional hours that are not paid by the client. Some other design firms have the reputation of wanting to make the world better with "good design." With this design philosophy, the management feels unconcerned with low profitability and income.

Style

Design firms differ in their management styles and in how they look at their environment. Successful design firms are extroverted, whereas the less-known focus on their direct competitors. Successful design firms know the members of the communities in which they are successful and are continuously striving to improve themselves. Being outward-looking, they are more prepared to take risks and act faster on new opportunities. They are continuously evaluating their strategies in terms of SWOT analysis (strengths, weaknesses, opportunities, and threats) and are continuously working on the strategy formulation of critical competitive factors.

Successful design firms adopt marketing methods that are selective and professional. They search for a potential client if it has an interesting profile that fits into the firm's skills and has long-term interest. The way a design firm selects its clients and diversifies its activity in different markets is proof of good management.

FITCH RS

"We projected ourselves to new 'platforms' by finding new customers, e.g., going to fairs and other meeting places, sourcing interesting firms, and even driving around their premises to see if they really cared. We made a list to 'eliminate from.' Afterwards we identified six strategically interesting future industries and then in each sector selected one prospect firm to pay a personal visit."

A business approach to design is an exception in most firms. Many firms lack professional design management skills. Industrial design firms react differently when confronted with a client of limited capabilities for managing the design process: well-reputed design firms will consider as a main task understanding their client and cooperating with them in order to manage the design process. They organize workshops with potential clients, place staff in client organizations, and allow client representatives to sit on the project team to ensure ongoing communications during the project.

The less-successful design firms have a more aloof attitude toward the client and are inclined to execute the design process based on their own insights, without including the client in the design process. (That is, they do not work with the client, but for the client.) As the successful design firms have continuous "mutually beneficial" relationships with their clients and have good contacts with all the relevant managerial levels, they are more often successful in helping the client to develop design management skills and coming up with concepts that satisfy the client's wishes.

CHECKLIST: HOW TO CHOOSE YOUR DESIGN FIRM

1. **What is the nature of the question the design firm will have to answer?**
   Define the design problem and its strategic positioning. A new concept and a redesign do not involve the same creative skills.
2. **What are the design services you are asking of the firm?**
   Some design firms offer a global marketing approach that can have an international scope or the strategic study of product positioning. In other cases, only creation is needed.
      Other potential services are name research, trend analysis, brand evaluation, prototyping, and graphic communications.
3. **What is the philosophy of the firm?**
   Analyze the firm's philosophy, potential for creation, and policy in terms of client relationships. The firm's marketing tools are a good test.
4. **Should you use a design firm that specializes in your market?**
   An experience in your market will reassure you, and the firm will understand the design brief more quickly. But the experience of the firm that has worked on similar consumer targets might be a more important criterion than the experience in your product.
5. **Can you demand exclusivity on a market?**
   No, or you will have to pay for it. Confidentiality and a reasonable exclusive period are negotiable agreement conditions.
6. **Should you put several firms in competition?**
   This is more and more the case, but you will have to limit the competition to the presentation of a work methodology and a budget estimate.
7. **What is the reputation of the design firm in the market?**
   Word of mouth is still the best means of making decisions on key points: design reputation, budget monitoring, and respect for planning. Complicity with the commercial-creative team is fundamental. It is a condition of the quality of dialogue and the design solution.
8. **Is the design firm used to working with technical services?**
   Organize a meeting in order to assess the firm's level of technical knowledge and cover all of the technical constraints, such as production and NPD project team management.
9. **Is the estimate clear?**
   The estimate has to follow the stages of the design process. Be sure to ask for a fully detailed budget of technical expenses such as models and prototypes.
10. **What does it cost?**
    Think of your project in terms of investment and make clear the ratio you will use to calculate the success: profit margin, sales, market share, brand image, etc.

CHAPTER 9

OPERATIONAL DESIGN MANAGEMENT

T HESE FINAL THREE CHAPTERS look at different management situations confronting design managers and firm managers, and offer tools for effectively putting design management into practice. We will look at the practice of design management on three decision-making levels:

- The operational level of the project, or the first step toward integrating design
- The functional level, or the creation of a design function in the company
- The strategic level, or the ability of design to unite and transform the company's vision

----

PETER PHILLIPS, 2002

Strategy Consultant
"The Value You Offer"

"My recommendation is for design groups to brainstorm and determine their value in business terms. Designers need to communicate their value in a manner that is both compelling and understandable.

"Management includes planning, organizing, coordinating, and controlling resources in such a way to accomplish the mission in the most profitable way possible. Ask yourself: How do I fit in the description? In three directions:

- Recognize the business role of design. Solve business problems with visual concepts, interpret the status quo, respond pragmatically.
- Establish and maintain mutually valuable relationships. Be proactive, needs-sensitive, business wise, mutually informed.
- Implement efficient work with processes: structured steps, ensured involvement, checkpoints, clear and measurable ratios."

In practice, design management controls three areas:

- The administration of design's added value
- The administration of relationships
- The administration of processes

Its objective is to build credibility and confidence vis-à-vis design in the long term.

CREATING A DEMAND FOR DESIGN

FIRST, IT IS IMPORTANT TO BE AWARE of those decisions that are made within the company that fall within design's domain but are the responsibility of people other than designers.

Once the business context has been investigated, a demand for design is initiated.

DESIGN AND CREATING A BUSINESS

IN AN ENTREPRENEURIAL CONTEXT, such as creating a business or merging multiple businesses into one, it is important to link design with the launch of the business, whether as a means of creating a visual identity or projecting the company's concept or particular positioning. In the case of a corporate identity, the problem to be solved by the designer is often twofold: to come up with a name for the company and a typography for that new name.

LUCENT TECHNOLOGIES

(Source Design Management Institute case study)

The identity of Lucent Technologies was created despite and because of four paradoxes, according to Patrice Kavanaugh, executive director of Landor Associates.

"The first paradox was that this instant 'start-up' company became a Fortune 40 company with more than 125 years of experience and $20 billion in revenues. Nevertheless, despite its heritage, size, and international scope, nobody had heard of this new company because it was, after all, a 'start-up.'

"The second paradox was that in order to effectively shape and articulate the new company's future, its identity needed to leverage, from its own history, powerful brand equities and assets such as Bell Labs.

"The third paradox was that the announcement of the new identity, normally a high-profile media event for large corporations, was staged under strict U.S. Securities and Exchange Commission (SEC) regulations because of the company's impending initial offering (IPO) of stock.

"The fourth paradox was that this was a start-up company operating without a name but with thousands of customers."

INITIATING THE FIRST DESIGN PROJECT

ALTHOUGH THERE IS A TENDENCY for "market triggers" to be the events that instigate a demand for design (Bruce, 2002), a demand for design can also be triggered by business strategy and technology.

A demand for design stems from a need to differentiate a product, launch a brand, develop design leadership, and, finally, from the implementation of new technology (Borja de Mozota, 2000). The initial design demand can be triggered by various business objectives (Table 9.1).

One mustn't believe that an initial design project only exists in a professional context of a small business or simple problem. The Eurotunnel project demonstrates the opposite. The plan for the project was complex because not only did it need to manage the design role in a bicultural context and a project that was technologically complex, but it also had to balance multiple design projects, products, and company logos.

PETER GORB AND RAYMOND TURNER, 1992

Eurotunnel

"Before design and corporate identity could be managed at the Eurotunnel—the tunnel linking the U.K. and France under the English Channel—the decision-making chain had to be organized and a structure developed that would facilitate the work. In phase one, a structure was set up under four points: advice, action, approval, and information:

⚜ Advice. Authoritative design and corporate identity advice was provided by an English-French team of external consultants (Wolff Olins and ADSA), who attended a series of working groups.

Business Objective	Design Demand
To start a company	Logo
To be a design leader	Global design
To launch a new product or a store	Concept development and NPD
To launch a brand	Name development and graphic design
To increase market share	Web and package design
To regain market share	Redesign
To diversify into a new market	Product design or brand extension
To improve R&D policy	Concept development

Table 9.1. The Business Triggers of Design

- Action. Working groups were established, each to look after the design
  management needs of discrete tasks. Their task was to identify design gaps,
  agree upon design direction, and recommend to the project managers action
  that should be taken.
- Approval. Where additional authority was needed to approve action agreed
  upon by the working groups, their chairmen had access to one of the two senior
  management groups, the Corporate Identity and the Design Management
  Steering groups. These two groups were agents of Eurotunnel's Management
  executive and as such were empowered to make top-level decisions. The
  Design Management group was also empowered to establish new working
  groups as required, or to dissolve ones when they were no longer needed.
  This was clearly not the case for the corporate identity group whose work
  was continuous.
- Information. It was necessary for the Board to guide, and to be kept
  informed about, major design and corporate identity decisions. In some
  instances the Board approved the significant directions being taken by the
  two senior management groups. In addition to this formal structure, there
  was also an informal one resulting from some common memberships in working
  groups and a free-roving commission which was allowed to the consultants'
  advisers."

Once the design demand has been initiated, two decisions must be made:

1. Who will be responsible for design in the company—a "design champion" at
   the level of general manager who will attend to defining the new design policy?
2. How will project design management tools be delegated within the company?

MANAGING A DESIGN PROJECT

IS IT NECESSARY TO RELY ON AN OUTSIDE DESIGNER? How do you select this
partner? How do you supervise the relationship between the design firm and the
company? These are the questions we will answer in this section.

Internal Design versus External Design

Selecting an outside designer is often the solution in a first project, because the
company will always want to minimize risks when developing design for the first
time. Despite his lack of experience in design, the design manager can be reassured
by putting faith in the reputation of the design firm.

Hiring an outside firm or designer guarantees a state-of-the-art creative level and
solutions. Externalizing design also facilitates its integration at a higher hierarchical
level, more flexibility, supervision by a design board, and more control over project
costs. Table 9.2 compares the advantages and disadvantages of the two methods.

	Advantages	Disadvantages

In-house	• cost efficiency
	• accessibility
	• easier coordination
	• company retains control
	• design develops intimate
	  understanding of company
		• lack of creativity/new ideas
		• keeping the design team
		  busy, e.g., ongoing development work
		• losing touch with external
		  developments

External	• new inspiration
	• access to specialists' expertise
	  relieves workload
	• accessibility of additional
	  skills/staff
	• options of changing and exploring
	  different options
		• lack of understanding of company-
		  specific issues
		• problems of everyday accessibility
		• problems of coordination with
		  in-house design and/or other
		  departments
		• potential lack of confidentiality
		• company needs skills to evaluate the
		  design work
		• "not-invented-here" syndrome
		• problems with industrializing the
		  externally developed design
		• loss of control and continuity in the
		  relationship
		• credibility gap if design is too far
		  removed from company's own style

Table 9.2. **Comparing Internal versus External Design**
      (von Stamm, 1993)

Other than the "not-invented-here" syndrome, the solution of externalizing design presents many disadvantages; one might then suggest opting for an external designer or design team that is closely associated with internal team in charge of supervising the added value of design. Furthermore, externalizing is not incompatible with fidelity (Bruce et al., 1994).

How Do You Select a Partner?

Besides the expense, finding a design firm that meets the company's requirements is the principal barrier in developing a design project (von Stamm, 1993). Many companies don't know where to begin to look for a suitable design firm. Thus, companies will often seek the recommendation of a third party or a client. The firm's reputation is key. More and more, the firm will contact the company directly. This makes the selection process easier and assures the company that the design firm is experienced in the field and well-equipped.

It is advisable that a company use every resource available in order to find the right designer. Design consultants and directories help in the selection process. The design manager might also have confidence in a particular designer who has been recommended to him or with whom he has worked in the past.

The next step is to verify the design firm's abilities, which can be complicated. If the company is looking for a creative firm, it will be disappointed by firms that emphasize their own methodology, fearing to start the creative process without a contract agreement or full understanding of the design problem being presented. As a result, the company will visit many different firms and listen to the same presentations over and over that give no guarantee of uniqueness or the necessary technological capabilities. Therefore, it is crucial to ask for examples of past collaborations that show the design problem given to the firm, the firm's approach to the problem, and the final solution. This way, the company will have a better grasp of the design firm's competency.

Before making a final selection, it is advisable to organize a meeting with the design firm at the company's premises to discuss the project with the potential collaborators. The chemistry between the people on both teams is a good indicator of the success of the collaboration. Finally, there is also the possibility of asking for estimates; such a call can spread the word to other potential applicants, especially for important or prospective projects.

The main factor in the firm-client company relationship is whether their visions are compatible. A design firm will often have only a short-term approach and will only see its role as limited to a certain amount of work. The client company, on the other hand, may have a more policy-oriented and ideological view of the design project.

LEE WYNN, 2000

Head of industrial design, Human Factors Xerox

"Our study of nine companies identifies the different design ideologies on both sides.

- ✿ Client ideologies: design as cultural (ecological focus), futurist (technological focus), human ware (lifestyle focus), elitist (dictator focus)
- ✿ Consultant ideologies: design as image differentiation (stylistic focus), as coherence (corporate identity focus), as service (project focus)....

Industrial design needs to widen its activities to ensure pre-specification involvement and to remain online with client ideology."

The relationship with an outside designer should be viewed as one of apprenticeship. This means the company should hire a manager who can supervise the relationship and make sure the design is well integrated into the company.

DESIGN CONTINUUM, 2000

"The most important aspect of the relationship contract is in planning the responsibility, budget, and time commitment for developing the design relationship as an asset."

The same goes for the design firm; the firm must select a contact person to be in charge of the relationship with its client. The client company will keep this person informed of its decisions and actions (for instance, by putting the design firm on information distribution lists).

FITCH, 2000

"We recommend that design consultants use 'relationship managers' to enhance communications and establish a shared understanding of priorities and goals. From the client perspective, another important strategy involves executives and design principals meeting periodically for candid, closed-door account reviews."

Externalizing is also sometimes a quasi-internalization because an agreement is made with the partner according to a "network management" logic. The company has its own designers but also develops alliances with outside partners to have access to complementary capabilities, or to balance out the workload of internal design services.

Today, the demand for design in business is evolving toward more variety. Businesses still need to develop overall design concepts, but also have the need for limited specialized resources such as CAD expertise or designers to assist an internal team, or for prospective design research.

MANAGING THE PROJECT BUDGET

FINANCIAL MANAGEMENT REVOLVES AROUND THREE POINTS: the type of payment, the project budget, and how to evaluate cost effectiveness. Certain companies, lacking confidence in design as a new process that they do not have experience in, choose to ask for the advice of several design firms and, even, their creative solutions while not paying them for their work. By doing so, they deliberately select less competent designers who spend less time on creative problem solving and do a more shallow analysis of the project. One must admit that while this practice—competition between consultancies with no payment agreed upon during the selection process—is common in advertising agencies, it can pollute the design sector, which is working on smaller budgets than advertising agencies.

There are many different ways to pay for design services: fixed fees, hourly fees, royalties, and rates that vary according to the complexity of the proposed design problem. The design firm envisions the amount of work involved in a project and defines in a precise manner the conditions of the contract in terms of payment, planning, and the number of proposed visual solutions. To ensure efficacy, the firm can add exclusivity and confidentiality clauses to the contract. Fabrication fees for models are computed separately. Design centers are a good source of judgment on the validity of a budget.

How Do You Define the Budget and Calculate Costs?

In determining the long-term costs of a project, it is important to calculate in the following:

- ✹ The cost of trust-building between parties, since a successful design policy depends on a long-term compatibility between the client company and the design firm (Bruce & Morris, 1995)
- ✹ The indirect costs of understanding the client company—knowledge of the working conditions, personalities of directors, and constraints in the company culture. In other words, the costs of becoming familiar with the company are indirect costs of externalization if the firm goes from integrated design to outsourcing.

CREATING THE PERFECT DESIGN BRIEF

THE COMPANY HAS THE RESPONSIBILITY of writing up the design brief, which will be kept as a reference for whoever participates in the process from beginning to end. A brief consists of three elements: the project objective, information about the company, and information about the project (Table 9.3). A final section defines the different phases of the project—analysis, creation, and manufacture—and their respective time estimates.

The design brief written by the firm is often reiterated in a document issued by the design firm explaining its representation of the problem. The firm draws up a brief in which it explains its vision for the project and lists its analysis of the problem, its plan for the different phases of the project, and any "visuals" to be developed.

This back-and-forth over the design brief is essential for the design firm to absorb and prioritize the information outlined in the brief and initiates the relationship. The success of the project depends on these documents and an effective use of visuals as tools for communication during the project. The designer describes his creative process according to the problem presented and the investigations he will make: drawings of the product, observations of the product users, and visual representations of the market. The company will want to discuss with the designer his visualization of the proposed problem (Davenport-Firth, 2000).

LUNAR DESIGN, 1999

"Associative and brand visual maps provide a bird's eye view of the target customer's products and concepts. The metaphor provided by this kind of map is unusually appropriate for successful product design. It provides a comforting road map for the journey into the fuzzy world of aesthetics, features, and brand attributes."

The success of the project depends next on the organization of the project team. Around the project manager, who can come often from the design firm, are gathered

Table 9.3. The Design Project Brief

---

1. The Design Project Objective
The company states its principal purpose in initiating the project and, by synthesizing its analysis, specifies the design performance required, measured in terms of cost decrease or improvement in image or sales.

The design project objective narrows down the role of design and delineates the impact the project will have and on what audience.

Next, the type of design is specified according to the objective.

- -

2. Information about the Client Company
This entails information about the company's activities, and its history, size, and place in its competitive environment. In addition, it is important to describe the operational structure of the company, the names of the persons who will be in contact with the designer, and information regarding the company identity and its internal and external image, in order to paint a picture of the company identity and business mission.

Also added here is the degree of attractiveness of the company's business sector and its business strategy and market development.

Following this is information regarding the global context of the product or service: the position of the company in its different markets, the economic and sociocultural evolution of its market, its brand positioning, price structure, market research, and lifestyle studies.

- -

3. Project Information
The design brief entails:

- Conceptual data (a definition of the form to be conceived, the degree of originality that can be used in conception, the project's importance in the overall plans of the company, and concept test results).
- Technical data (the type of technology and materials that will be used; the means of production; the methods of innovation management; technical constraints, including standards, dimensions, and components; a definition of the role of R&D versus design; and the role of suppliers and subcontractors).
- Commercial data (how the product will be distributed and publicized, including sales policy; wholesalers, representatives, franchise, logistics, and maintenance and merchandising policies).
- Marketing data (definition of target consumers, consumer preferences segmentation, market positioning, and brand policy). Financial data (project budget, level of technical and design investment, model costs, cost of pre-series, technical studies, and consumer tests).

- -

4. Strategy Information

- Time estimate for each phase of the project.
- Number of visuals necessary in each phase.

---

the different disciplines or expertise necessary for the project and the eventual support staff, such as model makers and suppliers.

MANAGING THE PROJECT TEAM

THE EMPHASIS PLACED ON PROBLEM SOLVING sometimes makes us overlook the fact that the development of a design team is a design project in itself. The keys to the success of a team are well known, but for a design team, it is important to take the time to select the right partners, internally and from the design firm, in order to attain an organizational balance. This interactive structure of the first design project will have to work within a business environment that might not be receptive, or may even be hostile. The relational qualities of the team members become as important for the success of the project as creative talent.

For the project leader, the design brief acts as a sort of contract between the team members. In outlining the different aspects of the project, the brief demonstrates the multidisciplinary character of design and, therefore, the necessity of managing the interactions between the many partner functions and their integration into design decisions, even if the respective importance of each function varies according to the phase in the creative process.

The success of the design project depends largely on:

- The makeup of a multifunctional team in which all of the constraints of the design-form being conceived are represented— that is to say, its technical, marketing, and communications dimensions
- Introducing specialized experts at certain stages of the project
- The integration of design from the beginning phase of the project

The design team is composed of people who fulfill different departmental responsibilities:

- Designers who search out and create the solution to the problem
- The project leader or senior designer who is in charge of the everyday administration of the project, as well as the adequate structure, cost control, and planning, and the relationships with the designers on the project
- The "design champion," or person the project leader has made aware of design success in the company
- The suppliers and subcontractors: the model makers, prototypists, printers, draftsmen, and CAD or CFAD (computer fabrication assisted design) conceivers

The project team is, in fact, composed of three units: a creative unit, a management unit, and an interface unit.

EVALUATING A DESIGN PROJECT

EVEN IF THE CONTROL PROCESS OF THE DESIGN PROJECT is difficult, it is advised that a means of measuring the results of the project can be agreed upon between the company and the design partner. The simplest procedure for creating evaluation tools for a design project is to look at the objective of the design project and measure the success according to whether the objective was met and to the resources that were allocated to the project in terms of:

- Design awards
- Design/product cost
- Design/sales
- Design/market positioning
- Brand and company image
- Design/innovation
- Design/company performance (export rates, action value)
- Design/ROI (return on investment)

VIVIEN WALSH, 1995

"The first possibility for the evaluation of design is an indicator of the output of the design process—rather like patents are an indicator of the output of the inventive process. It is a measure of design performance using prizes awarded for good design and other kinds of peer evaluation. But this is no satisfactory indicator of the total output of design activity.

"The second possibility is to measure inputs of investment in the design process and compare such costs with outcomes such as financial and other benefits at the level of the individual project. We found this more satisfactory."

It is useless to search for specific tools for evaluating design. Many common quantitative and qualitative tools used in marketing, management, and publicity can be transferred to the context of a design project (see chapter 3, a synthesis of studies on design and company performance).

DESIGN AND MARKETING STRATEGY

BY INTRODUCING DESIGN INTO ITS MARKETING POLICY, the company changes its nature. Product policy, brand policy, and marketing are modified by design input. The product marketing manager will often have the responsibility of defining the design objective.

DESIGN AND PRODUCT POLICY

IN PRODUCT MARKETING:

- Design is viewed as a supplementary attribute that is added to the sales level of the product (like the brand or logo). In this case, the marketer often ignores the link between the brand—another product attribute—and graphic design. However, this link is fundamental, since the graphic designer is a participator in the creation phase of the brand.

* Design is global and goes beyond changing the exterior, stylistic appearance of the product. Product differentiation occurs according to eight product dimensions: function, performance, conformity, durability, reliability, reparability, style (its exterior appearance), and service.

In marketing, one of the essential product elements is the packaging that facilitates the first interaction with the customer. Design, then, is often integrated into the product through its packaging. The packaging policy entails making decisions about the nature, form, and sales objective of the packaging that will affect the design objective.

Design is present in the product from the first level (Table 9.4) of the definition of the physical characteristics. Design enhances the product and its performances. This improvement concerns the product's exterior appearance, perceived quality, user satisfaction, functionality, and, finally, originality (Borja de Mozota, 2000).

The product is defined first by its material attributes, or its physical structure: its weight, life cycle, parts, and technology. These days, the "physical" definition of the product does little to make it stand out from other goods in its class; differentiation is more likely to come from branding, packaging, or special features. One would prefer a product to be defined by its functional and symbolic aspects, by its exchange or esteem value and its emotional impact, and by how it is perceived by the consumer. Design becomes a means of balancing the physical, functional, and symbolic visions of the product in order to improve global coherence.

The product is traditionally represented in marketing on three levels (Table 9.4):

1. Level 1: the technical product, described by its core physical characteristics
2. Level 2: the market product, which entails packaging, brand, and instructions for use
3. Level 3: the global product, which integrates services such as free delivery, after-sales maintenance service, installation, and warranty

In this new product schema, design can be integrated at all levels—on the physical and market levels, and on the global level of long-term product performance. The maintenance of a product cannot be separated from the quality of its conception.

Design's place in the product varies. The role of marketing is to choose on which level to integrate design and define the design attributes of the product in terms of marketing and the consumer's experience.

DESIGN AND MARKETING
POSITIONING AND SEGMENTATION

PRODUCT POLICY SEEKS TO DIFFERENTIATE the company's offer from its competition by valorizing its specific advantages. The concepts of positioning and segmentation are traditional tools used by marketers to differentiate their products. Design easily inserts itself into these concepts because it also creates differentiation. The concept

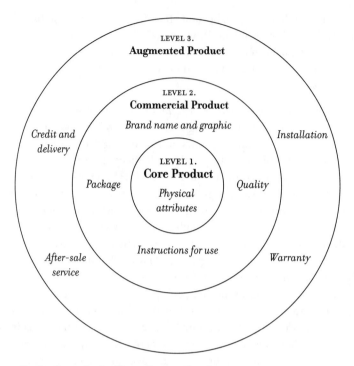

Table 9.4. **Design Input in the Three Product Levels**

of positioning is very close to the conceptual idea underlying the creative process of the designer. Design inserts itself into marketing strategy through the aesthetic definition of a market positioning and by new market segment research.

A market positioning can be defined by an aesthetic positioning: (1) either wanting to be different and unique or contrary; and (2) by copying leading brands in order to identify distributor products and help product categorization. The positioning approach clarifies for the designer the degree of liberty he has in the project and his objective in terms of the desired degree of differentiation, from a completely original concept to a product readjustment in the same range. For the same product, design can suggest alternative positionings that respond to the different preferences of chosen market targets.

Concerning the segmentation criterion, recent changes in consumer needs question the validity of traditional segmentation in terms of lifestyle, age, and sociological and professional categories, and suggest the development of niche segmentation and even the idea of aesthetics as a segmentation criterion.

The discovery of a new micro-segment becomes more important than the development of an existing market, and intuition is given more importance in market research, as in Japanese marketing. In product policy, the marketer asks the designer to develop new ideas for these mini-segments and to not put aside opportunities to win positions in the marketplace.

Design positioning becomes warlike; it implies being capable of searching out new ideas for beating the competition, but also being able to quickly adapt the ideas of the competition to its own market as well as the ideas of other markets.

DESIGN AND PRODUCT LIFE CYCLE

THE OBJECTIVE OF DESIGN depends on the phases of the life cycle of the product. Design helps to increase the longevity of the product, by adapting the product and adjusting its performance as it progresses through its life cycle. The design-form passes through a divergent phase (from the launch or introduction phase to the maturity phase) and a convergent (or growth phase). There is an aesthetic cycle of the product, and according to each phase, different design actions can be programmed. This entails studying the product phase before clarifying the design policy (Table 9.5):

- In the introduction phase, one searches out through various stages the optimal configuration between form and function by adapting to the remarks of the first customers. The aesthetic is divergent.
- In the growth phase, the objective is to innovate in order to be able to industrialize the product. The aesthetic becomes convergent and is integrated into the production process. Design is focused on the assimilation of form into the production process.
- In the maturity phase, the focus is on matching the attributes of the best competitive products or researching minor differentiations in order to enlarge the consumer's choice and/or reduce the consumer's price (detail design).
- In the decline phase, research is conducted to see whether a new technology or new needs can drive a complete reformulation of the product and, therefore, begin a new cycle (concept design).

The life cycle of the bicycle is a good example: from bicycles with different wheel sizes to the development of the standard bicycle to the present dynamism of the market because of a new aesthetic driven by leisure and competition bikes.

THE PRODUCT PORTFOLIO AND DESIGN POLICY

THE DESIGN POLICY VARIES according to a product's place in the product range. The company proposes a family of products that has, more or less, both breadth and depth in order to cover multiple market segments and spread the risks over multiple products. The product range reflects the goal of covering the market in terms of both volume and adaptability to changing behaviors. It responds to the necessity to attain a balance between activities in order to guarantee permanence and profitability. The range also divides products according to price targets.

The design policy is equally different according to the product's place in the company's portfolio. This place can be analyzed according to the classic methods of strategy formulation of the Boston Consulting Group (Table 9.6) or of Ansoff.

Table 9.5. Design Policy and Product Life Cycle

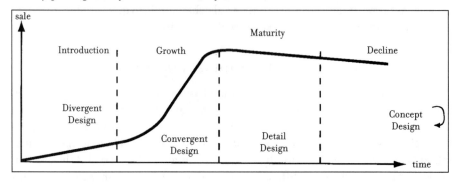

Table 9.6. Design Strategy and the BCG Product Portfolio

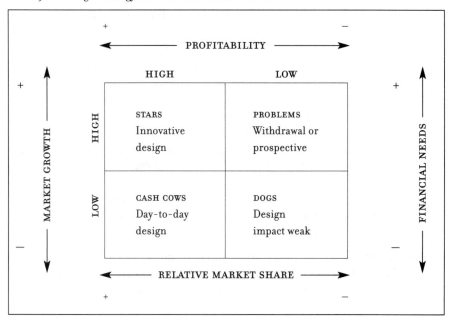

The Boston Consulting Group classifies a company's products according to two axes: the relative market share and the growth rate of the market. This creates four product types and, thus, four types of design policy:

1. "Star" products: strategic segment, rapid growth, and design innovation
2. "Cash cow" products: strong profitability but slow growth; day-to-day design
3. "Dog" or deadweight products: searching to sell, weak design impact
4. "Problem" products: low profitability but, eventually, future, potential, investing in order to become leader, re-segment, or abandon; strong impact of prospective design

Ansoff also divides the product portfolio into two axes—products versus markets and actual versus new—which create four design policy quadrants:

1. Actual product/new market: design responds by boosting sales in other countries or regions (adapting to local particularities) or adopting new forms (searching out new adaptations of the product for other uses; for example, the snowboard from the skateboard).
2. Actual product/actual market: design responds by extending the product range and diversifying packaging; design for extending product notoriety.
3. New product/new market: innovation design, calling for new strategies (new technologies for new needs).

New product/actual market: capitalizing design in the existing infrastructure.

Design and Brand Management

Design management goes through three phases as it evolves into a broader, more holistic commitment to brand supervision (Speak, 2000): from creating a brand to managing the brand image to managing the brand equity.

Creating a Brand Identity

After an analysis of the market needs and competition, creating a brand begins with the creation of the value proposition, followed by the name, the graphic, and the personality of the brand (Table 9.7).

ORANGE CASE STUDY

Wolff Olins started to explore four possible solutions, and for each one a "world" was constructed by putting together a combination of images and moods to reflect the essence of the position. The position "It's my phone" was meant to describe the way customers should experience the brand.

The value proposition, or brand essence, is a single thought that captures the soul of the brand. It holds the different identities of the brand together (the brand as product, person, company, and symbol), and resonates with customers in terms of functional, emotional, and self-expressive benefits.

From the set of five values and the core proposition about the "wire-free future" Wolff Olins began the name creation process. Hundreds were reduced to six names; it was time to begin designing, testing against the values. Orange was the one that stayed. It had everything, and owning the color orange could become a powerful symbol. In 1993 the company became Orange Persona Communications Limited, previously Hutchinson Microtel.

Designing the identity is seen as "brand strategy made visible," or customer relationships and benefits made visible.

The identity was set but not the brand. Only when a personality is added to a product can a brand genuinely exist. To do so Wolff Olins set about constructing the world of Orange. Creating manifestations of the brand in a range of media enabled Wolff Olins to bring the brand to life. Developing a set of visual identity guidelines was a basic part of the agency deliverables.

Managing the Brand Image

This tactical phase of brand management's focus on *brand image* is in order to:

❧ Develop brand image and diversify the brand options according to markets

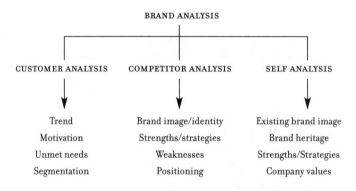

BRAND ANALYSIS

CUSTOMER ANALYSIS	COMPETITOR ANALYSIS	SELF ANALYSIS
Trend	Brand image/identity	Existing brand image
Motivation	Strengths/strategies	Brand heritage
Unmet needs	Weaknesses	Strengths/Strategies
Segmentation	Positioning	Company values

BRAND ESSENCE AND VALUE PROPOSITION			
Brand as product	**Brand as company**	**Brand as person**	**Brand as symbol**
Product scope	Company attributes	Personality	Visual image and
Product attributes	(innovation, consumer	Customer brand	metaphors
Quality/Value	concern, trustworthy)	relationships	Brand heritage
Use	Local versus global		
Users			
Country of origin			
Functional Emotional Self-expressive Benefits Benefits Benefits		Personal Relationship	Credibility Support other brands
Customer relationship			

Table 9.7. **Creating a Brand**
   (adapted from Aaker & Joachimstahler, 2000)

- Concentrate on a limited number of brands to create the structures of category-focused brands
- Work on the coherence of design decisions in a set of multiple communications options
- Initiate an internal dimension of brand communications
- Develop a global dimension of branding (Table 9.8)

Design tools are part of a formal brand strategy, a brand management decision support system that contains identity guidelines, brand definitions, brand usage guidelines, the brand management structure, and brand management responsibilities.

SIEGEL & GALE DESIGN AGENCY

"In the 1970s, we pioneered document simplification. In the 1980s we transformed traditional corporate identity into 'corporate voice' programs. In the 1990s the Internet began to change the business environment and we created new kinds of brand experiences."

The Landor capabilities process is a good example of how a design firm creates specific tools for the design and brand positioning processes (*www.landor.com*).

- Audit analysis through visual brand audits, management, and employee interviews, research including Image Power™ concepts and Brand Asset™ valuators, studies, and site surveys.

Using the information gathered, they then develop the branding strategy, system architecture, and recommendations, and move into the creative development phases.

- The Brand Driver™, in which they develop various conceptual options. At the core of the process is the development of a brand

	From	To
Product-market scope	Single products and markets	Multiple products and markets
Brand structures	Simple	Complex brand architectures
Number of brands	Focus on single brands	Category focus—multiple brands
Country scope	Single country	Global perspective
Brand manager	Coordinator of limited options	Team leader of multiple communication options
Communication focus	External/customer	Internal as well as external

Table 9.8. Managing the Brand Image

driver, created with their client through ideation workshops. Simply put, it is a unique, compelling insight that drives and unites all aspects of brand expression, which can underpin the development of the entire branding system.

Example: Client "e-business partners"; brand driver "Network anatomy" to reflect the observation that an understanding of the "biodynamics" of the e-B2B was critical to its brand-relevant differentiation.

- ❧ The concept: This phase blends the inspirational with the practical. Landor begins by scoping out all points of brand expression, including products, services, environments, and names. Within these, they identify the PowerApps™, which are applications or media that have the most power to influence brand perceptions. The design team then begins creative development, exploring a range of creative concepts that effectively communicate the Brand Driver™ and work well with the PowerApps™.
- ❧ Points of experience: Designing initially for the PowerApps™, they eventually extend the new design system to include all of a brand's points of experience and activity. This includes applications ranging from packaging, stationery, and corporate literature to retail environments, vehicles, and Web sites.
- ❧ Realization: Making the vision a reality, which can include implementation and launch planning, fine art development, design specifications, prototype development, on-press supervision, and environmental installation support. The company provides comprehensive brand guidelines and/or asset management systems to help clients maintain integrity after implementation.

Managing Brand Equity

This strategic phase of brand management focuses on brand equity. Design decisions are made with top-level management and have a more long-term perspective. Design is no longer considered "reactionary" to the fundamentals of brand positioning and promise but, rather, as an integrated component of the genesis of the offer. Design is "visionary." The best thing a brand can do is help create a vision of what the future can bring. Design can play a significant role by being the choreographer.

Brand equity is strategic. It is an asset that can be the basis of competitive advantage and long-term profitability. The goal of brand leadership is to build brand equity rather than brand image (Aaker & Joachimstahler, 2000). Design must identify brand equity elements that differentiate and drive long-term brand vision and staff-customer-brand relationships, and center company mythology around stories revealing the brand values.

Design tools include: an interactive brand management decision support system accessible to all employees, which acts as a knowledge management system; corporate

	TACTICAL BRAND MODEL	STRATEGIC BRAND LEADERSHIP MODEL
Perspective	*Tactical and reactive*	*Strategic and visionary*
Brand manager status	*Less-experienced* *Short-time horizon*	*Higher in the company* *Long-time horizon*
Conceptual model	*Brand image*	*Brand equity*
Focus	*Short-term financials*	*Brand equity measures*

Table 9.9. Managing Brand Equity

identity guidelines; brand-use guidelines; online training; real-time brand news tracking; brand success stories; "brand moment" celebrations; news about current brand promotion efforts; comprehensive training programs; and reward and recognition programs that celebrate brand behaviors.

Strategic brand management calls for new design tools: visionary and relational.

Creating a Vision

IDEO

"Today's design consultancy strategic services tend towards opportunity exploration, concept discovery in order to strengthen the connection between business needs and user needs."

Companies with a strong attitude or belief have something shared by insiders and customers: "a big idea" that goes deeper than any explicit statement of brand or vision.

- Big ideas are radical: Companies with big ideas want to change the world.
- Big ideas are social: They are the property of everyone, not just the chief executive. Examples: Saturn's idea of harmony; Apple users as fanatics.
- Big ideas are tangible: They are made out of actions, not words. Example: Herman Miller's idea of design.
- Big ideas magnify desire: They create a community of customers.

ROBERT JONES & WOLFF OLINS

"Design must be less about corporate identity (the way an organization looks) and more about corporate idea (what it stands for and what it does). In this new century ideas—radical, social, tangible—are all that will matter. Design has to get

The benefit a design firm brings now is the idea rather than the logo, though the
design is still central for two main reasons:

1. An idea is not an idea until it has been expressed and you can see and touch
   it in some way.
2. A big idea takes a mix of skills and needs synthesis. It needs people who can
   cut through a mass of details and pull out the one thing that matters. It
   needs people unafraid to be radical. That is the kind of thinking that comes
   naturally to designers.

The designer's responsibility is to nurture real ideas. His eyes are on the difference
he makes in the world, not just the difference he makes to a client's capitalization
(value share).

Managing Internal Branding

When brand management has risen to the level of a "best practice" in the company,
everyone in the company understands how his or her behavior can make a significant brand statement.

Internal branding is the goal in building brand equity. Internal role models are
stories, programs, events, and people that perfectly represent the brand identity.
Branding is not a function performed by one department. Every point of contact,
not just design, advertising, and promotion, must be on brand, and every individual
within the company should be charged with the responsibility of knowing exactly
what it means.

The brand is the soul of the company, and understanding its core values becomes the
responsibility of everyone in the company—from the human resources professional
who is recruiting new talent to the customer service representative who is a direct link
to the consumer, to the R&D engineer who is considering new technologies.

SIEGEL & GALE

"Today, more and more companies understand that brand is no longer the exclusive property of the marketing department."

How can a brand be infused into company culture? Aligning company culture
and employee behaviors with the promise made by the brand is easier said than
done. Design decisions must try to:

- Build partnerships and generate involvement with other functions
  (human resources)

- Rearticulate the brand in terms of internal beliefs and the corporate mission or vision
- Create targeted messages for internal audiences
- Balance a budget between external execution and internal implementation requirements

---

JEAN LÉON BOUCHENOIRE

Brand management consultant

"Sound brand management has a positive impact on a corporation's financial results. . . . Brand management has an excellent ROI ratio compared to other activities because of its low cost and substantial benefits.

"We can only hope that in the future more brand equity executive directors and vice presidents will be responsible for brand character, identity, design, and nomenclature, and will command the same authority as communications, advertising, and marketing VPs. Brands are valuable assets that should be managed at the highest level.

"Building brand equity calls for a higher position of brand managers and a strategic vision of design in marketing strategy."

Evaluating the Brand

Evaluation systems should be based on statistics. Only evaluations that are based upon quantifiable amounts will bring about concrete changes. Therefore, design managers must consider their major responsibility to create brand evaluation systems.

There are two main focus points for design managers:

1. Infusing design variables in brand image and brand equity measurement systems
2. Understanding and participating in the choice of brand evaluation system

Design/Image Evaluation and Equity

Most companies regularly test their brand image, but it might be difficult to isolate the impact of design because design decisions are integrated into a marketing plan. However, there are design projects that involve no advertising or promotion where design impact can be easily measured.

Tools like brand evaluation and perceptual maps allow for control of the consistency of the graphic design with brand positioning in its market segment, and for understanding consumers' interpretations of brand image. When one thinks about a brand, visual representations come to mind. However, most marketing studies are based on verbal explanations of brand values. This explains why it is helpful to work with pictures in order to draw the sensory profile of a brand (Coulter & Zaltman, 1994).

When a company changes its logotype, the situation is often difficult, so most companies use posteriori studies of the quality of a design solution in order to validate the top management decision to change a logo.

Building brand value is systemic, so it is important in terms of measuring design impact, not only to measure the perception of the quality of the sign but also to investigate whether the design change affects the perception of the company product range, the company corporate image, or the perception the consumer has of himself or herself and of those who buy the brand (Almquist et al., 1998).

In measuring design's impact on brand equity, design should reflect over time equity dimensions such as awareness, loyalty, perceived value, and associations.

Selecting the Brand's Value System

Creating strong brands does pay off, and brands create meaningful value. Interbrand™ studied brand value compared to market capitalization: ratio of brand value as percent of market capitalization. Nine of the top sixty brands over $1 billion had values that exceeded 50 percent of the whole company value. BMW, Nike, Apple, and Ikea had company brand value ratios of over 75 percent. The top ten brands in 2001 were: Coca-Cola, Microsoft, IBM, General Electric, Nokia, Intel, Disney, Ford, McDonald's, and AT&T.

Brands have different values according to their evaluation system:

- Evaluating according to the market price. The difference between net assets and the negotiated value during a transaction, which is indirectly the value of the brand according to licensing value
- Evaluating by costs. According to investments made over history or for recent brands or by replacement costs, evaluating what it will cost to recreate a brand with the same notoriety and fidelity
- Evaluating by potential benefits. Brand evaluation according to separate income directly attributed to brand; brand premium; all brand capital assets (notoriety, fidelity, and image) that allow for selling the brand at a higher price than the competition; difference between the price of an equivalent product and the brand price
- Multi-criteria evaluation

Most models of evaluation rank brands according to benefits: the faithfulness of their consumers and the potential of the brand for internationalization. For example, the Interbrand™ model classifies brand values according to the earnings attributed to the brand using criteria such as:

- The market perspective on the brand
- The brand's market share dominance and of competing brands
- Brand image and notoriety
- Potential of brand extension
- Legal protection of the brand
- Potential of internationalization

But these models are criticized because:

- They produce brand value that changes, and rely on experts' subjective opinions. This volatility counters brand consistency
- They fail to improve understanding on how to manage a brand in the future

This explains why, in February 2002, Landor launched a new company, Brand Economics, which simultaneously uses analytical techniques for financial and brand profiling:

- Economic value creation. Stern Stewart EVA™ framework, widely recognized as the best technique for measuring and managing value creation
- Brand health measurement. Young & Rubicam Brand Asset Valuator™, the world's largest database of consumer attitudes toward individual brands

It is evidently fundamental that design managers understand which brand evaluation system is preferred by the company in order to better evaluate the effect of design on the brand.

DESIGN AND OTHER MARKETING POLICIES

THE INTEGRATION OF DESIGN CHANGES THE POLICIES in the marketing mix (communications, promotion, pricing, distribution, and sales)—not just in product policy. Beyond the brand as communication, a design policy seeks to ensure cohesiveness between product design, publicity, and promotion, and to emphasize permanent media, such as products or commercial spaces in a world saturated with publicity.

Design is referred to as "another form of communication," which implies that there needs to be collaboration between design and communications because:

- Added price value generated by good product design can generate opportunities for investing in communications. Example: Swatch.
- The product concept imposes itself on the creativity of both design and publicity as the company's product offer represented by a certain slogan. A product concept implies placing the aesthetic in its global context. This is what justifies a connection between marketing, design, and communications. A graphic object or sign is a permanent medium for both external and internal communication. An original aesthetic will be reproduced by the press and will valorize the investment outside of publicity media. Within internal communications, an object is a communal object that is shared by company.

Therefore, the design manager is often responsible for both product policy and communications policy.

VINCENT CRÉANCE

Alcatel, Brand Director, Mobile Phone Division

"Design and communications both give value to a brand. But differently:

* They are not in contact with the same people in the company.
* Their intervention periods are not linked. Design acts upstream, communications downstream.
* Their philosophies are different. Design is concerned with a 'good product,' communications with selling the product.
* They differ in regards to creativity. Design creates internally, communications subcontract creation.
* Finally, their budgets do not have the same proportions.

For all these reasons our brand department is divided into two distinct departments: the design department (twenty-four persons in four design disciplines) and communications (twenty-one persons in five different techniques)."

Design might also participate in another part of the marketing mix: the price policy. Two design policies are possible in regards to the price policy.

1. Price differentiation according to cost. Cutting costs drives a "design to cost" policy. The design function participates in cost structure by shaping the production structure so it reduces cost and time:

   * Managing design alongside the buying policy. Inverse design, or pushing design innovation among the suppliers in order to manufacture components that are less expensive and better adapted to the product's final shape.
   * "Target costing" encompasses several techniques, including design alternative analysis (Coughlan, in Bruce & Bessant, 2002).
   * Value engineering involves interdisciplinary and systematic examination of factors affecting the cost of a product. The objective is to devise a means of achieving the required standard of quality and reliability at target cost. The product is divided into components and subassemblies, and value engineering can lead to redesigning some in order to increase the manufacturability of the product.

   Functional analysis divides a product into its several functions, then generates a target cost for the components that is realistic but may be difficult to achieve. Target costs of all components are added together and compared with the expected cost of the product, and either component costs must be reduced or functionality improved.

In productivity analysis, the major steps in the product process for a proposed subassembly are analyzed and the sum of their costs is compared with the subassembly target cost. When the expected cost is too high, the manufacturing and engineering staff need to identify a cost reduction target for each step.

2. Price differentiation by aesthetic appearance. Design to justify a price differentiation for a similar product or service. Design helps the company control demand (using "limited edition," for example). This differentiation can just as easily be used to gain negotiating power with distributors.

The integration of design in the distribution policy is even more subtle. The designer does not participate in deciding on distribution channels. Instead, this selection has an evident impact on the terms of the product design by blending together the product's additional services, such as the instructions for use, packaging, point-of-sale promotion, and, above all, the logo. The objective is to optimize the package design to reduce the costs of transport and limit the risks of breaking or deteriorating. Distribution companies also have a design policy and are sensitive to a design strategy that involves branding and retail space design.

A design policy can contribute to extending the efficiency of sales policy:

- On the exterior. Training or presentation tools that use aesthetic force and graphic visualization to maximize vendors' talents.
- On the interior. In the relationships between designers and salespeople, the salespeople can sometimes put a false façade on the original design form that is thought to be too risky in certain markets. The job of the designer, then, is to identify, in its creative statement, the real power of the sales force and its permeability to new concepts, and initiate actions in favor of accepting new concepts, like free gifts and other compensations.

In the relationships between designers and personnel, it is important to "sell" design internally by using design expertise to facilitate access to the new needs employees and executives have in terms of autonomy and individualization. Design will be best understood if it identifies with and brings together the values that permeate the company and its products. Design management implies having an internal scanning that also allows for reducing risks of the design being rejected, by investigating how the product is received in the outside world as well as within the company.

BUILDING TRUST IN DESIGN IN THE COMPANY

THIS LAST ASPECT OF THE DESIGN MANAGER'S ROLE looks at the management process decisions that build credibility and trust in design in the company in the long term. It puts into practice Peter Phillips's model (see the introduction to this chapter).

How do you capitalize on a first experience to achieve a favorable view of design within the company? Which methods and tools can you use to anchor the design dimension in other departments of the company?

VINCENT CRÉANCE

Alcatel, Brand Director, Mobile Phone Division

"The prerequisite for good design management is trust. Trust at two levels:

- The team must have confidence in their boss and this confidence has a lot to do with his ability to incorporate a 'pleasure dimension' in the creative process. And it is the design manager's role—and main difficulty—to make sure that this dimension expresses itself in the company strategy.
- The company confidence in the relevance of its design solutions. This has a lot to do with the behavior of the design department and of the members of this design direction within the firm."

Building confidence in design necessitates weaving together new liaisons that aspire to build a network of persons who are sympathetic to design within the business structure:

- A liaison with marketing studies. The design project might incite the company to change its marketing research tools, either by inserting design questions into traditional tools of brand evaluation or market opportunity analysis, or by using other methods, including those that observe consumer use situations, sensory analysis, or studies on the aesthetic sensibility of a given market.
- A liaison with technology management. Often, a design project incites technology transfers or new innovation solutions in the design process; it is important to keep rejuvenating this input in order to envision other applications and new ideas.
- A liaison with human resources management. The design firm selection process ends with defining design skills so they are comprehensible to those responsible for recruiting in the company.
- A liaison with information management. A successful relationship with the design firm occurs when the design partners have a strong understanding of their clients' business goals. There must be a concrete "pedagogy" of what the company stands for to creators. At the same time, the relationship will only endure if documents are established that detail all of the steps of the project and specify the tools of control and evaluation that have been selected for the

project. These documents can be used as formulas for developing procedures for selecting and paying design agencies.

- ❧ A liaison with communications management. If the project is a graphic design project or creation of a visual identity, it is likely that graphic guidelines will have been established. These guidelines will act as a means of communication internally and externally. Communication about visual identity will be integrated into the general communications policy of the company. If the project is a product design project, it might be preferable to establish specific communications throughout the design community: communications with the design profession press or with design schools, and participation in design competitions.

OPERATIONAL DESIGN MANAGEMENT CHECKLIST

Strategy:	Define the design policy in the product and communications policies. Define brand policy and design's role in the brand.
Planning:	Write design briefs.
Structure:	Select designers. Define teams and liaisons with the designers. Designate a design champion at the top management level.
Finances:	Manage the design project budget. Estimate design costs.
Personnel:	Define design skills.
Information:	Develop an understanding of business goals among designers. Write project documentation and regulations.
Communications:	Develop liaisons with design schools. Create graphic guidelines.
R&D:	Develop technology transfers.
Project Management:	Manage relationships with design agencies—information, evaluation meetings.
Brand:	Visualize design's place in the brand policy. Modify marketing research to accommodate design input.
Evaluation:	Evaluate the results of the design/design brief. Evaluate the results of the design/market/brand.

CHAPTER 10

FUNCTIONAL DESIGN MANAGEMENT: MANAGING THE DESIGN DEPARTMENT

I n this area of design management, the nature of design changes: No longer a product or project, design becomes a function or department and acquires its independence from the other departments in the company. The design department participates in the company's success in the marketplace.

HENRY DREYFUSS, 1950

"The Industrial Designer and the Businessman"

"One cardinal point which should be made unmistakably clear on both sides of the fence is that industrial designers are employed primarily for one simple reason: to increase the profits of the client company. That may sound unduly crass and materialistic—inartistic, if you wish—but it just happens to be true."

At this point, the company has gained experience in design and may also have had some experience in a succession of different design projects. In order to develop design internally, the most important issues are supporting design at the top-management level and being involved in the development of a brand strategy (Borja de Mozota, 2002).

From the start and throughout the development of the design department in the company, there are a number of examples that illustrate the difficulty of working with creators in an effective and well-balanced way. The following is a list of ten commandments to follow in order to successfully integrate design into the company (Table 10.1).

The issue becomes giving both the designer and the manager methods and tools for successfully integrating design.

THE IN-HOUSE DESIGN DEPARTMENT

DIFFERENT DEPARTMENTS THAT TAKE ON DESIGN have the tendency to favor the design dimension that fits most closely with their specialties. For R&D, this is technology, and for marketing or communications, this is most often user-interface or brand symbols. Design can be viewed differently depending on the department that integrates it into its decision-making processes.

1. A design champion at the top-management level.
2. The overt and consistent support of top management.
3. One or several persons responsible for design.
4. A clear design policy, possibly with norms.
5. A brand policy.
6. A rolling succession of design projects.
7. A financial budget for design.
8. Control tools for design.
9. Staff training in design.
10. A balance between design innovation and communication projects.

Table 10.1. The Ten Commandments of Efficient In-House Design

Therefore, design management takes on the coordination of these different visions of design. Whenever design has a place in the organizational structure, it takes part in decision making and, thus, plays the role of a catalyst.

Creating the In-House Design Department

Why Integrate Design?

The creation of an in-house design department offers many advantages (see chapter 9 also). It allows the company to:

- ❧ Regulate the designer's ideas. An outside design consultant only gives selected solutions to one given design problem.
- ❧ Optimize and standardize the process for a new product launch. This is particularly important for those businesses that have several product ranges and renew them frequently.
- ❧ Guarantee confidentiality, and protect ideas and innovations.
- ❧ Improve the coherence of design decisions concerning the project by entrusting all decisions from the beginning to a responsible designer or team. This applies to product design as well as graphic design (from a brochure to a Web site to the realization of an exposition stand).
- ❧ Entrust the aesthetic thinking of the company to an in-house design department.

However, this in-house design department also presents certain risks that must be counterbalanced by the management quality of the design department, such as:

- ❧ The limiting of a designer's creativity by a hierarchy that forces him to moderate his views.
- ❧ Apathy on the part of the designer because he is limited to one type of product or service. It is difficult for companies to encourage

searching for ideas outside their fields, but it is possible through the implementation of mixed design (in-house and external).

❖ Difficulties in recruiting. The objectives of a design service are often unclear at the beginning and evolve rapidly. The recruited person, often a junior because of a lower salary, will have more difficulty adapting to the company than an experienced designer.

❖ Increasing costs compared to outside design. In-house design costs include departmental expenditures and salary budgets, models, and other design tools.

Therefore, the job of the design manager takes on three different dimensions: creativity management, personnel management, and financial management. A company will create a design department once it becomes aware of the managerial value of design—particularly product design or retail design—and the necessity to effectively manage its expense plan, as well as the objectives assigned to this department.

If a company considers design to be a strategic element in its overall structure and planning, in-house designers will be recruited at the business' inception. The designer's place in the company hierarchy will affect how the designer works and how the company uses design capabilities.

Recruiting a Designer

Recruiting an in-house designer is the first step toward creating a design department and, as in any hiring, relies on the evaluation of the candidate's potential competencies and his or her motivations.

The competencies of an in-house designer must include abilities in design, as well as in driving change. The competencies of a designer can be divided into five categories: design, relational qualities, business sense, project management, and the capacity to generate a perspective (Cooper & Press, 1995).

The psychological profile of the in-house design candidate is as important as her intrinsic competence: Her ability to generate concepts must be complemented by management abilities and, finally, by relational abilities. The most important qualities of a manager are her sense of dialogue, her creative imagination, and how demanding she is. Her capacities to influence and listen are just as fundamental for bringing design into the company (Borja de Mozota, 2000).

It is also necessary to verify that the candidate is motivated with regards to integrating design into the company, is capable of talking about design in a way that is understandable to the manager, and is interested in an in-house position—because of the perspective she can bring to it, the business-world knowledge she can gain, and the challenge of creating a new department.

For a first recruitment, there are two different scenarios: either an in-house designer—most often a young graduate—is chosen by the R&D engineers, or, in the case of creating a design department, a senior designer is hired who has several years of experience in a design firm. But does hiring one designer instantly create a

THE FIVE DESIGN COMPETENCIES	RELATED SKILLS
DRIVING THE PROCESS COMPETENCIES	• *commitment, enthusiasm, self-confidence* • *results orientation* • *team orientation* • *high standards*
DESIGN COMPETENCIES	• *objective creativity* • *technical, color, and conceptual ability*
BUSINESS ORIENTATION COMPETENCIES	• *organizational, planning, problem solving* • *commercial skills*
PERSPECTIVES AND FRAMEWORK COMPETENCIES	• *gathering and using information* • *strategic thinking* • *consumer/customer focus*
INTERPERSONAL COMPETENCIES	• *relationship building* • *influence* • *presentation skills* • *flexibility*

Table 10.2. Competency Model for Designers

company wide design policy? No; the design department must reach a critical size before it will be able to influence ideas and procedures.

> **Crown Equipment DMI case study, discussing whether the new competitive environment and the recent purchase of their long-standing design consultancy called for an in-house design group:**
>
> "Crown had become large enough and required enough industrial design services to make this option viable. This would entail a group of six to eight designers, the critical mass for this type of endeavor. To provide an attractive environment for this in-house design group would involve redoing a historic building about five blocks from the engineering staff and equipping a model shop."

Empirically, a single employed designer will be able to hire outside consultants to do work on projects, but those consultants will not participate in any internal strategic decision making. The change from one to three or more designers is important for design integration—first, because the more they meet with designers, the more marketers and engineers understand the diversity of design and, second, because the design facilities and a design center can give the company a new opportunity for communication and decision making. It is more fun and easier to experiment with different solutions, and working more closely with different designers means engineers tend to ask themselves new kinds of questions, and new working procedures emerge (Svengren & Johansson, 2002).

Design in the Company Structure

DESIGN'S PLACE IN THE STRUCTURE and "reporting" of the department illustrates the design mission in terms of business strategy. Either design responsibilities are assigned to a department that imposes its vision on other departments, or cooperation between departments is encouraged, as well as the design department's independence within the business structure.

There are four roles the design department can play in the company structure that correspond to the different missions design has in the company and are linked to the different economic sectors.

Design as an R&D/Production Department

This link is frequent in evolving technology businesses where the products are complex and require several adjustments. The technological culture is often dominant and is illustrated by an undeniably large number of engineers and technicians in the company.

In this context, the designer is expected to possess creative talents that meet the technical constraints of the product. These jobs most often concern the conception or reconception of products and their packaging. Sometimes, the designer is asked to work with the R&D department on radical innovations.

The designer's innovative power is often diminished by the influence of engineers and an overall resistance to change in the company. But it can bring an important dimension of human and sociological interface to technological innovation. Depending on the technology department, the designer can establish a strategy based on technology that has equal weight with the business plan when his job is dominated by technological demands.

Example: Braun AG. The technical operations division has four departments: product design, R&D, manufacturing, and quality.

BRAUN (DMI CASE STUDY)

"10 Principles of Good Design"

1. Good design is innovative.
2. Good design enhances the usefulness of a product.
3. Good design is aesthetic.
4. Good design displays the original structure of a product: Its form follows its function.
5. Good design is unobtrusive.
6. Good design is honest.
7. Good design is enduring.
8. Good design is consistent right down to details.

9. Good design is ecologically conscious.
10. Good design is minimal design.

Design as a Marketing Department

This is a frequent situation in businesses dominated by commercial preoccupations in highly competitive markets. The role of design is controlled by the brand and selling power of the product and its attributes (packaging, labeling, etc.). This situation is also encountered in service industries in terms of the management of commercial space and signage.

Here, too, design has two levels of responsibility according to its role in marketing strategy:

1. A tactical level, in which design supplies are at the service of a certain style, depending on the trends of the moment. This tactical view of the creative process is often driven by brand management.
2. A more strategic level, in which design integrated upstream in projects takes advantage of its connection to marketing because it can participate in innovation. By contrast, if a prospective design approach is not included in its mission, it is likely that creativity will risk being hindered.

Design as a Corporate Communications Department

In service industries, this scenario is most commonly used in the management of visual identity. In this scenario, the product design department will be separate from the communications design department.

Because design is part of the communications function, it is often seen as nothing more substantial than a sign or graphic. Therefore, design is rarely considered seriously when executives evaluate business performance. However, if there is a change of management or a merger or restructuring of the company, design is usually given its strategic value.

Design as an Independent Department

Undeniably, this last route is an interesting solution in regards to the preceding constraints. It is most often the preference of directors who consider design a strategic rather than subordinate department. The weight given design, and the power it holds, is directly related to its degree of independence in relation to marketing and technical functions.

Linked to general management, design participates very early on in product conception and the defining of product specifications; it defines and guides the long-term design policy of the business; it is part of the innovation process; and it coordinates all visible manifestations of the business in order to instill consistency. The design function is on the same level as other departments; it is horizontal and global in its approach. But, such a global approach to design is rare.

In reality, the dependence of design on marketing or R&D services poses frequent problems in power and coordination, and a hierarchical engagement with general management often exacerbates this. To diminish the risk of failure in integrating design into the company, it is essential to clearly explain to the peripheral functions the prerogatives of a design service, its mission, its area of intervention, and its objectives. The internal microcultures, often fiercely independent and little-integrated into a common business project, otherwise risk making design the new scapegoat.

Design, as an independent department in the business structure, will have in-house customers, like those responsible for the brand management. A course in design should be organized for these in-house customers in order to avoid conflicts between pleasing the in-house customer's wishes, which often push for short-term initiatives, and the wishes of "good design," which necessitate a long-term coherence.

DEFINING THE DESIGN MISSION

First, the design function has as an objective:

- To define the design strategy in relation to the business strategy
- To coordinate the design strategy with the marketing, innovation, and communications functions
- To infuse the design strategy in the implementation phase of the business strategy

----

MARK OLDACH

Partner, VSA Partners

"Design is not an end, it is a means to an end. Our success is dependent on our ability to not stand out, but instead, become integral to a business, its products and services, its value, its positioning and its connection to customers, employees, investors, and partners.

"We must advocate for the audience, user, or stakeholder. We must connect sound business goals to user goals. (Believe it or not, this drives innovation.) We must be disciplined managers—managers of business, process, people, programs, and projects. And we must bridge the gap between strategy and implementation (conceive strategies that are doable). Our focus is on solutions, not on artifacts."

Coherence between the design mission and its place in the company organizational structure is fundamental. One cannot require the designer to be the sole guarantor of unity between different product lines, for example, or link to a specific activity or range of products.

Further, the design department's goal is to create a favorable managerial context for the development of design practice in the company, and seek to develop its own management tools (Midler, 1993). This is illustrated by the following decisions:

- The definition of a global design policy that is consistent with the image strategy and strategic positioning of the company
- The research of concepts for new products, in keeping with the different strategic positioning and segmentation
- The enlivening of the innovation process in relation to the marketing and technical departments
- The proposition of design in the visual and formal systems of the company (of products and other visible manifestations of the business: buildings, stationery, and commercial spaces), and the control of their homogeneity and unity
- Overseeing the realization of projects after they have been accepted, checking in the manufacturing stage that the design conforms to the initial project
- The treatment of quality and total-quality management issues

The in-house design department needs to set up its own budget, as well as outside assistance, such as the help of a design firm to tackle cultural resistance and be able to ensure the best service.

MANAGING THE DESIGN DEPARTMENT

THE MANAGEMENT OF THE DESIGN DEPARTMENT should be organized around a double objective: the performance of the design department and the integration of design into company management procedures.

The Structure of the Design Department

The structure of the design department is organized into four departments: product design service, prospective design service, creative support, and administration (Figure 10.3).

A design department's structure grows more and more complex over time. Today, in-house design departments are made up of designers divided between product design, advanced design, graphic design (those responsible for product logo and packaging), personnel administration, quality control, and model making. Computer-assisted conceptual development can also require the recruitment of CAD experts in rapid prototyping and virtual imagery.

Concept teams now welcome user-interface and ergonomic design specialists. Social science experts—in psychology, sociology, and ethnology—reinforce the design teams when user-interface improvement is more and more critical to product performance. The department administration strengthens and specializes in different support tasks: administration, human resource management, and communications.

- -

RCA THOMSON MULTIMEDIA

DMI Case Study

"A Human Factors group was launched in late 1990, and renamed 'User Interface Design' three years later. The professional backgrounds of the rapidly growing

Figure 10.3. The Structure of the In-House Design Department

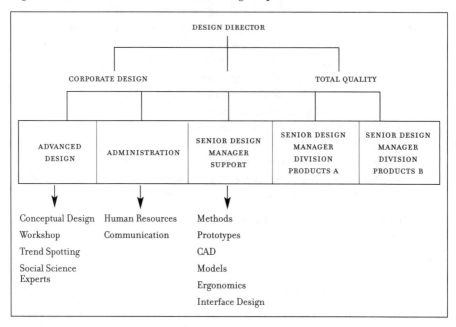

group included cognitive psychology, human factors, visual communication, graphic design, industrial design, electrical engineering, computer sciences, fine arts, journalism, and anthropology."

The structure of a design department reveals the tasks the design function must take on within the company through the design manager:

- ✱ Traditional departmental management tasks, such as defining a policy, budget, personnel management, and departmental interface management
- ✱ Tasks specific to better integrating design into the company, such as selecting communications methods, managing relationships with outside designers, and representing design at the strategic level

The specific nature of every company's design management is determined by the kinds of experts that are placed in the department structure. For example, a business can differentiate itself by the level of importance it gives to interface or advanced design. Other companies, such as Renault, choose to emphasize the optimization of the creative process and departmental interface management by naming project leaders, new virtual technology specialists, a total-quality policy, and a communications policy.

Graphic design varies between a supportive position, such as prototyping or ergonomics, and the more global position of brand design, including environmental (exposition stand design).

Finally, in more advanced companies, the structure is a matrix of design disciplines and the contributions of project and quality-control managers.

The Leadership Style of the Design Department

Managing a design department requires leadership:

- To develop competency in three different directions; creativity, user interface, and technology
- To build a team of specialists from advanced design to redesign, requiring different personalities and competencies
- To search for congruence in goals, tasks, and time

Managing creative teams demands a transformational leadership style (TLS). TLS leaders achieve a level of transformation among their team members by enhancing their awareness of the significance and value of their projects, getting them to transcend their self-interest for the good of the group and the project, inspiring them toward self-fulfillment, achieving their potential, and motivating them to do more than originally planned. All managers of creative work should be familiar with the four dimensions of TLS: charisma, inspiration, intellectual stimulation, and personal attention.

Design managers identify themselves as using a highly transformational leadership style, and those who score high in TLS think the quality of the effectiveness and creativity of their teams is higher. Design managers who use a transformational style of leadership perceive a positive influence on the outcomes of their efforts in terms of creativity, productivity, and efficiency.

Challenge and support are the two work environment attitudes that are the most important for productivity and efficiency (Ryan, 2002). Practical implications for design managers are:

- Recruitment strategies that identify management candidates who are highly transformational
- The formulation of training programs based on TLS behaviors and key intervening variables
- Performance evaluation and the organization of a reward system

Design Department Methods and Tools

Outside of decisions regarding the design mission and leadership style, the design manager must, in the end, define procedures and methods for strengthening the design department's performance.

In deciding on the most appropriate structure, the design manager has many issues to consider:

- Flexibility versus consistency. The design manager must invent processes that provide consistency or a certain amount of rigidity in terms of how things are done and flexibility in terms of creative thinking.

- Autonomy versus control. Manager must choose in terms of where the lines of discretion are drawn between senior and relatively junior members.
- Centralization versus decentralization. Who is allowed to make which decisions?

Planning and Budgeting

The design manager first outlines the schedules for design projects to be completed and the management procedures to be followed. For instance, he will define procedures for outside agency competition, and the selection of project teams—in-house designers or mixed design teams.

In order to make these procedures smoother over time, the design manager can opt to make a policy of alliance with certain outside partners. For example, he can build a list of suppliers authorized in different fields of work, such as publishing, prototyping, or model-making, or select a list of possible design firm partners according to their specialty. These partners will be routinely consulted first for this or that design problem. This planning stage is reinforced by negotiating a budget necessary for realizing these programs.

Performance Evaluation

Design management also seeks to evaluate the return on investment and define the tools that will be used to assess the performance of the design department. These evaluation tools aim to reconcile design department costs in terms of the value it adds. Design's value creation is assessed by looking at its impact on the activities that support company value. Design's performance is evaluated according to how it affects processes such as:

- The change in the mind-set of the company that becomes more innovative
- The improvement of decision-making processes and innovation management
- The circulation of information within the company
- Relationships with suppliers
- Time reduction of new product development
- Customer value
- Design's role in total quality

Other tools are then put in place to evaluate the quality of design in terms of its "peer reputation," which has the double advantage of protecting the company against imitation and drawing better talent and younger designers (Gemser & Wijnberg, 2001). The design manager will then have the heart to enter the company in design competitions and awards, and to cultivate relationships with the media.

DISSEMINATING DESIGN KNOWLEDGE

THE UNDERLYING OBJECTIVE OF DESIGN MANAGEMENT is to establish a design know-how internally. This first happens with the recruitment of competent collaborators into the design department who are supported by technical and specialized skills.

However, a competent team is not enough to disseminate design knowledge within the company. A partner network must be put together in both the upstream and downstream creative processes. This means that the design manager has to be involved everywhere. She must reiterate whenever she can that design can be of assistance to every department in solving its problems. From the legal department to logistics to finance, the design manager is involved in every task and shows other departments how design can help them.

Disseminating Design in the Company

In order for design to play its role as coordinator, it should be brought up in discussions of subjects that have a philosophical basis, such as ethics and how that relates to sustainable development, corporate values, customer value, aesthetics, etc. This way, the dissemination of design occurs by bringing its philosophy into policy meetings in marketing, R&D, and quality.

Depending on design's structure and its reporting to this or that department or general management, this "presence" of design competence is made natural or pro-active by the design manager. Disseminating design occurs through procedures of training, contact, listening, and communication.

In innovation, certain decisions take place on an implicit level, in the domain of perceived quality and, thus, of design: the choice of style, or acoustic quality. They motivate supporting professions to develop knowledge in response to concrete situations. Design management can help to change mentalities and eliminate cultural blockages in front of downstream competencies.

In order to optimize the design approach, the design manager must drive it upstream. This implies investing in relationships with suppliers. If a company has in-house innovation management, the relationship with suppliers changes and suppliers become coworkers, or partners in co-conception.

The concept of codesign affects every member of the network. Relationships change from contracts to trust between the partners: Each supplier has a monopolistic situation, which guarantees a new industrial civility. This drives the design department (and other innovation functions) to be interested in the management of the components and the multigenerational developments of products and managing the conflicts of new product development in perspective.

Example: An advanced concept design for the inner high-tech mechanism can be contrary to a design servicing product integrity.

Among design's most effective skills is its participation in the implementation of a total-quality policy in the company. This active participation allows design to impact upon:

1. The definition of customer satisfaction. This entails implementing evaluation and testing tools; for example, joint marketing and design groups for consumer testing, acting like codesigners working with the company to define customer satisfaction.
2. The optimization of technology, R&D, and production processes; for example, whether or not to choose certified suppliers and design agencies as external partners.

The other way design competence is disseminated is the joint management of brand valorization between marketing, communications, and design:

* By giving design power over the communication of the brand name
* By orchestrating the relationship between design and brand strategy by hiring outside partners, such as communications or design agencies that will, at the same time, manage the global brand image

It is important to continue to supervise the coordination of the people involved in brand management globally, through either a hierarchical relationship or common decision-making teams.

Lastly, design's dissemination occurs through coordination with human resources management, since it can help locate the tools needed to support an understanding of design, first among the design partners, then among the rest of the collaborators in the company. Thus, familiarity with design in the company culture can be facilitated by the recruitment policy on two levels:

1. In the recruitment of each new collaborator, so there is a consistency in the selection criteria for creativity and design culture and the company's design policy.
2. In the recruitment of the in-house designer, so there is verification that he is able to assert himself within the group. Since product development is more and more the responsibility of independent, multidisciplinary groups based in decision-making processes that are largely informal, the presence of the designer, his charisma, and his ability to dominate without being obtrusive will have an influence on the presence of design in innovation (Owens, 2000).

Communication on Design

The integration of design knowledge into the business process happens next through the communications policy regarding design. For this, one could use the company newsletter, create a design department bulletin, or create a Web site for the design department that can be accessed through the company intranet.

Design knowledge is also spread by instigating awareness and design training. Intensive internal communications efforts around design are planned in order to involve everyone in the company, such as an informative display in the hallway or press relations on concept design activities. This dissemination of design knowledge happens within the company through collaboration with the communications department and the joint management of the company's graphic signs and communication spaces.

IMPROVING PROCESS MANAGEMENT THROUGH DESIGN

INNOVATION CAN BE STIMULATED THROUGH INCREASED KNOWLEDGE of the nature of creative and innovative problem solving in a company. Increased awareness of the habitual nature of the ways in which designers approach problems generates insights into new approaches.

Example: Changing the vision of the child toothbrush market.

BERTRAND BARRÉ, 2001

"The Signal Croissance saga 'life scenario' offers the perfect example of the benefits of a permanent innovation strategy based on seeking these oblique visions that enable us to turn needs into desires."

Process-focused design management is a performance issue for an in-house design department. There are four ways to create value through the integration of design capabilities in the management process (Table 10.4).

IDEA MANAGEMENT AND CREATIVITY

WHAT ARE THE TOOLS a design department can set up in order to make the company more creative?

Fostering Creativity in the Design Department
One of the disadvantages of in-house design is the risk of a lack of creativity due to repetitive design projects. The design manager must find methods to limit this risk. Various solutions have been developed, including:

DESIGN CAPABILITIES	CHANGE IN PROCESS MANAGEMENT
DESIGN CREATIVE METHODS	*Idea and creativity management*
THE DRYADIC DIMENSION OF DESIGN	*Coordination in NPD management*
USER-CENTERED DESIGN PROCESS	*User-centered business*
USER OBSERVATION RESEARCH	*Ethno-marketing research* *Consumer as codesigner*
VISUALIZATION SKILLS	*Communication and information systems* *Decision systems*

Table 10.4. **Changing Process Management through Design**

- Developing an advanced design section with creative workshops on concepts: Philips or Hallmark
- Implementing a design scanning system and documentation center, and subscribing to design trend publications
- Organizing creative outings: visiting international fairs, trade shows, and exhibitions
- Choosing a vibrant urban environment for the in-house design department (such as in the automobile industry)
- Invigorating creativity through design competitions with students in design schools (such as the Braun Design Prize)
- When the company is international, rotating the staff between one office location and another
- Introducing outsiders: working with design consultancies on specific projects, or "internalizing" them for a certain period
- Networking with the most advanced abilities in technology in order to stay informed, whether with institutions or leading-edge customers of the most advanced technology
- Break through and stimulate concepts and scenarios, building on technological paths for future products
- Using design creativity techniques to develop ideas and link these ideas with strategy analysis

"Educating" Other Departments in Design Creativity Methods

Another solution is to elevate designers in the company to the rank of "creativity specialists." Ideas arise from two sources: an intrinsic source based on ideation and an extrinsic source based on market and technological data. But the ability to elicit truly original concepts through outside research has been questioned recently, and, moreover, all companies now have equal access to market research techniques.

Designers are educated in creativity techniques. Therefore, the design manager should investigate "ideation" management:

- See if there is a process for managing ideas in the company
- Work with it if it exists; create it if not
- Allocate resources and time to creativity
- Develop creativity programs that can be applied to all functions

Example: Sony "Blue Sky" projects

Design managers should think of methods to improve the key factors of creativity in the business context:

- Work with human resources in training program on reducing mental blocks to individual creative thinking.
- Improve group creativity performance.

Example: Brainstorming. The efficiency of brainstorming has been questioned. Various factors explain this: production blocking, distractions, deferred judgments, fear of assessment, and the illusion of group effectiveness. But still, there is widespread adoption of the method. Perhaps brainstorming is not very effective for the generation of new ideas, but it exposes previously nonexploited ideas. In order to reap the benefits of brainstorming while avoiding its relative shortcomings, electronic versions of brainstorming ("virtual brainstorming") are developing.

- Work on the motivation to innovate in the company, fostering a culture that values and rewards ideas. No creative expertise will ever compensate for the lack of motivation to do the job. Design managers in the most innovative companies should systematize the process for generating and testing new ideas.
- Capture good ideas. Systematically transform design's "cross-fertilization" creative system into a management process.

HARGADON & SUTTON, 2000

"The best innovators systematically use old ideas as the raw materials for one new idea after another. We call their strategy 'knowledge brokering'; companies that do it serve as intermediaries or brokers between otherwise disconnected pools of ideas."

- Keep ideas alive. Spreading information about "who knows what" and embedding ideas into objects that people can look at and bring to brainstorming meetings are powerful ways to keep ideas alive. Databases are useful in helping people find out who to talk to about how the knowledge was really used and might be used again.

Example: IDEO Tech boxes are maintained by a local curator, and each piece is documented on IDEO's intranet. Curators have a weekly meeting to talk about new additions and the uses to which items are being put in new projects.

- Imagine new uses for old ideas. Use analogical thinking to develop an innovative pulse. Give the group a good deal of practice in the use of analogies to spontaneously relate brain activity to the problem (mind mapping).
- Hire people with the right attitude—relentlessly curious, open to others' ideas, possessing a personality that is a mixture of confidence and humility. They create a collaborative culture, and financial rewards are used to further support collaborative behaviors.
- Put promising concepts to the test—putting ideas into tangible outputs and testing prototypes or models and benefits by learning through the process—even through ideas that do not work.

"Designers as knowledge brokers have the 'nothing-is-invented-here' attitude. It means they reach out early and often, to anyone who might help them solve problems and test ideas."

Designers have good experience in developing templates for design projects, especially for graphic and identity projects. This "template" attitude can be used in idea management. Ideation needs surprise—even chaos—and regularity. Templates provide regularity. Creativity templates for creative thinking from the past may be used for accelerating thinking about new ideas in the present (Goldenberg & Mazursky, 2002).

Design methods used in the divergent phases become templates or tools for creativity and decision processes. These include:

- Removing mental blocks by searching for new relationships between parts of an existing unsatisfactory solution. Attribute lists or the "forced relationship" method (mental associations sought by juxtaposing each part of a group in pairs), or finding two independent variables and creating a new dependency between them.
- Morphological charts defining the functions, listing a wide range of sub-solutions or alternative means of performing each function. Select an acceptable set of sub-solutions, one for each function.
- Interaction matrix to permit a systematic search for connections between elements within a problem, search for dependency of variables between internal and external variables, and make a new link between components in the internal environment of the product and in its external environment.
- Analysis of Interconnected Decision Areas (AIDA) to identify and evaluate all of the compatible sets of sub-solutions to a problem and display the pattern of connection (decision mapping).
- Shifting the boundaries of an unsolved problem so outside resources can be used to solve it, removing an intrinsic component from the configuration in order to cause a qualitative change.
- "Alexander's method" of determining components used to find the right physical components of a structure, such that each component can be altered independently to suit future changes (production modularity). Identify all the requirements that influence the shape of the physical structure, then decide whether each pair of requirements is independent or not and record each decision in an interaction matrix.

COORDINATION IN NPD MANAGEMENT

DESIGN MANAGEMENT HAS THE RESPONSIBILITY of creating a structure for innovation management and a cooperative of projects and disciplines. The new integrated and competitive management model for innovation takes advantage of design's input in the company because it resembles the design profession's methods and creative processes.

The role of the design department is to support the dissemination of the new integrated innovation management model into companies. Working in multidisciplinary groups channel innovation from a profession logic into a project logic. Concurrent engineering is integrated into the design management process, and should also be integrated into interdepartmental coordination. Design management has to choose between the optimization of the design expertise and the optimization of project management, meaning a designer's interests shift from trying to do his or her job better (professionally-oriented) to managing the project better (project-oriented).

The design manager establishes the project culture of a company by instigating a project leader position or project team and organizing a project matrix and professional specifications within the design department structure. This project model can take different organizational forms (Table 10.5). Design management seeks to increase the involvement of design agents in projects and avoid rigid expert discourse that can lead to a standstill. Project management questions the hierarchical regulations of a vertical structure, and also inverts the flow of functioning from bottom to top and in a transversal way.

Project functioning guarantees the need for autonomy but, also, a capacity for design's collective involvement in the project. Joint development cultivates professionalism in design, and the design manager encourages an understanding of the impact of every design decision on the golden triangle of the project: cost, lead time, and quality. In practice, this implies nominating a quality manager in the design department.

DESIGNING A CUSTOMER-ORIENTED BUSINESS

DESIGN MANAGEMENT IS RESPONSIBLE for improving customer management in the company and helping to make sure the company is customer-oriented. The integration of design into the innovation process changes the management of customer processes. Even if design's role is limited to an expertise in user interface, the system of interaction and market perception has already been transformed (Veryzer, 2000).

The design manager is responsible for supervising operations in order to emphasize customer perception in the creative process, minimize risks perceived by the customer, reinforce the role of customer interface in the design process, have the customer participate as codesigner, and establish a customer-oriented system of information and evaluation tools.

Functional Organization

STRENGTHS	WEAKNESSES	EXAMPLES	MAJOR ISSUES
Specialization and expertise	Coordination between different functional groups slow and bureaucratic.	Packaging customization development.	Integration to achieve a common goal.

Lightweight Project Organization

STRENGTHS	WEAKNESSES	EXAMPLES	MAJOR ISSUES
Coordination and administration of projects explicitly assigned to a single project manager. Maintaining development of specialization and expertise.	Requires more managers and administration than non-matrix organization.	Traditional automobile, electronics, and aerospace companies.	How to balance functions and projects

Heavyweight Project Organization

STRENGTHS	WEAKNESSES	EXAMPLES	MAJOR ISSUES
Provides integration and the benefit of speed to the project organization. Some of the specialization of a functional organization is retained.	Requires more managers and administrators than non-matrix organization.	Recent successful projects in automobile, electronics, and aerospace.	How to evaluate project and functional performance simultaneously.

Project Organization

STRENGTHS	WEAKNESSES	EXAMPLES	MAJOR ISSUES
Resources can be optimally allocated within the project team. Technical and market trade-offs can be evaluated quickly.	Individuals may have difficulty maintaining cutting-edge functional capabilities.	Start-up companies. Companies competing in extremely dynamic markets.	How to maintain functional expertise over time. How to share technical learning from one project to another.

Table 10.5. Choosing between Different Organizational Structures for Innovation (Ulrich & Eppinger, 2000)

Develop User Observation Techniques

The designer becomes the "voice of the user" (not always the customer or the consumer) through the development of a user database of videos, photos, problem identifications, and models. Project leaders are systematically put in contact with market experts. These meetings encourage inspiration and comprehension of the commercial aspects of the product, as well as the cultivation of more constructive relationships with consumers (Bailetti & Guild, 1991).

In businesses dominated by technology, the penetration of user care requires the company to make an effort. The design team realizes a prototype for conducting tests. The test results encourage customer concerns to be entered into every step of the process, so team members train themselves on usage value through the analysis of test results. Improved response to user needs, therefore, becomes a collective training process, a tacit knowledge gained from experience and through the interaction between individuals (Walsh et al., 1996).

Design for Minimizing Resistance to Change

Minimize behaviors that resist change because of two major risks—perceived and cognitive. In order to overcome resistance to change, design strategies should incorporate:

1. Communication. If the perceived risk is social or psychological, create a network with consumers.
2. Altering the innovation in the conceptual stage to make it more acceptable, if the risk is cognitive (Ram, 1989). Cognitive resistance is a function of the consumer's real beliefs. But, consumers also need stimulation, and their tendency to take risks is a personality trait.

Developing User-Interface Knowledge

Ergonomics and the human-machine interface is a main field for many designers and is often design's port of entry into the company.

Example: The design department at Thomson RCA illustrates that the remote control is perceived by the consumer as a product in itself and not as an accessory, and should be conceived as a new product.

Design management is based on a cognitive ergonomic approach, in which the conceptual process consists of the progressive construction of representations of the problem and its solution. It implies defining the problem from the user's point of view, which introduces user knowledge into the creative process in design schools (Marinissen, 1990). In effect, the demand for well-made products that are ergonomic implies that the user immediately perceives an improvement (Franzen et al., 1994).

Design management develops skills that go beyond ergonomics adapted to the body: It adapts design to the mind and, thus, constructs conceptual models and system images (Mitchell, 1996)—hence, for example, the concept of universal design (Story, 1995).

The User as Designer

The role of the design manager is, therefore, to make the design process more interactive. This is accomplished by welcoming individual customers, answering every customer request, and keeping a customer database, but, also, by constantly developing customer experimentation (Bucci, 1994; Woudhuysen, 1990).

The design management function must place the customer in the position of co-producer of the offer. Two examples are:

1. At Nortel, there is an interactive methodology of conception in that the design helps the user develop his self-esteem by giving him opportunities to better understand himself or others through using the product (Campbell et al., 1996).

2. At Nissan, design management altered the traditional context for marketing studies. Before, consumers were asked to evaluate new concepts which were shown to them as two-dimensional pictures of the car viewed from the front, side, and back. In order to better understand their needs, the design department changed how studies were conducted. Now, studies no longer take place in a clinical setting but, rather, in the design studio. First, the consumer is asked her opinion about the earlier model and her personal experience. Then, she is asked, in front of a regular-size model, what she thinks of the concepts now. (Coughland et al., 1996).

Designing a User-Centered Information System

The design management position is responsible for integrating information about user needs into the different phases of innovation launch and the marketing information system:

- Formal information about specifications
- Information coming from tests, especially in complex projects
- Informal information generated by designers during the creative process. A comparison of the performance of existing solutions in order to complete the specs, a heterogeneous synthesis of consumer needs, and a hierarchical organization of those needs

User-Oriented Evaluation Methods

Controlling product costs of tomorrow through today's product design entails managing the costs according to consumer segments in the upstream stage; if the cost objective cannot be attained, the product must be redesigned (Cooper & Chew, 1996). Interactive processes become iterative.

COOPER ROBIN & BRUCE CHEW, 1996

"Market leaders have no choice but to manage costs from the design phase forward: target costing. Senior managers need to approach New Product Development controlling tomorrow's costs, not just today's."

All companies are in the "perception business." They live for their customers and regularly take an active part in their evaluation processes. This entails inventing a way to measure the perception of value-added design.

Example: Transfer the tools of analysis scales of consumer emotions used in publicity to design (e.g., the scales of Holbrook & Batra and the Consumption Emotion Set by Richins).

USING VISUALIZATION IN DECISION MAKING

THE NEW FIELD OF "SCIENCE DESIGN" encourages designers to better communicate their choices and explain their aesthetic involvement. Visualizing the aesthetic is a tool in design management for optimizing the management of ideas, by coordinating partners in an innovation around the same mental image in order to make the design tangible to them ("A block of wood speaks" [Leonard Barton, 1991]).

Visualization in Project Management

The role of drawing in the process is fundamental. A study in the field of graphic design shows that designers use drawing in every stage of the process, from the briefing stage through to the design solutions, but, also, that drawing is used to conduct management procedures, stimulate creative behavior, and vary the forms of communication between design team members (Schenk, 1991).

Sketches in the design process must act as a visual dialogue or argument between the different points of view in the design team. The sketch is a language capable of generating an emotion, explaining the thought process of the designer, testing conceptions, and providing a more concrete image of an original idea (Temple, 1994).

Because of visualization, all of the steps in the chain of innovation become simulation. This accelerates process-oriented fabrication (Freund et al., 1997). Once the innovation takes shape, the physical symbols provide a powerful aid in the communication process. The images pass from two-dimensional drawings to forms that resemble the final product more and more, such as nonfunctional and functional models. These models serve as visible and accessible symbols of the final product; they help to unify the design team and reveal any possible technical flaws.

LEONARD BARTON, 1991

"Another valuable use of physical models is to capture the current understanding of a problem solution in order to reveal the next set of questions. Physical representations often uncover technical flaws, and they communicate the partially-formulated innovation to potential users during the process of empathic design. As the community of stakeholders in the development of new products and processes broadens, physical objects that help bridge disciplinary and functional boundaries become more important."

Models are also useful because they display the ways in which design and production problems have been solved, and reveal new issues that have arisen. Design is a dynamic process of adaptation and transformation of knowledge from past experiences that one adapts to current contingencies. These experiences are coded and stored in the designer's memory. The prototype is a tool for structuring design knowledge, a practical base for organizing different classes of complex associations. The prototype is a means for representing this complex structure of knowledge (Oxman, 1990).

Design is the interaction between making and seeing, acting and discovering. When a designer looks at what he has drawn, he makes discoveries. He discovers characteristics and relationships in the design-form that ultimately lead to a deeper understanding of it. A design prepares the way for another design. Designers remember what they have discovered in past projects and bring this to new design situations in which the characteristics are similar (Schon et al., 1992).

Achieving commercial success for new products implies that their potential was not compromised by neglecting to test them. Through visualization, tests are easy: rough drawings, detailed drawings, large models, model tests, prototype testing, and final form testing. Companies place the prototype performance test first, but there is a correlation between the number of tests done with visual design tools and the chances of success of the product (Hise et al., 1989).

Visualization in the Decision Process

Design management optimizes visual input in order to contribute to the dissemination of design knowledge and, thus, reinforce the circulation of valuable information in the new product launch model (Clark et al., 1991).

Optimizing the circulation of information necessitates new visualization skills. Beyond classical skills of sketches and models, charts are constructed that resemble "visual trend mapping" or "cognitive charts" and act as representations of a problem. They help to resolve connection problems—for instance, the connections between the product and its technology.

At Philips, for example, the management considers these new visual tools a good way to eliminate bureaucratic reports, as well as to induce change in employee behavior, which can support a cultural shift (Van de Kraats & Thurlings, 1997). A matrix can be created to organize the circulation of data and allow for the grouping and visual restructuring of the information (Austin et al., 1996).

FUNCTIONAL DESIGN MANAGEMENT CHECKLIST

Strategy: Coordinate the design strategy with marketing, innovation, and communications
Infuse the design strategy into the implementation of the business strategy

Planning:	Define procedures/programs
	Define the standards of design performance
	Define the relationship between design and total quality
Structure:	Define the role, place, and tasks of the design manager in the structure
	Create a matrix structure for innovation and projects
	Establish an in-house design department
Finances:	List selected suppliers and designers
	Secure a budget for these programs
Human Resources:	Cultivate design understanding among partners
Information:	Distribute plans for marketing/design/production
	Distribute design knowledge in the company
Communications:	Supervise the relationships between graphic and architectural norms
	Organize outside or internal communications about design
R&D:	Manage relationships with suppliers
	Quality policy
Project management:	Integrate design into idea management and conception processes
	Supervise key decision phases
	Manage the visualization of the conception and decision processes
Branding:	Design and valorize the brand
	Create test groups of customers and design
	Make alterations to marketing research
Evaluation:	Evaluate the process of design and improve it
	Evaluate the impact of design on the customer-oriented culture
	Evaluate return on investment

Chapter 11

STRATEGIC DESIGN MANAGEMENT

A T THIS LEVEL OF DESIGN MANAGEMENT, the manager must, ultimately, create a relationship between design, strategy, and the identity and culture of the company. The objective is to control the consistency of design work in the company and to instill design into strategic formulation processes.

The design manager, then, becomes a strategy consultant. This role can also be taken on by a design firm that provides the design ideology for the business mission. It is important to elect a long-term design vision and a mind-set that is ecological, technological, humanistic, and dictatorial (Xerox, 2000).

At the strategic level, design management has four essential roles (Seidel, 2000):

1. Visualizing the business strategy
2. Searching for core competency
3. Gathering market information
4. Innovating in management processes

These roles imply a visual planning of strategy, in which clients and designers become coconspirators (Davenport-Firth, 2000).

In practice, strategy is more like a trajectory than a succession of major decisions. Strategic design management methods vary in function according to the configuration of strategy development:

1. "Constructed strategy" through incremental strategic planning, rational personification, politics, or cultural influence
2. "Imposed strategy" through dependence on the external environment or group strategy

This final level of design management echoes the strategic process of the company with methods of strategy formulation, selection, and implementation.

DESIGN MANAGEMENT STRATEGY FORMULATION

DESIGN MANAGEMENT MUST FIRST PARTICIPATE in the strategy formulation and selection processes by making an effort to bring design knowledge into the transformative vision of the market, but also by supervising the penetration of the design spirit into business objectives. Design management participates in all of the different stages of strategic formulation (Table 11.1).

Table 11.1. The Design Management Strategy Process

Phases	Issues to analyze	Tools
1. Strategy formulation Competitive analysis External	Industry attractiveness Opportunities & threats	"PEST" analysis "Porter five forces" model Scenarios Strategic group Segmentation Matrix attractiveness/assets
Competitive analysis Internal	Strategic capacity Key success factors Strengths & weaknesses	Value chain Benchmarking Portfolio analysis
Organizational objectives	Synthesis	SWOT analysis
	Corporate governance Stakeholders' expectations Business ethics Culture	Matrix power/interest Identity focalization
	Mission vision	Design management strategic audit
2. Strategy selection	Balance between governance objectives and SWOT analysis	Porter generic strategies · volume/price · differentiation
3. Strategy implementation	Strategy development routes	Vertical integration Diversification Internationalization

Note: Column 1 of table 11.1 lists the steps that are involved in deciding upon a strategy for the company to follow in order to achieve its aims (column 2). Column 3 lists the tools that are necessary to implement each stage of strategizing, and achieve the company's goals.

DESIGN MANAGEMENT AS COMPETITIVE ANALYSIS

COMPETITIVE ANALYSIS SEEKS TO DETERMINE INDUSTRY ATTRACTIVENESS, measured first by the profitability margin of invested capital and then by key success factors, which every business needs to know and master in order to survive. It takes the form of two successive evaluations and a synthesis of SWOT analysis (strengths, weaknesses, opportunities, and threats).

External Analysis: Opportunities and Threats

Analysis of the company's external environment is conducted on two levels: the environmental opportunities, and threats for the company and design function. To analyze industry attractiveness, design management examines:

* The environmental influences that were important in the past and their impact on the future. This "PEST" approach takes into account key political, economic, social, and technological factors.
* The national competitive advantage of the market using the "Porter diamond" tool: business strategies, specific conditions, local demand, and mutual stimulation between industries.
* The forces that determine the nature of the competitive business environment (the "five forces" Porter model) through barriers to entry, the intensity of the rivalry between present competitors, threats of potential new competitors, the power force of customers and suppliers, and, finally, the threat of substitute products.

This analysis ends with constructed scenarios based on identified key influences and factors of change. Planning with scenarios hinges on a plausible representation of what can be envisioned five years ahead.

Next, the design manager analyzes the competitive situation of the company:

* By determining strategic clusters made by regrouping companies within an industry that have similar strategic characteristics.
* By determining the company's strategic domains of activity. The design manager will question this analysis; the potential input of design is in the way the company perceives its activity.
* By determining market segments that have similarities or differences in terms of customers and users. The segmentation criteria are:
  * Demand criteria: customer type, functions of use, distribution mode, and geographic zone
  * Supply criteria: type of technology, cost structures, and control of competencies according to the key success factors

The design manager finds the best criteria to determine pertinent market segments and the right allocation of resources.

Finally, the matrix of attractiveness and assets positions each domain of strategic activity according to the industry attractiveness and competitive assets of the company.

Internal Analysis of Strengths and Weaknesses

An analysis of the strengths and weaknesses in terms of a company's resources or its strategic capability also has two levels: the strengths and weaknesses of the company and those of the design function in the company. This analysis consists of:

* *Resources audit* that identifies and classifies resources a company can acquire internally and externally in order to support its strategies—physical, human, financial, and intangible—and distinguishes those resources that are unique.

* *Core competency analysis* through an analysis of the value chain: What are the functions underlying the competitive advantage of the company? What are the sources from which these core competencies can be developed?
* *Benchmarking*, which is the strategic capability of a company, is always a relative notion and, therefore, it is useful to conduct a comparative analysis, known as benchmarking. Past analysis and sectorial norms are already a source of information, but it is instructive to compare the company's capabilities with the best practices implemented in other industries.
* *Balanced business portfolio*, a tool that helps verify the pertinence of the company's activities portfolio.

The company can be divided in a number of ways. Thus, it is necessary to divide the company into a number of homogenous subsets or strategic segments. A strategic segment is a homogenous domain of activity identified by a combination of key success factors specific to this domain and independent of others in which the company is involved. Each strategic segment mobilizes a particular knowledge in which the company has experience and searches for competitive advantage.

Once the company's different domains of activity are divided into strategic segments, it becomes necessary to analyze them along two variables: the company's competitive position in each of these segments and the value of each segment. The matrix models of strategic segments, like those developed by the consultancy offices BCG, Arthur D. Little, and McKinsey, generate one design strategy per strategic segment.

The last step in internal auditing consists of a selection of key success factors that a company must master in order to outdo the competition. This raises a fundamental question for design management: What is the place of design in these key success factors? The most common key success factors are: the company's position in the marketplace, the company's position in terms of costs, commercial image and distribution, technical capabilities and control of technology, and profitability and financial power. All of these criteria help define a design strategy.

Finally, competitive analysis is summarized according to external and internal SWOT analysis. The SWOT analysis is a basic strategic analysis tool that is perfectly adaptable to design management strategy. It synthesizes the company's situation in its context and determines the key success factors to consider in design management.

DESIGN ANALYSIS AS AN ORGANIZATIONAL GOAL

STRATEGY FORMULATION DOES NOT ONLY DEPEND ON THE SUITABLE RESULTS of the two external and internal analyses; it also depends on the importance of the role played by individuals in procedural strategy. It is important to understand the mixture of influences that determines the goals of a company.

The Forces Influencing Company Goals

The design manager must look at four determining forces:

1. The corporate governance that determines which interests the company should serve and in what ways its goals and priorities should be established. Corporate governance has become more and more complex due to the separation between ownership and management, and the tendency to make companies more and more indebted to stakeholders.
2. The "power/interest matrix," which distinguishes investors according to the power they hold and the interest they have in company strategy. Even if there is an agreement on general objectives, there are often differences in the expectations of stakeholders, and it is useful to analyze these differences.
3. Business ethics determine the global positioning of a company vis-à-vis its responsibilities to the community. This position can change from a narrow view, in which short-term interest of investors are emphasized, to a larger view, in which the company wants to change society.
4. The cultural context at different levels: national and professional culture. There are many conflicting influential forces on the definition of company goals.

Company Goals: Mission, Vision, and Identity

The company mission is to support its main vocation, its raison d'être. The mission has to be visionary, clarify its strategic intent, and assert its core values.

Design participates in developing a vision by issuing concepts that unify company communications and strategic values. This is particularly true when a company changes its business.

Example: E-commerce seen not as a new distribution channel, but as a new way to define a company.

MARK DANZIG

Vice president, creative director, BlueLight.com, 2002

"The presence of 'blue light specials' in K-Mart stores continued for more than twenty years, from 1965 to 1984. By the late nineties, K-Mart felt the company needed some sort of Web presence to stay in the game. They went for talent and ended with a deal from Soft Bank. Once the deal was done, the management team turned to the question of what to name this new venture. Kmart.com was the obvious choice, but at that time the K-Mart brand had negative associations for many consumers.

"Within this sea of poor brand equity, there was a pearl left resting at just about arm's length. Extensive consumer research showed that despite its absence for almost ten years, people still had fond memories of the Old Blue Light special. It had managed to fix itself in the minds of consumers as something associated with fun, surprise. Thus the name BlueLight.com was born. In addition to leveraging the only good equity available from K-Mart, using the BlueLight name gave the company some latitude about what it could offer: an opportunity to sell items that would not necessarily be found in a K-Mart store.

"Developing the logo, we selected a solution by Michael Osborne Design in San Francisco, a simple image with a bulb that was a clear echo of the original blue light. Concurrently, we hired Addwater Design to design the first version of the Web site. One of the most important things we did was to create a unique organizational structure, a staff organization centered on the overall customer experience of the Web site, a path for repositioning the whole brand and stores in 2000."

In this visionary strategic process, design managers develop an increased interest in the cognitive structures and thinking processes of decision-makers. Design input is integrated into the social construction and representation process of strategy formulation. Design managers develop tools for identifying the social "anchoring" of mental representations. They anchor strategy in representations related to figurative elements and existing beliefs (Durand et al., 1996).

Strategic design management is about "interactionism." Through language, design managers are involved in a constructivist approach to reality building. Design is a key process for both generating and diffusing representations, whether abstract or visual. Representations are made visible through a visual identity and the company's choice of identity focus.

The components of an identity are the company's culture and its three elements:

❧ The symbolic elements: corporate values, myths, rites, and taboos

----
NOVO NORDISK A/S

DMI case study

"Corporate Visual Identity is a tool that asserts Novo Nordisk's identity worldwide. What we do:

❧ the way we market our products
❧ the way we organize our working environment
❧ the way we communicate

should signal:

❧ what we stand for
❧ where we are going
❧ the demands we make on ourselves

supported by the Corporate Visual Identity program."

- The company imagery, divided into three elements: the company image, the professional image, and the power chart
- The leadership style can vary from narcissistic to possessive, seductive, or wise

Focusing a company's identity is a dynamic process in which all of the aspirations of the employees unite in a common goal that incites their enthusiasm. Design strategy is shaped according to the focus of the company identity:

- Focus on the leader. Executives and employees identify themselves with the president's image, internally and externally.
- Focus on business activity. The directors and employees of the company see themselves as professionals, as specialists in a certain industry. This poses a problem when the competitive context necessitates a downsizing of certain activities or the creation of others, or diversification.
- Focus on behavior, either bureaucratic, with a focus on clearly defined business actions, often restricted by precise rules that allow for little initiative (administrations or companies in stable industries), or flexible, with a focus on the ability of the directors and employees to adapt quickly to new tasks and occupations.

Finally, design management participates in the building of a consistent identity, so the external image is a good indicator of the internal image of the company.

DESIGN MANAGEMENT STRATEGIC AUDITING

ONE LAST CONCERN is the evaluation of the design department in order to analyze the strengths and weaknesses of the company's design management, as well as the consistency between the design and business strategies. It is important to assess the effectiveness and coherence of the company's design decisions (Table 11.2).

A design audit strives to integrate design into the strategic formulation process and is organized much like a strategic audit. After a brief that summarizes the company mission, its domains of activity, competitive market, product strategy, and communication strategy, the documents sent out to different public contingencies over the past three years are gathered together.

The design audit means comparative analysis of the results of design on product strategy, the information system, and the communication strategy. If the analysis reveals a weak or nonexistent synergy between these three elements, further analysis is conducted.

An audit committee is created out of the different department heads (office spaces, facility management, market research, human resources, finance, communications, and design). The committee plans different operations and divides up

COHERENCE EVALUATION	Is there a visible unity between the design strategy and the business strategy?
	Is there a visible coherence between the product, information, and communications strategies?
	Is there a global design strategy?
PRODUCT STRATEGY	What is design's role in product strategy?
	Who oversees the role design plays in new product launch committees or product strategy committees?
	How are investments divided according to different types of design?
	What is the ratio of investments in design in the phase of identification of new business opportunities?
	What are design costs compared to R&D costs?
	Is there a cost control of components bought externally?
	What is the ratio of design costs to expenditures on packaging, labeling, and paper documents?
INFORMATION SYSTEMS	What role does design play in information systems?
	Is there a systematic procedure for observing the competitors' design on retail sites?
	What kinds of sales materials are given to the sales force, and what is their value in terms of how the information is designed?
	What role does information design play in internal communications?
COMMUNICATION STRATEGY (VISUAL IDENTITY)	*What is the relationship between expenditures on graphic design and architecture and those for corporate communications?*
	What is the percentage of design expenditures in different communications techniques?
	Who is responsible for graphics and the coherence between graphic signage and corporate communications?

Table 11.2. Design Management Strategic Audit

the work. Actions include meetings with marketing, production, and R&D, meetings with the sales force on points of sale, and visits to all of the company's retail outlets, factories, and offices. These different meetings and visits allow for gathering the necessary information to make a final assessment, with the help of targeted questionnaires.

A design audit this complete is rare, but a partial audit can be conducted, such as an audit of design management practices, including inventory of working procedures with outside design firms, procedures for selecting designers, and project management using a standard contract, evaluation sheet, and balance sheet. This sometimes leads to benchmarking, or a comparison of design management's best practices.

DESIGN MANAGEMENT STRATEGY SELECTION

THE MAJORITY OF COMPANIES ADOPT the "acquired" strategic design management model through successive levels of apprenticeship and experience curves (Borja de Mozota, 2001). The design strategy will vary depending on the type of business:

- ❧ One where design always plays a strategic role, often because of the will of the founder
- ❧ One where design plays a progressively more strategic role.

YO KAMINAGAI, 2002

Design manager, RATP (Paris metro and bus service)

"The life of the design entity called today 'Unity Design Management' was until now determined by its adaptability to the firm's strategic positions.

"In the beginning, design management was rather in the hands of marketing. At the time of the big-bang management change of RATP in 1990, conducted by Christian Blanc, a first unit of 'design and spaces' was born, which did not last more than eighteen months because of the confusion about the word 'design' used in a cosmetic sense and the launch of RATP's new identity. For three years design management activity was assigned to a team called 'Transport Spaces,' a title that describes the objective: spaces.

"When in 1995 a direction for project management was initiated, the first design management unit was created simultaneously. This unit was called 'Design and Standards'; it was responsible for the architectural program or project management activities that were more technical and functional. Since October, 2001, the design unit has migrated up to the users services direction and is now finally called 'Design Management.'

"In other words, adaptability in design management is necessary not only so it can survive but so it can develop."

MAKE THE STRATEGY VISIBLE

ONE OF DESIGN'S JOBS IS TO MAKE THE BUSINESS STRATEGY VISIBLE. A design strategy is based on a global image of all aspects of the company in terms of its communications, products, and locations. This is organized around two objectives.

The Objective of Coherence

Managing the visual system of the company (communications, buildings, and products) entails an effective and consistent use of design by every decision maker in the company. But the obligation toward consistency does not imply being boring; it is important to define design standards for the company, to inform about and apply them, but also to accept digressions from the norm in order to generate variation.

The design management system must manage the overseeing of coherence on three levels: consistency between the elements in the visual system, consistency of the visual system and the business strategy, and consistency of the visual system with design positioning.

The Definition of a Design Standard

To define the company's design "standard," or its philosophy in regards to design, means specifying:

- Design's place in the key success factors in each strategic business unit.
- The design department's responsibility in front of other departments in the company. In other words, it is important to clarify the driving role given to designers in front of the other creative forces in the company, particularly corporate communications, R&D department, and the committee on new product development.

The extent of design's responsibility as a key success factor for building a competitive advantage is determined by the extent of its influence on innovation, information, and communications strategies. This determines the resources allocated to design, the design positioning of the company, and the selection of the design-mix.

CHOOSING A DESIGN STRATEGY

BY DEFINITION, "DESIGN STRATEGY" IS A PLAN that helps diffuse design throughout the company.

The Designer-Entrepreneur Model

Many companies conform to the designer-entrepreneur model, as in fashion design, retail, and furniture design. This list is not exhaustive. This model is becoming more and more common in textile, luxury items, jewelry, and decoration, because creation automatically plays a strategic role, but there are also designer-entrepreneurs in other industries. The story of James Dyson and the vacuum cleaner is a good example.

JAMES DYSON, UNITED KINGDOM

"One day when James Dyson was vacuuming, he realized that the bag vacuum cleaner he was using had stopped working. Thinking the bag was full, he changed it. But again after a short period of time the cleaner lost suction. He had seen a cyclone cleaning air in sawmills, and adapting the idea, he began developing his product.

"He strongly believed the idea would work because there was no choice for the consumer. His early experiments were not entirely successful, but he applied for a patent in 1980 for a vacuum cleaning appliance using cyclone technology. It took another four years and 5,127 prototypes, but even having proved the technology, he found little interest on the part of the existing vacuum cleaner industry.

"Eventually, Dyson began the hard work of raising funds to start his own business and it gradually paid off. Launched in 1993—fourteen years after the initial idea—Dyson employs 1,800 staff, producing around 10,000 cleaners every day in its factory in Wiltshire. The Dyson empire is worth £530 million and has a number of product variants in its vacuum cleaner range." (Bruce & Bessant, 2002)

The design-entrepreneur strategy is "innate" to the founder's idea and close to the business strategy. For a design strategy and "constructed" competitive design advantage we will look at three strategies based on those of Michael Porter—three generic design strategies with three different aesthetic positionings in an industry (Table 11.3).

These strategies express the relationship between strategy from the point of view of top level management and the strategies of different operational activities—between vision and implementation. Every strategy privileges one of the three "form dimensions": the cost-driven strategy privileges the structural dimension; the image-driven strategy, the symbolic dimension; and the market-driven strategy, the functional dimension.

In sum, choosing a design strategy means choosing an aesthetic positioning that will be the expression of the company's approach to design. That choice will determine the position that design has in the company structure.

The Cost-Driven Strategy

This is convenient for companies that give priority in their competitive advantage to advanced technology. This technology-driven development creates a design position that is close to R&D, qualified by design policies driven by product design, and supported by user-interface and environmental design (particularly for production

Cost-driven design strategy	Image-driven design strategy	Market-driven design strategy
Strategy dominated by costs	Strategy of differentiation	Strategy of concentration
Design's role is to improve productivity	Design's role is to reinforce the company's market share through the quality of its image and brands	Design's role is to help position the company as a specialist that appeals to a certain kind of user
The company's aesthetic positioning favors the structural (or technical) dimension of the corporate design system	The company's aesthetic positioning favors the semantic dimension of the corporate design system	The company's aesthetic positioning favors the functional dimension of the corporate design system

Table 11.3. Design Strategies According to Porter Generic Strategies

units). The objective assigned to designers is to innovate and lower production costs in order to maintain technological leadership, which includes working on fabrication processes, technical documentation of products, and production architecture.

The Design Differentiation Strategy

This concerns enterprises that base their competitive advantage on the power of their marketing and the quality of image. The important aspects of this strategy are the positioning of company brands and their market shares. The design strategy must reinforce chosen market positionings and contribute to reformulating them in the competitive environment in order to maintain leadership in terms of image.

This development through marketing leads to:

- A differential aesthetic positioning that emphasizes the symbolic dimension of the product and its communicative impact
- A design position close to marketing, publicity, and communications departments
- A design strategy that insists on brand equity across all design disciplines and customer-oriented value creation

---

YO KAMINAGAI
Design manager, RATP

"The objective of RATP is to give a maximum of possibilities so that every user can have a positive sensory experience. The design-oriented approach has allowed the building of a progressive response fitted to different process and project levels:

- to consolidate the design management unit by infusing design into every project—transportation, information, space, repairs, modernization—by striving to minimize bad surprises for customers.
- to enrich its service with more functions, pleasures, and emotions through cultural actions. 'Tactical' introduction of good surprises enriches basic transportation service.
- finally, to have the opportunity to manage large development projects RATP created and to bring to life new models of service. These ambitious realizations, though limited in number, bring hope to the public in proving the strategic intent of the company."

There are also hybrid design strategies that rely on both cost advantage and differentiation.

The Market-Driven Strategy

This concerns companies that specialize in one segment or use a strategy of concentration. Their competitive advantage is guaranteed by their leadership in understanding a particular market or a certain type of user. Design must then reinforce this leadership in finding improvements and differences in the functional dimensions of the product, adapting to its uses but also anticipating new uses.

This development leads to:

- A differential aesthetic positioning that emphasizes the functional dimension of design: use, user interface, and user experience
- A design positioning between production and marketing
- A design strategy that privileges product design and consumer behavior research

The cost-driven design strategy concentrates on economies and the reduction of costs in the company system. The other strategies focus on the creation of qualitative value in the company system.

Design strategy and its corollary aesthetic positioning offers a direction to design management that must be infused in the decision-making systems of the company:

- Across the systems of financial allocation of investments and ratios, budgets affected by design, the definition of design evaluation tools, design performance measurement in terms of the company's performance
- In the communications and training systems, meaning to diffuse design knowledge in the company through a connection with the human resources management department
- Through the management of design's role in information systems

SELECT A DESIGN STRATEGY DEVELOPMENT ROUTE

AS WITH STRATEGY FORMULATION, the design department participates in the selection of a route for implementing the chosen strategy, then develops design actions that will cohere to that route. The principal development routes are:

1. Upstream and downstream integration
2. Innovation
3. Diversification
4. Internationalization
5. Withdrawal
6. Alliances

These different routes can be followed by the progressive acquisition of new knowledge internally through innovation, integration, and internationalization, but also, more and more often, externally through fusion, acquisition, alliance, and withdrawal.

Whatever the chosen route, design can anticipate new routes consistent with strategic analysis or play a role in implementation:

- By taking the internationalization route; for example, by creating a design center in different countries or assembling a multicultural design team

- By conceiving a new offer in the innovation route or diversification phase
- By choosing a visual identity in the fusion and acquisition route or by an innovation strategy that develops alliances

Design Management Strategy Implementation

STRATEGIC DESIGN MANAGEMENT adopts specific methods to diffuse design as a key success factor in the company.

Strategic Design Management Tools

Defining a Design-Mix

The design-mix is the allocation of design resources and budget amongst the different design departments of the company. It expresses the division of the design budget between different design disciplines according to the design strategy.

If the company considers its most important visual components to be its business documents, graphic design will be favored. If the company puts most of its energies into the products, packaging, and product design, or "user design," interface is put at the forefront. If priority must be given to the shops and workspace, investment in environmental design should be favored.

Therefore, the integration of design into the company implies determining a priority every year and establishing a middle-term coherence between these different investments by examining the consistency between the design-mix and the marketing-mix, or the design-mix and investments in corporate communications.

In participating in strategic analysis, the design manager defines the goals toward which the design department works, then selects design investments and the budgets necessary for the programs. The efficiency of budget allocation comes from the trust given to design and the coordination between the design budget and that of the other departments in the company.

Controlling Design Performance

Controlling design performance and its efficiency depends on the tools used to evaluate strategic objectives, such as the return on investment of design and its impact on company performance. Strategic design management implies financial auditing. This necessitates that design management work with the financial department to help designers insert their work into company management ratios.

The integration of the design function implies the establishment of criteria to measure the strategic value of design. For example, measuring the impact of design on company vision, the creation of a market, and the value chain of the industry, or measuring design's influence on the stock market value of the company.

Control should not be limited to the final results; it must take into account the degree of design diffusion in the company. It must measure the impact of design policies in every department of the company and on every decision-making level, and find the points of entry for design issues in human resources management procedures and competencies.

Human Resources Design Management

Design is an instigator of behavioral and mental change. The design department can aid the human resources department and internal communications in:

- ❧ Creating and maintaining internal and external information networks and establishing places for information exchange.
- ❧ Building long-term relationships externally and internally, particularly through building relationships with design schools, enacting recruitment favorable to design diffusion, and valorizing of the "creative" profiles of collaborators in their careers.
- ❧ Identifying the reciprocal expectations of the collaborator, customer, and designer. Design can facilitate new expectations of personnel in terms of autonomy and individualism.

The creation of a climate favorable to design cannot be realized without stressing design influence in recruitment decisions or career management decisions—for example, ideas valorized by remuneration.

Design Management and the Law

Design management should constantly rethink and improve every aspect of design protection. Intellectual property rights are intangible rights that have value, and can be transferred and licensed with royalty payment. It is important to recognize these rights and to take the appropriate steps to protect them. Intellectual property rights prevent others from stealing new designs, and they form a framework within which new designs can be exploited to their full potential.

Intellectual property rights include copyright, design rights (unregistered and registered), patents, and trademarks. If the design has novel and inventive qualities, obtaining a patent is possible; if the features of the design configuration are novel, they are subject to copyright. If the articles are being sold under a particular trade name or sign, they can be protected by a registered trademark (Bruce & Bessant, 2002).

INFUSING DESIGN IN THE
ORGANIZATIONAL DECISION-MAKING SYSTEM

IN ORDER FOR DESIGN TO BE CONSIDERED A KEY SUCCESS FACTOR, it must consider tools for infusing design into the decision-making system.

Design at Top-Level Management

Design is represented at the board of directors by a design director (a position sometimes assumed by a designer-entrepreneur or founder), by the design manager, or by a joint director of quality control and design or communications and design. But the importance of design will also be shared by general management as a whole.

Structuring the Design Department
Large companies with in-house design departments will specify the role of different teams and dedicate some teams to long-term visionary design missions, either externally or internally.

YO KAMINAGAI

Design manager, RATP, 2002

"Methods are concretized by three teams adapted to the company's strategic evolution:

- ❧ a product development team that sets procedures in which architecture and design intervene upstream in projects, and a global design plan that translates stable and trend fundamentals, issued from company memory.
- ❧ an entity in charge of the diffusion of a 'sensible culture' in the RATP, whose objective is to transmit a need for design that is assumed by every employee in charge of the travelers' spaces.
- ❧ an entity of cultural engineering for a limited series of cultural and artistic projects reporting directly to top management, which steers design activity to be more visible."

The role of design management is, therefore, to create a mind-set that supports design in every department in the company. This is accomplished by:

- ❧ Defining a design department that evolves alongside strategy building
- ❧ Creating specific management skills in each department, particularly in accounting and finance, human resources, and quality control

Infusing Organizational Culture
The goal is to align design with the rites of the company, which is done naturally either because the founder is a designer himself, the founder's legacy and the values he represents, or because the design director has a certain charisma that exceeds the design management department.

Transforming the Information Systems
Design management cannot dissociate itself from the implementation and improvement of information systems in the company on many levels. The choice of computer systems influences design management in innovation and communications management, and in the different stages of managing a new product launch.

It is particularly important when design co-opts customer competence (Pralahad & Ramaswamy, 2000).

Still other computer choices can be equally useful to design management, such as decisions made in terms of information systems and, in particular, the documents used for communicating the corporate financial and performance results to all stakeholders. Information design helps everyone understand and share strategic decisions, because statistics and figures are organized in the most effective manner. Information design also creates a standard, so that all company documents are consistent and well-designed—not just those documents that are external, but also meeting reports, memos, notes, or internal electronic messages.

Data presentation and information design in the company has an impact on decision-making processes. To oversee the consistency of design and company strategy entails the visualization of an information system that is optimized by design.

Transforming the Company Vision

When design is considered a key success factor, it is likely that design management will participate in the strategic diagnosis that aims to transform and anticipate new visions of the company's business context.

Selling Design Expertise

Firms like Philips began by developing internal design capabilities, design management, and concept design. They also gathered information by surveying fashion and design trends. This knowledge is part of key company resources and becomes a means of penetrating other markets by transforming the design department into a subsidiary that can then work in other market segments. This diversification of the design function can also become a tool for enriching its competitive and technological research and observation.

Prospective Design Trend Spotting

By observing the slight changes in outside world, the designer can forecast how these will affect the environment and the goals of the company. Design management acts as counselor in times of uncertainty, advising the company on where to find innovative areas from which useful information can emerge. Companies that are involved in fluctuating environments put more and more confidence in their designers to formulate new product opportunities and competitive visions.

The design department must then organize in order to clearly assert its vision for future products and markets. Design management seeks to:

- Delimit space dedicated to creation. For example, set aside a room where prototypes are exhibited and discussed on a regular basis with general management or "premium" compensation policy makers, or have contests for the best design of the month from within the design department, or systematically distribute articles on selected creations and design trends among strategy directors.

* Ensure prospective design research for product concepts. The development of product concepts is surely the most effective tool for envisioning the future and gaining reactions from other departments in the company and outside markets. But it is difficult to validate this in the management plan; why mobilize resources on an activity that is not immediately valued by the market? How do you pilot research if it isn't connected to a project?
* Utilize trend spotting, as well as technological research. One of the responsibilities of design management is to be aware of design trends through the research of pertinent sources, and to synthesize this information visually.

The company might subscribe to trend books from styling offices. Visual trend mapping helps the company build a representation of its perception of the environment, and to anticipate prospective changes. It also helps define relationships between an object and its context and harmonize its discourse with psycho-sociological trends and values.

Hence, the idea to create trend maps for new design-forms. This tool goes beyond communications or concept generation, since it aims to standardize the conceptual process and deduce a prescriptive method for trend spotting and strategic formulation (Bouchard, 1997).

This meta-model demonstrates a standard for spotting trends based on the study of:

* Specific design skills—for example, user-interface systems
* Global design as created by the manufacturers
* Design as perceived by consumers
* Design as created by suppliers

The automobile industry, for example, relies upon trend spotting in design and technology, and, from that, a new vision of strategic design management has emerged. Its objective insists on managing alliances, creating systemic co-conception relationships, and encouraging a change of vision in an industry.

STRATEGIC DESIGN MANAGEMENT CHECKLIST

Strategy: Define a business strategy that incorporates design goals.
          Define a design strategy.
          Ensure that the design strategy regroups products,
            communications, space, and information.
Planning: Schedule design projects.
          Instigate design tests.
          Define design standards; graphic, product architecture,
            and structural norms.
Structure: Represent design at the top-management level.
          Create a mind-set favorable to design.

Finance:	Define design ratios for accountancy and audit.
	Ensure a budget is available for design strategy implementation.
Human Resources:	Create a favorable climate for design.
	Influence recruitment and career management.
Information:	Communicate the design mission to the company.
	Utilize trend spotting.
Communication:	Create design contests.
	Communicate about product concepts.
R&D:	Create relationships between design, marketing, and technological trend spotting.
Project Management:	Supervise key decision phases.
	Integrate design upstream, at the ideation phase.
Branding:	Insert design research into strategic marketing.
	Create prospective brainstorming on brands.
Evaluation:	Compare design performance with company performance.
	Verify the coherence of the design system.

Table 11.4 summarizes the design manager's position and the different levels on which design enters into the decision-making system of the company.

OPERATIONAL DESIGN	FUNCTIONAL DESIGN	STRATEGIC DESIGN
Strategy: · Define design policy in the product and communications policies · Define a brand policy and the role design plays in the brand	**Strategy:** · Coordinate design strategy with the marketing, innovation, and communications departments · Instill a design strategy into the implementation of the business strategy	**Strategy:** · Define a business strategy that incorporates design goals · Define a design strategy · Ensure that the design strategy regroups products, communications, space, and information
Planning: · Draft design briefs	**Planning:** · Define procedures/schedules · Define standards of design performance · Define relationships between design and total quality	**Planning:** · Schedule design projects · Launch design tests · Define design standards: graphic, product, and structural norms
Structure: · Select designers · Define teams and people who are connected with the designers · Nominate a "design champion"	**Structure:** · Define the role, workspace, and tasks of the design manager in the business structure · Create a matrix model for innovation and projects · Implement an in-house design service	**Structure:** · Represent design at the top management level · Create a mind-set that is favorable to design
Finances: · Manage design project budgets · Estimate design costs	**Finances:** · List suppliers and collaborating designers · Ensure that the budget is scheduled	**Finances:** · Define the design management regulations · Ensure that there is a budget for implementing the design strategy
Human Resources: · Define design competencies	**Human Resources:** · Create design understanding among the firm partners	· Create a climate that is favorable to design · Influence hiring and management of design careers
Information: · Develop an understanding of company goals among designers · Draft project documentation and control	**Information:** · Draft marketing, design, and production plans · Disseminate design know-how in the company	**Information:** · Communicate the design mission in the company · Implement trend spotting
Communications: · Form relationships with design schools · Create a graphic chart	**Communications:** · Manage the relationship between graphic and structural charts	**Communications:** · Create design contests · Communicate product concepts
R&D: · Support technology transfers	**R&D:** · Manage relationships with suppliers · Form quality policy	**R&D:** · Create a relationship between design and technological trend spotting

Table 11.4. The Design Manager's Toolbox

CONCLUSION

This book suggests the ways in which a design manager needs to develop value creation through design, by:

- Creating value through difference in aesthetics and perception
- Creating value through coherence with "gestalt"
- Creating value through metamorphosis in systems

These ideas of differentiation, coherence, and metamorphosis remind us of management concepts such as difference or heterogeneity in companies, conflict coordination and management, vision and organizational change, and competitive advantage.

Design management encourages an inclusive approach: The principal characteristics of design management probably rest in the fact that it tends to involve a large number of people to create the company offer. However, design management is also a tool for change. For certain companies, design contributes to the implementation of a new strategic core in order to reposition the company.

In fact, investing in "design management" is also investing in the detection of how the design knowledge of the creative team can inspire the company internally.

Every design activity implicitly necessitates the mastery of problem-solving know-how. In order to envision solutions and options for resolution, it is important to "draw" the context. Therefore, design helps the company structure its environment and make it understandable. It is a way of thinking and a "process" that "imagines" the relationship between the company and its environment. This structuring mechanism develops a worldview among company employees. The employee is no longer only a problem solver; his role is to represent, to "shape," his own environment.

Conception know-how helps management in two principal ways: by contributing to "reality construction" (the way in which the company constructs its relationship to its environment), and by helping strategic management, because the mastery of design skills can contribute to a better understanding of complex situations.

A three-part design management model is developed in this book. This model, defined by Patrick Hetzel in the fashion industry in 1993 and validated in our European study of the "33," can be applied to any type of business. The following is a final table summarizing the key parts of the book, presenting "3" basic design policies at each of the "3" decision-making levels.

In his thesis, Patrick Hetzel (1993) concludes that design influences:

1. The offer. It gives a sense to the offer that is, at the same time, an object and a means of discourse.
2. People. It helps mobilize and motivate buyers, facilitates the circulation of information, and unifies employees working in different departments around a common project.

Design ACTION	Design FUNCTION	Design VISION
The Differentiating Value of Design	**The Coordinating Value of Design**	**The Transforming Value of Design**
Design is an economic competency that changes the primary activities in the value chain.	Design is a management competency that changes in the support activities in the value chain.	Design is a core competency that changes the value chain of the sector and the vision of the industry.
"3" Brand marketing Production Communication	"3" Structure Technology management Innovation management	"3" Strategy Knowledge management Networking management
Operational Design Management	**Functional Design Management**	**Strategic Design Management**

Table 11.5. The Three Levels of Design Management

3. The company. It facilitates the formulation of a mission statement and encourages a strategic intent in the core strategic team.

These three levels of design management correspond to the three decision-making levels of the design manager: operational, functional, and strategic design management. They also coincide with the three levels of value creation through design:

1. Design action. Design's impact on the company's offer, or on the creation of differences valued by the market.
2. Design function. Design's impact on the company and its coordination methods.
3. Design vision. Design's impact on the company environment, or the transformative function.

Each design management strategy represents a choice in design scope and corporate goals:

1. Design action, or design as economic competence. The goal of design is to create value in the company's primary functions: production and marketing.
2. Design function, or design as managerial competence. Design will create value in the company's support departments, and, in particular, in innovation and technology management.
3. Design vision, or design as a core competency. Design improves the understanding of the company environment and changes its scope and the representation of its competition.

The organization of design in three strategic choices reinforces the idea of "designence," developed in this book in the example of *total quality*. Design and management have points in common, and the design management field, as defined in this book, is not only enriched by management concepts, but also opens a door to management by design.

It is the relationship between the concrete situation (perceived reality) and the projected situation (desired reality) that is shaped by design. Therefore, design know-how is used not only to create a product or service, but also to serve a better construction of the perceived reality of the moment and the desired reality.

In conclusion, the process of creating, judging, deciding, and choosing is the new intellectual commerce of scientific cultures and disciplines. It encourages the possibility of creating what Nobel prize–winning economist Herbert Simon has termed "a new science of design."

BIBLIOGRAPHY

Aaker, David, and Joachimstahler, Erich, 2000, *Brand Leadership*, New York: The Free Press.

Ackrich, M., M. Callon, and B. Latour, 1988, *A quoi tient le succès des innovations, Gérer et comprendre*, nos. 18 & 19.

Afuah, Allan, 1998, *Innovation Management*, Oxford University Press.

Alessi, Alberto, 1998, *The Dream Factory, Alessi Since 1921*, Köneman, Cologne.

Alleres, Danielle, 1990, *Luxe . . . Stratégies-Marketing*, Paris: Economica.

Allen, Dave, 2000, "Living the Brand," *The Design Management Journal*, Winter, 35.

Allouche, José, and Géraldine Schmidt, 1995, *Les outils de la décision stratégique*, La Découverte.

Amit, R., and P. Shoemaker, 1993, "Strategic Assets and Organizational Rent," *Strategic Management Journal*, vol. 14, no. 1, 33–46.

Anders, Robert, 2000, "Defining, Mapping and Designing the Design Process," *Design Management Journal*, Summer, 29–37.

Arbonies Ortiz, Angel, 1996, "Product Design and the Role of External Design Consultants," Sixth International Forum on Design Management Research and Education.

Argyris, Chris, 1999, *On Organizational Learning*, Basil Blackwell, Second Edition.

Arnheim, Rudolf, 1976, *La pensée visuelle*, Flammarion.

Aubert-Gamet, Véronique, 1996, *Le Design d'environnement commercial dans les services*, Thèse de Doctorat en Sciences de Gestion, Université d'Aix Marseille III.

Austin, Simon, Andrew Baldwin, and Andrew Newton, 1996, "A Data Flow Model to Plan and Manage the Building Design Process," *Journal of Engineering Design*, vol. 7, no. 1, 3–26.

Ayral, Suzanne, 1994, *L'intégration du design dans les stratégies de développement des industries de matériaux polymères*, Thèse de Doctorat en Sciences de Gestion, Université de Montpellier 1.

Badawy, M.K., 1996, "A New Paradigm for Understanding Management Technology: A Research Agenda for 'Technologists,'" *International Journal of Technology Management*, vol. 12, nos. 5–6, 717–32.

Bailetti, Antonio J., and Paul D. Guild, 1991, "Designers' Impressions of Direct Contact Between Product Designers and Champions of Innovation," *Journal of Product Innovation Management*, 91–103.

Bailetti, Antonio J., and Paul F. Litva, 1995, "Integrating Customer Requirements into Product Designs," *Journal of Product Innovation Management*, vol. 12, 3–15.

Baker, J., and Levy M. Grewald, 1992, "An Experimental Approach to Making Retail Store Environmental Decisions," *Journal of Retailing*, Winter, vol. 68, no. 4, 445–60.

Baker, 1987, *The Role of the Environment in Marketing Services: The Consumer Perspective in the Service Challenge: Integrating for Competitive Advantage*, Czepiel, J. and Shanahan, J., American Marketing Association.

Baldwin, Carliss, and Kim Clark, 1997, "Managing in an Age of Modularity," *Harvard Business Review*, September/October, 84–93.

Balmer, J.M.T., 2001, "Corporate Identity, Corporate Branding, and Corporate Marketing," *European Journal of Marketing*, vol. 35, 248–91.

Bamossy, Gary, Debra Scammon, and Marilyn Johnston, 1983, "A Preliminary Investigation of the Reliability and Validity of an Aesthetic Judgment Test," *Advances in Consumer Research*, vol. 10, 685–90.

Barkan, Philip, 1991, "Strategic and Tactical Benefits of Simultaneous Engineering," *Design Management Journal*, Spring 1991, vol. 2, no. 2, 39–42.

Barre, Bertrand, and Francis Le, 2001, *Vision Oblique*, Les Presses du Management.

Barthes, 1970, *L'empire des signes*, Editions A. Skira.

Bassereau, Jean-François, T. Lageat, and R. Duchamp, 1997, "From Semantic Differential to Sensorial Profile," paper prepared but not presented, Second European Academy of Design Conference, Stockholm, April.

Baudrillard, Jean, 1981, *For a Critique of the Political Economy of the Sign*, St. Louis Telos, 1972, in French, Gallimard.

Bauhain-Roux, Dominique, 1992, *Gestion du Design et Management d'Entreprise*, Chotard.

Bauer, Christine, 2001, *Le cas Philippe Starck ou de la construction de la notoriété*, L'harmattan, Paris.

Beckwith, Deanne, 2000, "Design Leadership at Herman Miller," *Design Management Journal*, Winter, vol. 11, no. 1, 54–64.

Belk, Russell, and Wendy Bryce, 1993, "Christmas Shopping Scenes: From Modern Miracle to Postmodern Mall," *International Journal of Marketing*, vol. 10, 277–96.

Belk, R.W., 1975, "Situational Variables and Consumer Research," *Journal of Consumer Research*, vol. 2, 157–64.

Belk, R.W., 1974, "An Exploratory Assessment of Situational Effects in Buyer Behavior," *Journal of Marketing Research*, vol. 11, 156–63.

Bellizi, J. A., A.E. Crowley, and R.W. Hasty, 1983, "The Effects of Color in Store Design," *Journal of Retailing*, Spring, vol. 59, no. 1, 21–45.

Bergadaa, and Nyeck, 1992, *Recherche en marketing: un état de controversies*, RAM 7.3, 23–44.

Berlyne, D.E., 1971, *Aesthetics and Psychobiology*, New York: Meredith Corporation.

Bernstein, David, 1984, *Company Image & Reality*, Holt, Rinehart and Winston.

Berkowitz, Marvin, 1987, "Product Shape as a Design Innovation Strategy," *Journal of Product Innovation Management*, vol. 4, 274–83.

Bernsen, Jens, 1987, *Design Management in Practice*, EEC European Design Editions, *12 principles in Design Management*, Danish Design Council.

Berton, Pierre, James Hulbert, and Leyland Pitt, 1999, "To Serve or to Create? Strategic Orientations Toward Customers and Innovation," *California Management Review*, Fall, vol. 42, no. 1, 37–55.

Bessant John, Caffyn, 1997, "High Involvement Innovation through Continuous Improvement," *International Journal of Technology Management*, vol. 14, no. 1, 7–27.

Birren, F., 1969, *Light, Color and Environment*, New York: Van Nostrand Reinhold.

Bitner et al., 1987, *Consumer Responses to the Physical Environment in Service Settings*, from *Creativity in Services Marketing*, Venkatesan, Schmalensee, Marshall, eds., Chicago, 89–93.

Bitner, Mary Jo, 1990, "Evaluating the Service Encounter: The Effects of Physical Surroundings and Employee Responses," *Journal of Marketing*, April, no. 54, 69–82.

Bitner, Mary Jo, 1992, "Servicescapes: The Impact of Physical Surroundings on Customers and Employees," *Journal of Marketing*, April, vol. 56, 57–71.

Blaich, Robert, and Janet Blaich, 1993, *Product Design and Corporate Strategy: Managing the Connection for Competitive Advantage*, New York: McGraw-Hill.

Bloch, Peter, 1995, "Seeking the Ideal Form: Product Design and Consumer Response," *Journal of Marketing*, July, vol. 59, 16–29.

Bloch, Peter, and Marsha Richins, 1983, "A Theoretical Model for the Study of Product Importance Perceptions," *Journal of Marketing*, Summer, vol. 47, 69–81.

Bohemia, Erik, 2000, "Suitability of Industrial Designers to Manage a Product Development Group: Australian Perspective," *Academic Review Design Management Journal*, no. 1, 40–53.

Boisot, Max, and Dorothy Griffths, 1999, "Possession is Nine Tenths of the Law: Managing a Firm's Knowledge in a Regime of Weak Appropriability," *Journal of Technology Management*, vol. 17, no. 6, 662–76.

Borja de Mozota, Brigitte, 2002, *Design and Competitive Edge: A Typology for Design Management Excellence in European SMEs*, Academic Review of the Design Management Journal, September, no. 2.

Borja de Mozota, Brigitte, 2002, *Un modèle de management du design*, Revue Française de Gestion, Avril-Juin, vol. 28, numéro 138, 75–95.

Borja de Mozota, Brigitte, 2001, *Design Management*, Editions d'Organisation, Seconde édition corrigée, Paris.

Borja de Mozota, Brigitte, 1998, "Structuring Strategic Design Management: Michael Porter's Value Chain," *Design Management Journal*, Spring, vol. 9, no. 2, 26–31.

Borja de Mozota, Brigitte, 1998, *Challenge of Design Relationships: The Converging Paradigm*, Management of Design Alliances, John Wiley and Sons.

Borja de Mozota, Brigitte, 1992, "A Theoretical Model for the Future of Design Education and Research," *Design Management Journal*, Fall, vol. 3, no. 4.

Borja de Mozota, Brigitte, 1990 a, *Design & Management*, Editions d'Organisation, Paris.

Borja de Mozota, Brigitte, 1990 b, *Design Management: Handbook of Issues and Methods*, editor: Mark Oakley, advisory editors: Brigitte Borja de Mozota and Colin Clipson, chapter 9: *Design as a Strategic Management Tool*, Basil Blackwell Reference: Oxford.

Borja de Mozota, Brigitte, 1985, *Essai sur la fonction du Design et son rôle dans la Stratégie marketing de l'Entreprise*, Thèse de Doctorat en Sciences de Gestion, Université de Paris I Panthéon Sorbonne, Juin.

Bouchard, Carole, 1997, *Modélisation du processus de style automobile: méthode de veille stylistique adaptée au Design du composant d'aspect*, Thèse Docteur en génie Industriel, ENSAM.

Bourdieu, Pierre, 1984, *Distinction: A Social Critique of the Judgment of Taste*, Cambridge: Harvard University Press.

Briggs, Bonnie, and Jill Dorjath, 2001, "The CAT Rental Store," *Design Management Journal*, vol. 12 , no. 4, Fall, 24.

Bruce, Margaret, and John Bessant, ed., 2002, *Design in Business*, Design Council & Pearson Education.

Bruce, Margaret, and Richelle Harun, 2001, *Exploring Design Capability for Serial Innovation in SMEs*, Proceedings 4th European Academy of Design Conference, University of Aveiro, Portugal, April 10–12, 280.

Bruce, Margaret, and Birgit Jevnaker, ed., 1998, *Management of Design Alliances*, Wiley.

Bruce, Margaret, and Barny Morris, 1995, *Approaches to Design Management in the Product Development Process*, John Wiley and Sons.

Bruce, Margaret, and Barny Morris, 1994, *Managing External Design Professionals in the Product Development Process*, Technovation, vol. 14, no. 9, 585–98.

Bruce, Margaret, and Barny Morris, 1994, *Evaluation of Design Management Practices: A Diagnostic Tool*, 6th International Forum on Design Management Research & Education, Paris.

Brun, Monique, 1998, *Design management: les PME aussi*, Revue Française de Gestion, Janvier-Février, 31–42.

Brun, Monique, and Philippe Rasquinet, 1996, *L'identité visuelle de l'entreprise*, Les Editions d'organisation.

Bucci, Ampelio, 1998, *Quand les idées mènent l'entreprise*, Dunod.

Bucci, Ampelio, 1994, *From Design Management to Design Direction*, 6th International Forum on Design Management Research & Education, Paris.

Bukowitz, Wendi, and Gordon Petrash, 1997, "Visualizing, Measuring and Managing Knowledge," *Research Technology Management*, 24–30.

Butcher, John, 1988, *The Macroeconomic Value of Design, 1988, Design talks!*, ed. Peter Gorb, The Design Council, London Business School.

Caron, Gérard, 1996, *L'avenir des marques*, Futuribles, Février, 27–43.

Cellini, R.J., and F.W. Hull, 1996, "Beyond Work on Hire: Results-based Compensation in the Client Consultant Relationship," *Design Management Journal*, Spring, 7, 2, 48–53.

Chandler, 1990, *Scale or Scope: The Dynamics of Industrial Capitalism*, Cambridge: Harvard University Press.

Childers, Terry, et al., 1985, "Measurements of Individual Differences in Visual versus Verbal Information Processing," *Journal of Consumer Research*, Sept., vol. 12.

Clark, Kim, and Takahiro Fujimoto, 1991, *Product Development Performance*, Harvard Business School Press.

Clark, Kim B., and Takahiro Fujimoto, 1990, "The Power of Product Integrity," *Harvard Business Review*, November–December, 107–118.

Claeys, C., A. Swinnen, and Abeele P.Vanden, 1995, "Consumers' Means-End Chains for 'Think' and 'Feel' Products," *International Journal of Research in Marketing*.

Coates, Del, 1997, "Analyzing and Optimizing Discretionary Information," *Design Management Journal*, Spring, vol. 8, no. 2, 58–65.

Coates, Joseph F., 1997, "Long-Term Technological Trends and Their Implications for Management," *International Journal of Technology Management*, vol. 14, nos. 6/7/8, 579–95.

Cooper, Rachel, and Mike Press, 1997, "Design as a Strategic Resource for Management," *Revue Gestion 2000*, Sept.–Oct., 91–108.

Cooper, Rachel, and Mike Press, 1995, *The Design Agenda*, John Wiley & Sons.

Cooper, Rachel, Alison Prendiville, and Tim Jones, 1995, "High Technology NPD," *Co-Design*, April-May-June, vol. 3, 14–22.

Cooper, Rachel Davies, 1995, "Setting a Research Framework," *Co-Design*, January-February-March, vol. 2, 14.

Cooper, Rachel Davies, and Tim Jones, 1994, *Successful Design Interfaces in New Product Development*, Sixth International Forum on Design Management Research & Education, Paris.

Cooper, Rachel, 1993, *Perceptions of Design: A Study of the Attitude and Perceptions among European Buyers of the Design of a Range of Products*, 5th International Forum on Design Management Research & Education, MIT, July 14–16.

Cooper, Robert, 1998, *Product Leadership*, Perseus Books.

Cooper, Robert, Scott Edgett, and Elko Kleinschmidt, 1999, "New Product Portfolio Management: Practices and Performance," *Journal of Product Innovation Management*, vol. 16, 333–51.

Cooper, Robert, and Elko Kleinschmidt, 1996, "Winning Businesses in Product Development: The Critical Success Factors," *Research Technology Management*, July–August, vol. 39, no. 4, 18–30.

Cooper, Robert, and Elko Kleinschmidt, 1986, "An Investigation into the New Product Process: Steps, Deficiencies and Impact," *Journal of Product Innovation Management*, vol. 3, 71–85.

Cooper, Robin, and Bruce W. Chew, 1996, "Control Tomorrow's Costs through Today's Designs," *Harvard Business Review*, January–February, 88–97.

Corfield, K.G., 1979, *Report on Product Design*, National Economic Development Office (NEDO), London.

Coughlan, Peter, and Nick Backlund, 1996, "Fostering Design Consciousness within a Marketing Research Paradigm: A Case Study in Automotive Design Research," 8th International Forum on Design Management Research and Education, Barcelona.

Coulter, Robin Higie, and Gerald Zaltman, 1994, "Using the Zaltman Metaphor Elicitation Technique to Understand Brand Images," *Advances in Consumer Research*, vol. 21, 501–7.

Cova, Bernard, and Christian Svanfeldt, 1993, "Societal Innovations and the Postmodern Aestheticization of Everyday Life," *International Journal of Research in Marketing*, vol. 10, 297–310.

Cowell, D., 1983, *The Marketing of Services*, Institute of Marketing and the CAM Foundation.

Cox, Dena, and Locander William, 1987, "Product Novelty: Does It Moderate the Relationship Between Ad Attitudes and Brand Attitudes," *Journal of Advertising*, 16, 3, 39–44.

Credoc Entreprise, 1992, *Design et forme naturelle de l'objet: la mise au point d'un outil de design et d'ingénierie de l'immatériel*, Etude financée par Ministère de la recherche et de la Technologie.

Creusen, Marielle, and Jan Schoormans, 1998, "The Influence of Observation Time on the Role of the Product Design in Consumer Preference," *Advances in Consumer Research*, vol. 25, 551–56.

Crossan, Mary, 1998, "Improvisation in Action," *Organization Science*, September–October, vol. 9, no. 5, 593–99.

Csikszentmihalyi, M., and R. Robinson, 1990, *The Art of Seeing*, Malibu, California: Jean Paul Getty Museum.

Damak, Leila, 1996, *Corps du consommateur et design du produit: recherche d'une similarité ou d'une complémentarité*, Thèse de Doctorat Sciences de Gestion Université Paris Dauphine.

Dandridge, Thomas, 1983, "Symbols, Function and Use," in L.R. Pondy, P. Frost, and T.C. Dandridge: *Organizational Symbolism*, Jay Press, Greenwich, 69–79.

Dandridge, Thomas, Ian Mitroff, and Joyce William, 1980, "Organizational Symbolism: A Topic to Expand Organizational Analysis," *Academy of Management Review*, vol. 5, no. 1, 77–82.

Danger, E.P., 1969, *How to Use Colors to Sell*, Boston: Cahners.

Danzig, Mark, 2002, "By Design: The BlueLight Brand Story," *Design Management Journal*, Winter, vol. 13, no. 1, 26.

Dano, Florence, 1994, "Contribution de la sémiotique à l'Etude des attentes et représentations des consommateurs à l'égard du Packaging," Thèse de Doctorat ès Sciences de Gestion, 4 juillet, Université de Paris-Dauphine.

Darmon, Françoise, 1992, *Le sens dans l'utile: 9 entreprises 9 créateurs*, Chêne.

Davenport, Thomas, 1993, "Process Innovation: Reengineering Work through Information Technology," Boston: Harvard Business School Press.

Davenport-Firth, David, 2000, "Visual Planning: Design and Clients as Co-conspirators," *Design Management Journal*, Spring, vol. 11, no. 2, 57–62.

Davis, M., 1987, *Visual Design in Dress*, Englewood Cliffs, NJ: Prentice Hall.

Davis, Tim, 1984, "The Influence of the Physical Environment in Offices," *Academy of Management Review*, vol. 9, no. 2, 271–83.

De Bono, Edward, 1970, *Lateral Thinking: Creativity Step by Step*, New York, Harper and Row.

Debord, Guy, 1983, *Society of Spectacle*, Detroit: Black & Red.

Demirbilek, Oya, and Miles Park, 2001, "A Survey of Criteria for the Assessment of 'Good Product Design,'" Fourth European Academy of Design Conference, University of Aveiro, Portugal, April 10–12, 370.

De Noblet, Jocelyn, éditeur, 1993, *Design, Miroir du Siècle*, Flammarion/APCI.

Design de A à Z, Mode d'Emploi, 1998, Ministère de l'Economie, des Finances et de l'Industrie, DPI, rédaction Jean-Charles Gaté.

Design Continuum Inc, 2000, "Getting Design: Bringing External Design Resources into an Organization," *Design Management Journal*, Spring, vol. 11, no. 2, 53.

Design Policy, 1982, "GK Industrial Design Japan. Smallness as an Idea," Proceedings International Conference, Royal College of Art.

Dess Management du Design et le la Qualité, 2000, Enquête professionnelle sur la profession de Design Intégré, *Annuaire du Design Intégré*, Université de Nancy 2, publié par Design Fax.

Djelic, Marie-Laure, and Antti Ainamo, 1999, "The Coevolution of New Organizational Forms in the Fashion Industry: A Historical and Comparative Study of France, Italy, and the United States," *Organization Science*, September–October, no. 5, 622–37.

Donovan, R.J., and J.R. Rossiter, 1982, "Store Atmosphere: An Environmental Approach," *Journal of Retailing*, Spring, vol. 58, no. 1, 34–57.

Donovan, R.J., J.R. Rossiter, G. Marcoolyn, and A. Nesdale, 1994, "Store Atmosphere and Purchasing Behavior," *Journal of Retailing*, vol. 20, no. 3, 283–94.

Dormer, Peter, 1990, *The Meanings of Modern Design*, Thames and Hudson.

Dosi, G., S. Teece, and G. Winter, 1990, *Les frontières des enterprises*, Revue d'Economie Industrielle, 1er trimestre.

Droste, Magdalena,1990, *Bauhaus*, Taschen.

Dreyfuss, Henry, 1950, "The Industrial Designer and the Businessman," *Harvard Business Review*, November, vol. 28, no. 6.

Drucker, Peter, 1998, "The Discipline of Innovation," *Harvard Business Review*, November–December, 149–157.

Dubois, Bernard, 1987, "Culture et Marketing," *Recherche et Applications en Marketing*, vol. II, no. 1/87, 45–63.

Dubuisson, Sophie, and Antoine Hennion, 1996, *Le Design: l'objet dans l'usage*, Presses de l'Ecole des Mines de Paris.

Dumas, Angela, and Henry Mintzberg, 1991, "Managing the Form, Function and Fit of Design," *Design Management Journal*, Summer, 26–31.

Durand, Thomas, Eléonore Mounoud, and Bernard Ramantsoa, 1996, "Uncovering Strategic Assumptions: Understanding Managers Ability to Build Representations," *European Management Journal*, August, vol. 14, no. 4, 389.

Durgee, Jeffrey, 1996, "Design Research Implications of Adrian Forty's 'Objects of Desire': Merging Consumer Culture with Design Culture," 8th International Forum on Design Management Research and Education, Barcelona.

Durgee, Jeffrey F., et al., 1995, "Why Some Products 'Just Feel Right,' or, The Phenomenology of Product Rightness," *Advances in Consumer Research*, vol. 22, 650–2.

Dyson, James, 1997, *Against the Odds: An Autobiography*, London: Orion Business Books.

Eckman, Molly, and Janet Wagner, 1994, "Judging the Attractiveness of Product Design: The Effect of Visual Attributes and Consumer Characteristics," *Advances in Consumer Research*, vol. 21, 560–4.

Eckman, Molly, and Janet Wagner, 1995, "Aesthetic Aspects of the Consumption of Fashion Design: The Conceptual and Empirical Challenge," *Advances in Consumer Research*, vol. 22, 646–49.

Eco, Umberto, 1992, *Les limites de l'Interprétation*, Paris: Grasset.

Eco, Umberto, 1988, *La structure absente*, Mercure de France.

Ehrnberg, Ellinor, and Staffan Jacobsson, 1996, "Managing Technological Discontinuities—A Tentative Framework," *International Journal Technology Management*, vol. 11, nos. 3/4, 452–65.

Eisenhard, K. M., 1989, "Building Theories from Case Study Research," *Academy of Management Review*, vol. 14, (4), 532–50.

Ellis, Willis D., 1950, *A Source Book of Gestalt Psychology*, London: Routledge.

Evans, W., J. Fellows, M. Zorn, and K. Doty, 1980, "Cognitive Mapping and Architecture," *Journal of Applied Psychology*, vol. 65, no. 4, 474–78.

Everett, Peter B., G.M. Rik Pieters, and Philip A. Titus, 1994, "The Consumer-Environment Interaction: An Introduction to the Special Issue," *International Journal of Research in Marketing*, vol. 11, 97–105.

Faruque, Omar, 1984, *Graphic Communication as a Design Tool*, Van Nostrand Reinhold Company.

Ferry, Luc, 1990, *Homo Aestheticus*, Paris: Grasset.

Feldman, Laurence, 1995, *Design Research and the Usability of High Tech Products*, 7th International Forum on Design Management Research & Education, University of Stanford

Fitch, Agence, 2000, "Building and Fostering Long-Term Client Relationships," *Design Management Journal*, vol. 11, no. 2, Spring, 41–45.

Firat, Fuat, and Alladi Venkatesh, 1995, "Liberatory Postmodernism and the Reenchantment of Consumption," *Journal of Consumer Research*, December, vol. 22, no. 3, 239–67.

Firat, Fuat, and Alladi Venkatesh, 1993, "Postmodernity: The Age of Marketing," *International Journal of Research in Marketing*, 227–49.

Floch, Jean-Marie, 1989, "La contribution d'une sémiotique structurale à la conception d'un hypermarché," *Recherche et Applications en marketing*, vol. IV, no. 2/89, 37–59.

Forty, Adrian, 1986, *Objects of Desire*, London, Pantheon.

Franzen, Stefan, et al., 1994, "The Inappreciative Market. Marketing Ergonomic Design," Sixth International Forum on Design Management Research & Education, Paris.

Frery, Frédéric, 2000, *Benetton ou l'entreprise virtuelle*, Vuibert Collection Management.

Freund, Bruno, et al., 1997, "Impact of Information Technologies on Manufacturing," *International Journal of Technology Management*, vol. 13, no. 3, 215–28.

Fry, Tony, 1995, "Ecologic Crisis and Design," in *Discovering Design*, Buchanan and Margolin, eds. University of Chicago Press.

Fujimoto, Takahiro, 1991, "Product Integrity and the Role of 'Designer as Integrator,'" *Design Management Journal*, Spring, vol. 2, no. 2, 29–34.

Garber, Lawrence L., 1995, "The Package Appearance in Choice," *Advances in Consumer Research*, vol. 22, 653–60.

Gato, J.A., and A. Porter, et al., 1987, *Exploring Visual Design*, Worchester, Mass.: Davis Publications.

Gemser, Gerda, 1997, "Industrial Design and Competitiveness," 2nd European Academy of Design Conference, Stockholm, April.

Gemser, Gerda, and Eric Van Zee, 2002, "Benchmarking Industrial Design Services, *Design Journal*, United Kingdom.

Gemser, Gerda, and Nachoem Wijnberg, 2002, "Industrial Design Awards and Competitive Dynamics," Academic Review, *Design Management Journal*, no. 2.

Gemser, Gerda, and Nachoem Wijnberg, 2001, "Effects of Reputational Sanctions on the Competitive Imitation of Design Innovations," *Organisation Studies*, EGOS 22/4, 563–91.

Gemser, Gerda, and Mark Leenders, 2001, "How Integrating Industrial Design in the Product Development Process Impacts on Company Performance," *Journal of Product Innovation Management*, vol. 18, 28–38.

Gobe, Marc, 2001, *Emotional Branding*, Allworth Press.

Goldenberg, Jacob, and David Mazursky, 2002, *Creativity in Product Innovation*, Cambridge University Press.

Gombrich, E.H., 1979, 1984, *The Sense of Order*, Phaidon Press.

Goodrich, Kristina, 1994, "The Designs of the Decade: Quantifying Design Impact over Ten Years," *Design Management Journal*, Spring, vol. 5, no. 2, 47.

Goodsell, C., 1977, "Bureaucratic Manipulation of Physical Symbols," *American Journal of Political Science*, February, XXI, 79–91.

Goodwin, C., 1994, "Private Roles in Public Encounters: Communal Relationships in Service Exchanges," Proceedings 3rd International Research Seminar in Service Management, LaLonde les Maures (cité par Aubert Gamet 1996).

Goodwin, C., et al., 1992, "Social Support through the Service Interaction," Actes du 2ème séminaire International de recherche en management des activités de services, IAE Aix Marseille.

Gorb, Peter, 1995, "Managing Design in an Uncertain World," *European Management Journal*, March, vol. 13, no. 1, 120–27.

Gorb, Peter, 1990, *Design-management et gestion des organizations*, Revue Française de Gestion, Septembre–Octobre, numéro 80, 66–72.

Gorb, Peter, and Raymond Turner, 1992, "A Design Frontier: Corporate Identity and Design Management at Eurotunnel," *Design Management Journal*, Winter, 21–32.

Gorb, Peter, and Angela Dumas, 1987, "Silent Design," *Design Studies*, July, vol. 8, no. 3, 150–56.

Goto, Kelly, and Emily Cotler, 2002, *Web Redesign: Workflow that Works*, NewRiders, traduction française Editions Eyrolles.

Grange, Thierry, and Loïck Roche, 1998, *Management et technologie: pour un développement de l'imaginaire en entreprise*, Collection management technologique ESC Grenoble, Diffusé Maxima.

Greimas, A.J., and J. Courtes, 1979, *Sémiotique, dictionnaire raisonné de la Théorie du Langage*, Paris: Hachette.

Grewal, Dhruv, and Julie Baker, 1994, "Do Retail Store Environmental Factors Affect Consumers' Price Acceptability? An Empirical Examination," *International Journal of Research in Marketing*, vol. 11, 107–15.

Griffin, Abbie, and John R. Hauser, 1996, "Integrating R&D and Marketing: A Review and Analysis of the Literature," *Journal of Product Innovation Management*, vol. 13, 191–213.

Groppel, A., 1992, "Store Design and Experience-Orientated Consumers in Retailing," *Advances in Consumer Research*, vol. 20.

Grossbart, S.L., R.A. Mittelstaedt, W.W. Curtis, and R.D. Rogers, 1975, "Environmental Sensitivity and Shopping Behavior," *Journal of Business Research*, vol. 3, no. 4, 281–94.

Gulmann, Steffen, 1987, *Design Management in Practice: Image Management*, EEC Design Publications (SG4).

Guimaraes, Luiz, John Penny, and Stanley Moody, 1996, "Product Design and Social Needs: The Case of North East Brazil," *International Journal of Technology Management*, vol. 12, no. 7/8, 849–63.

Hamel, Gary, and C.K. Pralahad, 1994, *Competing for the Future*, Boston: Harvard Business School Press.

Hamel, Gary, and C.K. Pralahad, 1993, "Strategy as Stretch and Leverage," *Harvard Business Review*, March–April.

Hansen, R.A., and T. Deutscher, 1978, "An Empirical Investigation of Attribute Importance in Retail Store Selection," *Journal of Retailing*, Winter, vol. 53, no. 4, 59–72.

Hargadon, Andrew, 1998, "Firms as Knowledge Brokers: Lessons in Pursuing Continuous Innovation," *California Management Review*, vol. 40, no. 1, 209–27.

Hargadon, Andrew, and Y. Douglas, 2001, "When Innovations Meet Institutions: Edison and the Design of the Electrical Light," *Administrative Science Quarterly*, September, vol. 46.

Hargadon, Andrew, and Robert Sutton, 2000, "Building Innovation Factory," *Harvard Business Review*, May–June, 157.

Hargadon, Andrew, and Robert Sutton, 1997, "Technology Brokering and Innovation in a Product Development Firm," *Administrative Science Quarterly*, vol. 42, 716–49.

Harris, K., S. Baron, and J. Ratcliffe, 1994, "Oral Participation of Customers in a Retail Setting: An Empirical Study," Actes du 3ème séminaire international de recherche en management des activités de services, IAE Aix Marseille III, 347.

Hart, Susan, and Linda Service, 1988, "The Effects of Managerial Attitudes to Design on Company Performance," *Journal of Marketing Management*, vol. 4, no. 2, Hivers, 230.

Hart, Susan J., Linda M. Service, and Michael J. Baker, 1989, "Design Orientation and Market Success," *Design Studies*, April, vol. 10, no. 2, 103–8.

Hatchuel, Armand, and Benoit Weil, 1999, *Design Oriented Organizations: Towards a Unified Theory of Design Activities*, Ecole des Mines de Paris, 6th International Product Development Management Conference, Cambridge, July.

Hayes, Robert, Steven Wheelwright, and Kim Clark, 1988, *Dynamic Manufacturing*, New York: The Free Press.

Hayes, Robert, 1990, Design: Putting Class into 'World Class,'" *Design Management Journal*, Summer 1990, vol. 1, no. 2, 8–14.

Henderson, Pamela, and Joseph Cote, 1998, "Guidelines for Selecting or Modifying Logos," *Journal of Marketing*, April, vol. 62, 14–30.

Henry, Jane, ed., 1991, *Creative Management*, Sage Publications, 319.

Herbruck, Diane, and Steven Umbach, 1997, "Design Management and New Product Development: Linking People and Process," *Design Management Journal*, Spring, vol. 8, no. 2, 44–50.

Hertenstein, Julie, Marjorie Platt, and David Brown, 2001, "Valuing Design: Enhancing Corporate Performance through Design Effectiveness," *Design Management Journal*, Summer, vol. 12, no. 3, 10–19.

Hertenstein, Julie H., and Marjorie B. Platt, 1997, "Developing a Strategic Design Culture," *Design Management Journal*, Spring, vol. 8, no. 2, 10–19.

Hetzel, Patrick, and Gilles Marion, 1995, "Contributions of French Semiotics to Marketing Research Knowledge," *Revue Marketing and Research Today*, February–May, vol. 23, nos. 1 and 2.

Hetzel, Patrick, 1995, *Le rôle de la mode et du design dans la société postmoderne*, Revue Française du Marketing, Numéro 151, vol. 1, 19–35.

Hetzel, Patrick, 1995, *Pour renouveler les processus d'innovation en entreprise*, Revue Française de Gestion, Mars-Avril-Mai, Numéro 103, 87–97.

Hetzel, Patrick, 1994, *Design Management, constitution de l'offre et "néo-marketing": les contributions du design au renouvellement de la "construction" des processus d'innovation en entreprise*, Sixth International Forum on Design Management Research & Education, Paris.

Hetzel, Patrick, 1993, *Design Management et Constitution de l'Offre*, Thèse de Doctorat Sciences de Gestion, Université Jean Moulin Lyon 3.

Hirschmann, Elisabeth, and Morris Holbrook, 1992, *Postmodern Consumer Research*, Newbury: Park Sage Publications.

Hise, Richard T., Larry O'Neal, James McNeal, and A. Prasuraman, 1989, "The Effect of Product Design Activities on Commercial Success Levels of New Industrial Products," *Journal of Product Innovation Management*, vol. 6, 43–50.

Holbrook, Morris, 1986, "Aims, Concepts, and Methods for Representation of Individual Differences in Esthetic Responses to Design Features," *Journal of Consumer Research*, vol. 13, 337–47.

Holbrook, Morris, and Elisabeth Hirschmann, 1993, *The Semiotics of Consumption*, New York: Mouton de Gruyter.

Holbrook, Morris, and Elisabeth Hirschmann, 1982, "The Experimental Aspects of Consumption: Consumer Fantasies, Feelings and Fun," *Journal of Consumer Research*, September, vol. 9, 132–40.

Holland, Ray, 1995, "Integrated 'R' Us: Multidisciplinary Team Design of Education Toys," 7th International Forum on Design Management Research and Education, Stanford University.

Hollins, Bill, 1995, "Managing Concurrent Engineering," *Co-Design*, April-May-June, vol. 3, 22–30.

Hollins, Bill, and Stuart Pugh, 1990, *Successful Product Design*, London: Butterwoths.

Hollins, Gillian, and Bill Hollins, 1991, *Total Design: Managing the Design Process in the Service Sector*, London: Pitman.

Holt, Knut, 1991, "The Impact of Technology Strategy on the Engineering Design Process," *Design Studies*, April, vol. 12, no. 2, 90–5.

Holt, Knut, 1990, *The Nature of the Design Process*, in *Handbook of Design Management*, edited by Mark Oakley, Basil Blackwell, 195–98.

Hubel Vello, Diedra, and B. Lussow, 1984, *Focus on Designing*, McGraw-Hill, Ryerson Limited.

Hughes, David G., and Don C. Chafin, 1996, "Turning New Product Development into a Continuous Learning Process," *Journal of Product Innovation Management*, vol. 13, 89–104.

Ingram, Jack, and Richard Heppenstall, 1996, "Design Management Strategy and Concurrent Engineering," 8th International Forum on Design Management Research and Education, Barcelona.

Itten, Johannes, 1970, *The Elements of Color*, Van Nostrand Reinhold Company.

Jenkins, S., et al., 1997, "Managing the Product Development Process (Part 1 & 2)," *International Journal of Technology Management*, vol. 13, no. 4, 359–77, 379–93.

Jensen, M., and W. Meckling, 1976, "The Theory of the Firm: Managerial Behavior, Agency Cost and Ownership Structure," *Journal of Financial Economics*, vol. 4, no. 3, 305–60.

Jevnaker, Birgit, 2000, "Championing Design: Perspectives on Design Capabilities," Academic Review, *Design Management Journal*, no. 1, 25–39.

Jevnaker, Birgit, 1996, "Fostering Strategic Design Directions in Business Firms: The Hidden Assets," 8th International Forum on Design Management Research and Education, Barcelona.

Jevnaker, Birgit, 2000, "How Design Becomes Strategic," *Design Management Journal*, Winter, vol. 11, 41–7.

Johne, Axel F., and Patricia A. Snelson, 1988, "Success Factors in Product Innovation: A Selective Review of the Literature," *Journal of Product Innovation Management*, vol. 5, 114–28.

Jonas, Wolfgang, 1997, "Viable Structures and Generative Tools," Second European Academy of Design, Stockholm, 23–25, April.

Jones, Christopher, 1992, *Design Methods*, Wiley & Sons, (first edition, 1970).

Jones, P., 1991, *Taste Today*, New York: Pergamon Press.

Kaminagai, Yo, 2002, *la stratégie de design d'une marque de transport urbain*, Eurosyn, lettre trimestrielle, juillet.

Kapferer, Jean-Noël, and Jean-Claude Thoenig, 1989, *La Marque*, Ouvrage Collectif, McGraw-Hill.

Katz, D., 1950, *Gestalt Psychology*, New York: Ronald Press.

Keeley, Larry, 1991, "Taking the D-team Out of the Minor Leagues," *Design Management Journal*, Spring 1991, vol. 2, no. 2, 35–8.

Keller, Kevin Lane, 1993, "Conceptualizing, Measuring, and Managing Customer-Based Brand Equity," *Journal of Marketing*, vol. 57, 1–32.

Keller, Kevin Lane, 1999, "Brand Reinforcement and Revitalization Strategies," *California Management Review*, Spring, vol. 41, no. 3, 102–23.

Kelley, Tom, 2001, *Prototyping is the shorthand of innovation, Design Management Journal*, vol. 12, Summer, 35–42.

Kelley, Tom, 2001, *The Art of Innovation*, New York: Doubleday.

Kelley, Tom, 1999, "Designing for Business, Consulting for Innovation," *Design Management Journal*, Summer, vol. 10, no. 3.

Keen, P.G.W., 1997, *The Process Edge*, Harvard Business School Press, 11.

Kogut, Bruce, and Udo Zander, 1996, "Why Firms Do? Coordination, Identity, and Learning," *Organization Science*, September-October, vol. 7, no. 5, 502–17.

Kotler, Philip, and Alexander Rath, 1984, "Design, A Powerful but Neglected Strategic Tool," *Journal of Business Strategy*, Fall 1984, vol. 5, no. 2, 16.

Kotler, Phillip, 1973, "Atmospherics as a Marketing Tool," *Journal of Retailing*, Winter, vol. 49, no. 4.

Kristensen, Tore, 1995, "The Contribution of Design to Business: A Competence-Based Perspective," Process of Change Laboratory, Stanford University/Copenhagen Business School; 22 February.

Landry, Roch, 1987, *Contributions du design industriel au processus d'innovation et de communication dans l'entreprise*, Thèse pour le Doctorat ès Sciences de gestion, Université d'Aix–Marseille, 3 mai.

Langrish, John, and Chiwu Huang, 1996, "Product Semantics and Ease of Use," 8th International Forum on Design Management Research and Education, Barcelona.

Lawson, B., 1983, *How Designers Think*, Westfield, NJ: Eastview Editions.

Lazarus, R.S., 1991, *Emotion and Adaptation*, NYK, Oxford University Press.

Lebahar, Jean-Charles, 1994, *Le Design Industriel*, Editions Parenthèses.

Leifer, Richard, C. McDermott, G. O'Connor, L. Peters, M. Rice, and R. Veryzer, 2000, *Radical Innovation*, Harvard Business School Press.

Leonard, Dorothy, and Sylvia Sensiper, 1998, "The Role of Tacit Knowledge in Group Innovation," *California Management Review*, Spring, vol. 40, no. 3, 113–31.

Leonard-Barton, Dorothy, 1991, "Inanimate Integrators: A Block of Wood Speaks," *The Design Management Journal*, Summer, vol. 2, no. 3, 61–7.

Le Quement, Patrick, 1994, "The Case of the Twingo," 4th International Forum on Design Management Research & Education, Paris, 1–3 June.

Lewasky, Z., 1988, *Product Esthetics: An Interpretation for Designers*, Carson City, NV: Design and Development Engineering Press.

Lester, Richard, Michael Piore, and Kamal Malek, 1998, "Interpretive Management: What General Managers Can Learn from Design," *Harvard Business Review*, March–April, 86–96.

Levin, Morten, 1997, "Technology Transfer is Organizational Development: An Investigation into the Relationship between Technology Transfer and Organizational Change," *International Journal of Technology Management*, vol. 14, nos. 2/3/4, 297–308.

Liedtka, Jeanne, 2000, "In Defense of Strategy as Design," *California Management Review*, Spring, vol. 42, no. 3, 8–30.

Linquist, J.D., 1974, "Meaning of Image," *Journal of Retailing*, Winter, vol. 50, 29–38.

Loken, Barbara, and James Ward, 1990, "Alternative Approaches to Understanding the Determinants of Typicality," September, *Journal of Consumer Research*, 111–26.

Loewy, Raymond, 1963, *La laideur se vend mal*, Gallimard.

Looschilder, Gérard et al., 1995, "A Means-End Chain Approach to Concept Testing, in Product Development," edited by Bruce and Biemans, Wiley & Sons, 117.

Lorenz, Christopher, 1986, *The Design Dimension*, Blackwell (édition française Editions d'Organisation 1990).

Lovering, Tim, 1995, "Corporate Design Management as an Aid to Regional Development," 7th International Forum on Design Management Research & Education, University of Stanford.

Lutz R., and P. Kakkar, 1975, "The Psychological Situation as a Determinant of Consumer Behavior," *Advances in Consumer Research*, 439–53.

McCracken, Grant, 1986, "Culture and Consumption," *Journal of Consumer Research*, June, vol. 13.

Macelroy, J.C., P.C. Morrow, and S. Eroglu, 1990, "The Atmosphere of Personal Selling," *Journal of Personal Selling and Sales Management*, Fall, 31–41.

Macneal, J.U., 1973, "An Introduction to Consumer Behavior," John Wiley & Sons, New York.

Madahvan, Ravindranath, and Rajiv Grover, 1998, "From Embedded Knowledge to Embodied Knowledge: New Product Development as Knowledge Management," *Journal of Marketing*, October, 1–12.

Maeda, John, 2002, "Design Education in the Post-Digital Age," *Design Management Journal*, Summer, vol. 13, no. 3, 39–45.

Maffessolli, Michel, 1990, *Au creux des apparences*, Paris Plon.

Magne, Stéphane, 1999, *Essai de mesure de l'attitude esthétique du consommateur envers la forme—design du packaging et d'une variable explicative, la sensibilité esthétique personnelle: une application au Design de couvertures de livres*, Université de Toulouse I, Thèse de Doctorat en Sciences de Gestion, 22 janvier, ESUG.

Maisseu, André, 1995, "Managing Technological Flows into Corporate Strategy," *International Journal of Technology Management*, vol. 10, no. 1, 3–20.

Manzini, Ezio, 1995, *Ecology of the Artificial*, in *Discovering Design*, Buchanan & Margolin, eds., University of Chicago Press.

Margulies, W.P., 1970, *Packaging Power*, World Publishing, New York.

Marinissen, A.H., 1990, *Effectivity of Ergonomics in the Design Process*, Delft University of Technology, Colloque recherches sur le Design, Compiègne, octobre.

Marion, Gilles, 1999, *La nouvelle crise des modèles rationalisateurs du marketing*, Revue Française de Gestion, Septembre-Octobre, 81.

Marchandet, Éric, 1994, *Les formes de la relation à l'objet: contribution à une sociologie de l'objet*, Thèse de Doctorat de Sociologie, Université Paris 5.

Markin, R.J., C.M. Lillis, and C.L. Narayana, 1976, "Social Psychological Significance of Store Space," *Journal of Retailing*, vol. 52, 43–54.

Marquardt, R.A., J.C. Makens, and R.G. Roe, 1979, *Retail Management*, The Dryden Press, Hinsdale.

Mehrabian, A., and J.A. Russell, 1974, *An Approach to Environmental Psychology*, MIT Press.

Meyers, Herbert M., 1994, "The Role of Packaging in Brand Line Extensions," *The Journal of Brand Management*, June, vol. 1, no. 6.

Meyers, Levy Joan, and Alice Tybout, 1987, "Schema Incongruity as a Basis for Product Evaluation," *Journal of Consumer Research*, 16, June, 39–54.

Mick, David Glen, and Fournier, Susan, 1998, "Paradoxes of Technology: Consumer Cognisance, Emotions and Coping Strategies," *Journal of Consumer Research*, September, vol. 25, 123–43.

Mick, David Glen, 1986, "Consumer Research and Semiotics: Exploring the Morphology of Signs, Symbols and Significance," *Journal of Consumer Research*, September, vol. 13, 196–213.

Midler, Christophe, 1993, *L'auto qui n'existait pas*, Intereditions.

Mintzberg, Henry, 1994, *Rise and Fall of Strategic Planning*, Prentice Hall.

Mintzberg, Henry, 1990, "The Design School: Reconsidering the Basic Premises of Strategic Management," *Strategic Management Journal*, vol. 11, no. 3, 171–95.

Mitchell, Thomas, 1996, *New Thinking in Design: Conversations on Theory and Practice*, Van Nostrand Reinhold.

Mitchell, Thomas, 1993, *Redefining Designing: From Form to Experience*, Van Nostrand Reinhold.

Mok, Clement, 1996, *Designing Business*, Adobe Press.

Moles, Abraham, 1992, *Qualité de vie et constance de l'environnement*, Design Recherche, Numéro 2, Septembre.

Moody, Stanley, 1982, "Role of ID in Development of New Science-Based Products Innovation," Design Policy, Proceedings International Conference, Royal College of Art, Design and Industry.

Morello, Augusto, 1995, *Marketing Design*, in Buchanan et al., ed., *Discovering Design*, University of Chicago Press.

Morin, Edgar, 1991, *La Méthode: 4 Les idées*, Seuil.

Morris, Charles, 1964, *Signification and Significance: A Study of the Relations of Signs and Values*, Cambridge: MIT Press.

Morrow, P.C., and J.C. Elroy, 1981, "Interior Office Design and Visitor Response," *Journal of Applied Psychology*, vol. 66 (5), 646–50.

Mueller, James, 1995, "Designing for Real People," 7th International Forum on Design Management Research & Education, University of Stanford.

Nadler, Gerald, 1991, "Design Teams: Breakthroughs for Effectiveness," *Design Management Journal,* Spring, vol. 2, no. 2, 5–9.

Nonaka, I., and N. Konno, "The Concept of Ba: Building for Knowledge Creation," *California Management Review,* Spring 1998, vol. 40, no. 3.

Nonaka, Ikujiro, and Hirotaka Takeuchi, 1995, *The Knowledge-Creating Company,* Oxford University Press.

Nussbaum, Bruce, 1993, "Hot Products," *Business Week.*

Oakley, Mark, editor, Clipson and Borja de Mozota, coeditors, 1990, *Design Management: A Handbook of Issues and Methods,* Oxford: Basil Blackwell.

O'Connor, William J., 1990, "The Package Design Imperative: Think Globally—Act Locally,"*Design Management Journal,* Summer, vol. 1, no. 2, 54–61.

Olins, Wolf, 1989, *Corporate Identity,* Thames & Hudson.

Olins, Wolf, 1974, *The Wolf Olins Guide to Design Management.*

Olson, Eric, Orville Walker Jr., and Robert Ruekert, 1995, "Organizing for Effective New Product Development: The Moderating Role of Product Innovativeness," *Journal of Marketing,* January, vol. 59, 48–62.

Olson, J., 1988, *Theoretical Foundations of Means-End Chains,* working paper at Penn State University.

Ornstein, Suzyn, 1986, "Organizational Symbols: A Study of Their Meanings and Influences on Perceived Psychological Climate," *Organizational Behavior and Human Decision Processes,* no. 38, 207–29.

Osborne, Harold, 1986, *What Makes An Experience Aesthetics in Possibility of the Aesthetics Experience,* Boston: Kluwes Academic Publishing.

Owens, David, 2000, "Structure and Status in Design Teams: Implications for Design Management," academic review of *The Design Management Journal,* no. 1, 55–63.

Oxman, Riuka, 1990, "Prior Knowledge in Design: A Dynamic Knowledge-Based Model of Design and Creativity," *Design Studies,* vol. 11, no.1, January, 17–28.

Pahl, G, and W. Beitz, 1988, *Engineering Design,* Design Council.

Papanek, Victor, 1991, *Design for the Real World,* Thames and Hudson.

Parasuman, A., V. Zeithaml, and L. Berry, 1985, "A Conceptual Model of Service Quality and Its Implications for Future Research," *Journal of Marketing,* vol. 49, 41–50.

Parasuman, A., V. Zeithaml, and L. Berry, 1988, "A Multiple Item Scale for Measuring Consumer Perceptions of Service Quality," *Journal of Retailing,* vol. 64, no. 1, Spring, 12–37.

Paul, Joseph, 2000, "Performance Metrics to Measure the Value of Design," *Design Management Journal,* vol. 11, no. 4, Fall, 71–5.

Paul, Joseph, and Patrick Fricke, 1999, *The Pursuit of Performance Metrics: Measuring the Value of Design at Eastmann Kodak,* 3rd European International Design Management Conference, March 14–16, Amsterdam.

Pavesi, Giovanni, and Michael Carlo Sommer, 1996, *Washing Machines: Users' Perceptions and Expectations as Input into the Professional Design Process,* 8th International Forum on Design Management Research and Education, Barcelona.

Peirce, Charles, 1931–58, *Collected Papers,* edited by Hartshorne, Weiss, and Burks, Cambridge: Harvard University Press.

Peter, P., and J. Olson, 1987, *Consumer Behaviour: Marketing Strategy Perspectives,* Richard Erwin Inc.

Peters, Tom, 2000, "Design as Advantage No. 1: The Design + Identity 50," *Design Management Journal,* Winter, 11–17.

Peters, Tom, 1989, "The Design Challenge," *Design Management Journal,* Fall, vol. 1, no. 1, 8–13.

Pettigrew, Andrew, Richard Woodman, and Kim Cameron, 2001, "Studying Organizational Change and Development: Challenges for Future Research," *Academy of Management Journal,* vol. 44, no. 4, 697–713.

Phillips, Peter, 2002, "Lessons from the Trenches: Insights from Design Management Seminars," *Design Management Journal,* Summer, vol. 13, 53–7.

Pinson, Christian, N.K. Malhotra, and A.K. Jain, 1988, *Les styles cognitifs des consommateurs,* Recherche et Applications en Marketing, vol. III, no. 1/88.

Piore, Michael, and Richard Lester, 2001, *Language, Interpretation, and the Understanding of Economic Processes,* in Management de l'Innovation, Management de la connaissance, ouvrage collectif séminaire Condor, Lharmattan.

Pirkl, James, 1994, *Transgenerational Design,* Van Nostrand Reinhold.

Porter, Michael, 1998, "What is Strategy?" in *The Strategy Reader*, edited by Susan Segal-Horn, Basic Blackwell.

Porter, Michael E., 1990, *The Competitive Advantage of Nations*, New York: The Free Press.

Porter, Michael E., 1980, *Competitive Strategy*, New York: The Free Press.

Potter, Norman, 1980, *What is a Designer?* (revised edition), Hyphen Press.

Potter, Stephen, and Roy Robin, et al., 1991, *The Benefits and Costs of Investment in Design*, The Open University UMIST report DIGG-03, Design Innovation Group, September.

Pralahad, C.K., and Venkatram Ramaswamy, 2000, "Co-opting Customer Competence," *Harvard Business Review*, January–February, 79–87.

Press, Mike, 1995, *From Mean Design to Lean Design and a Smarter Future: Design Management in the British Ceramic Tableware Industry*, 7th International Forum on Design Management Research & Education, University of Stanford.

Price, Alun, 1995, *Design Users' View of Their Design Experiences: Some Western Australian Evidence*, 7th International Forum on Design Management Research & Education, University of Stanford.

Quarante, Danielle, 1994, *Eléments de Design Industriel, Seconde edition*, Polytechnica.

Quinton, Philippe, 1997, *Design graphique et changement*, L'harmattan, Paris.

Ram, S., 1989, "Successful Innovation Using Strategies to Reduce Consumer Resistance: An Empirical Test," *Journal of Product Innovation Management*, vol. 6, 20–34.

RATP (entreprise), 1995, *La Métamorphose*, InterEditions et *Vous avez dit design? Yo Kaminagai*, RATP revue interne.

Reinhardt, Forest L., 1998, "Environmental Product Differentiation: Implications for Corporate Strategy," *California Management Review*, vol. 40, no. 4, Summer.

Rhodes, Ed, and Ruth Carter, 1995, "Emerging Corporate Strategies," *Co-Design*, April-May-June, vol. 3, 9.

Riedel, Johann, Robin Roy, and Stephen Potter, 1996, *Market Demands that Reward Investment in Design*, 8th International Forum on Design Management Research and Education, Barcelona.

Ring, Peter, 1999, *Using Trust to Promote Economic Growth, Innovation, and Entrepreneurship*, 2ème Colloque La Métamorphose des Organisations, Octobre, Université de Nancy 2, Grefige.

Rioche, Laurence, 2002, *On the Agenda: Design Management to Increase Cross-functional Integration in High-tech Companies*, 11th International Forum on Design Management Research and Education, Northeastern University, Boston.

Rogers, Everett, 1995, *Diffusion of Innovations*, 4th edition, New York: Free Press.

Rook, D.W., 1987, "The Buying Impulse," *Journal of Consumer Research*, no. 14, 189–99.

Rose, David, 2001, "Experience Architecture: A Framework for Designing Personalized Customer Interactions," *Design Management Journal*, Spring, 68.

Rothwell, Roy, et al., 1983, *Design and the Economy*, The Design Council.

Rothwell, Roy, and Paul Gardiner, 1983, "The Role of Design in Product and Process Change," *Design Studies*, vol. 4, no. 3, July, 161–69.

Rothwell, Roy, and Paul Gardiner, 1984, *The Role of Design in Competitiveness*, Design Policy, The Design Council.

Roy, Robin, and Stephen Potter, 1996, "Managing Engineering Design in Complex Supply Chains," *International Journal of Technology Management*, vol. 12, no. 4, 403.

Roy, Robin, 1990, *Product Design and Company Performance*, Design and the Economy, Design Council, London.

Roy, Robin, et al., 1990, *Design and the Economy*, The Design Council (récriture du rapport de 1983).

Roux, Dominique, 1995, *Design et Management: une revue critique de la literature*, Institut de recherche en Gestion Université Paris Val de Marne, Cahier de Recherche, numéro 95–09.

Roy, Robin, G. Salaman, and Vivien Walsh, 1986, *Research Grant Final Report, Design-based Innovation in Manufacturing Industry. Principles and Practices for Successful Design and Production*, Report DIG-02, Milton Keynes: Design Innovation Group, Open University.

Rufaidah, Popy, 2002, *Corporate Identity Management: The Comparison Between Verbal and Visual Models*, 11th International Forum on Design Management Research and Education, Boston, June 12–13.

Russel, J.A., and G. Pratt, 1980, "A Description of the Affective Quality Attributed to Environments," *Journal of Personality and Social Psychology*, vol. 38, no. 2, 311–22.

Rutter, Bryce G., Anne Marie Becka, and David Jenkins, 1997, "A User Centered Approach to Ergonomic Seating," *Design Management Journal*, Spring, vol. 8, no. 2.

Ryan, Laura, 2002, *The Transformational Leadership of Creative Work Teams: A Large Scale Survey of Design Managers,* Proceedings 11th International Forum on Design Management Research and Education, Boston, June 10–11.

Sanchez, Ron, 2000, "Modular Architectures, Knowledge Assets and Organisational Learning: New Management Processes for Product Creation," *International Journal of Technology Management,* vol. 19, no. 6, 610–29.

Sanchez, Ron, 1999, "Modular Architectures in the Marketing Process," *Journal of Marketing,* vol. 63, 92–111.

Schenk, Pamela, 1991, "The Role of Drawing in the Graphic Design Process," *Design Studies,* vol. 12 , no. 3, July 1991, 168–81.

Schewe, C.D., 1988, "Marketing to Our Aging Population: Responding to Physiological Changes," *Journal of Consumer Research,* vol. 5, 61–73.

Schmitt, Bernd, and Alex Simonson, 1997, *Marketing Aesthetics: The Strategic Management of Brands, Identity and Image,* New York: The Free Press.

Schmitt, Bernd, 2000, "Creating and Managing Brand Experiences on the Internet," *Design Management Journal,* Fall, 53.

Schmitt, Bernd, 1999, "Experiential Marketing: A Framework for Design and Communications," *Design Management Journal,* vol. 10, no. 2, Spring, 10–177.

Schön, Donald A., and Glen Wiggins, 1992, "Kinds of Seeing and Their Functions in Designing," *Design Studies,* vol. 13, no. 2, 135–56.

Schwach, Victor, 1994, *Micropsychologie du mode d'emploi,* Design Recherche, no 5, janvier, 63.

Seidel, Victor, 2000, "Moving from Design to Strategy: The 4 roles of Design-Led strategy consulting," *Design Management Journal,* vol. 11, no. 2, Spring.

Senge, Peter, 1999, *In the Dance of Change,* Interview with Fast Company, USA, May.

Sentence, Andrew, and James Clarke, 1997, *The Contribution of Design to the UK Economy,* Design Council, Research programme, Centre for Economic Forecasting, London Business School, 1–44.

Sewall, Murphy, 1978, "Market Segmentation Based on Consumer Ratings of Proposed Product Designs," *Journal of Marketing Research,* vol. 16, November, 557–64.

Siehl, C., D.E. Bowen, and C.M. Pearson, 1990, *The Role of Rites of Integration in Service Delivery,* Actes du 1er séminaire international en management des activités de service, IAE, Université Aix-marseille III, 617 (cité par Aubert-Gamet, 1996).

Simmel, Georg, 1986, *La tragédie de la culture,* Paris petite bibliothèque Ravage.

Simon, Herbert A., 1982, *The Sciences of the Artificial,* The MIT Press (first edition, 1969).

Simonson, Alex, 1997, "Affecting Consumers through Identity and Design," *Advances in Consumer Research,* vol. 24, 64–6.

Smith, Preston, 1996, "Your Product Development Process Demands Ongoing Improvement," *Research Technology Management,* vol. 39, no. 2, March–April, 37–44.

Solomon, Michael, 1983, "The Role of Products as Social Stimuli: A Symbolic Interactionism Perspective," *Journal of Consumer Research,* vol. 10, December, 319–29.

Solomon, O., 1988, "Semiotics and Marketing: New Directions in Industrial Design Applications," *International Journal of Research in Marketing,* 4, 3, 201–16.

Speak, Karl, 2000, "Beyond Stewardship to Brand Infusion," *Design Management Journal,* Winter, vol. 11, 45.

Speak, Karl, 1998, "Brand Stewardship," *Design Management Journal,* vol. 9, no. 1, Winter, 32.

Spies, Kordelia, Friedrich Hesse, and Kerstin Loesch, 1997, "Store Atmosphere, Mood, and Purchasing Behaviour," *International Journal of Research in Marketing,* vol. 14, 1–17.

Steiner, Carol J., 1995, "A Philosophy for Innovation: The Role of Unconventional Individuals in Innovation Success," *Journal of Product Innovation Management,* vol. 12, 431–40.

Story, Molly Follette, 1995, *Universal Product Design through Consumer Product Evaluations,* 7th International Forum on Design Management Research & Education, University of Stanford.

Sujan, Mito, and Christine Dekleva, 1987, "Product Categorization Inference Making," *Journal of Consumer Research,* 14, December, 378–92.

Svengren, Lisbeth, 1995, *Industrial Design as a Strategic Resource,* Proceedings, The European Academy of Design: vol. 4, April 11–13, University of Salford.

Svengren, Lisbeth, and Ulla Johansson, 2002, *One Swallow Doesn't Make a Summer,* 11th International Forum on Design Management Research and Education, Boston, June.

Sweeney, Gerry, 1996, "Learning Efficiency, Technological Change and Economic Progress," *International Journal of Technology Management,* vol. 11, nos. 1/2, 5–27.

Swift, Philip W., 1997, "Science Drives Creativity: A Methodology for Quantifying Perceptions," *Design Management Journal*, vol. 8, no. 2, Spring, 51–7.

Tabachneck, Hermina, and Simon Herbert, 1997, *Effect of Mode of Data Presentation on Reasoning about Economic Markets* (432–43), in Simon Herbert, 1997, *Models of Bounded Rationality*, MIT Press, vol. 3, *Empirically Grounded Economic Reason*.

Takeuchi, Hirotaka and Ikujiro Nonaka, 1986, "The New Product Development Game," *Harvard Business Review*, January–February, 137–46.

Tarondeau, Jean Claude, 1998, *Le management des saviors*, PUF Que sais-je, numéro 3407.

Teece, David, 1998, "Research Directions for Knowledge Management," *California Management Review*, vol. 40, no. 3, Spring, 289–92.

Temple, Sue, 1994, "The Value of Sketching," *Co-Design*, Oct.-Nov.-Dec., vol. 1, 16.

Thackara, John, ed. 1997, Winners !, BIS.

Thomke, Stefan, 2001, "Managing Digital Design at BMW," *Design Management Journal*, Spring, vol.12, no. 2, 20.

Thomke, Stefan, and Takahiro Fujimoto, 2000, "The Effect of 'Front-Loading' Problem Solving on Product Development Performance," *Journal of Product Innovation Management*, vol. 17, 128–42.

Topalian, Alan, 1986, "The Documentation of Corporate Approaches to Design Management to Share Experience and Improve Performance," *Engineering Management International*, no. 4, 54.

Tufte, Edward, 1983, *The Visual Display of Quantitative Information*, Connecticut: Graphics Press.

Ulrich, Karl, and Steven Eppinger, 2000, *Product Design and Development*, second edition, McGraw-Hill Higher Education.

Unghanwa, Davidson, and Michael Baker, 1989, *The Role of Design in International Competitiveness*, London: Routledge Ed.

Urban, G.L., and J.R. Hauser, 1980, *Design and Marketing of New Products*, Englewood Cliffs, N.J.: Prentice Hall.

Valkenburg, Rianne, and Kees Dorst, 1998, "The Reflective Practice of Design Teams," *Design Studies*, July, vol. 19, no. 3, 249.

Van De Kraats, Anthony H., and Lambert Thurlings, 1997, "A New Approach Towards Strategic Decision-taking in a Multi-product Innovative Organization," *International Journal of Technology Management*, vol. 13, no. 2, 93–109.

Van De Ven, A., and M.S. Poole, 1995, "Explaining Development and Change in Organizations," *Academy of Management Review*, vol. 20, 510–40.

Vervaeke, Monique, and Bénédicte Lefevre, 2002, "Design Trades and Inter-firm Relationships in the Nord-Pas de calais Textile Industry," *Regional Studies*, vol. 36, no. 6, 661–73.

Veryzer, Robert, 2000 a, *Design and Development of Innovative High-Tech Products*, 10th International Forum on Design Management Research and Education, Frankfurt, November.

Veryzer, Robert, 2000 b, "Design and Consumer Research," *Design Management Journal*, no. 1, 64.

Veryzer, Robert, 1998, "Discontinuous Innovation and the New Product Development Process," *Journal of Product Innovation*, vol. 15, 304–21.

Veryzer, Robert W., 1993, "Aesthetic Response and the Influence of Design Principles on Product Preferences," *Advances in Consumer Research*, vol. 20, 224–28.

Veryzer, Robert W., 1995, "The Place of Product Design and Aesthetics," *Advances in Consumer Research*, vol. 22, 641–45.

Veryzer, Robert, and Wesley Hutchinson, 1998, "The Influence of Unity and Prototypicality on Aesthetic Responses To New Product Designs," *Journal of Consumer Research*, vol. 24, March, 374–94.

Vitrac, Jean-Pierre, 1984, *Comment gagner de nouveaux marchés par le design industriel*, Editions de l'Usine Nouvelle.

Von Bertalanffy, L., 1973, *Théorie générale des Systèmes*, Dunod, Paris.

Von Krogh, Georg, 1998, "Care in Knowledge Creation," *California Management Review*, vol. 40, no. 3, Spring, 133–49.

Von Stamm, Bettina, 1993, "Whose Design Is It: The Use of External Designers?" *Design Journal*, vol. 1, issue 1, 41–52.

Walker, David, 1990, *Managing Design*, ESCP, Paris, June.

Wallart, Isabelle, 1996, *Structuration du flux de nouveaux produits, trajectoires et performance de PME de haute technologie*, Recherche et Applications en Marketing, vol. 11, numéro 3, 23–37.

Wallendorf, Melanie, and Eric Arnould, 1998, "My Favorite Things: Across Cultural Inquiry into Object Attachment, Possessiveness, and Social Linkage," *Journal of Consumer Research*, vol. 14, 531–47.

Walsh, Vivien, 1996, "Design, Innovation and the Boundaries of the Firm," *Research Policy*, vol. 25, 509–29, (reprint Academic Review, no. 1, *Design Management Journal*, 2000).

Walsh, Vivien, 1995, "The Evaluation of Design," *International Journal of Technology Management*, vol. 10, nos. 4/5/6, 489–509.

Walsh, Vivien, Carole Cohen, and Albert Richards, 1996, *Design for the User: A Case Study of Learning by Doing in the Telecom Industry*, 8th International Forum on Design Management Research and Education, Barcelona.

Walsh, Vivien, 1995, "The Evaluation of Design," *International Journal of Technology Management*, vol. 10, nos. 4/5/6, 489–509.

Walsh, Vivien, Robin Roy, Margaret Bruce, and Stephen Potter, 1992, *Winning by Design*, Basil Blackwell.

Walsh, Vivien, Robin Roy, and Margaret Bruce, 1988, "Competitive by Design," *Journal of Marketing Management*, vol. 4.

Walsh, Vivien, and Robin Roy, 1983, *Plastics Products: Good Design, Innovation and Business Success*, The Open University, Design Innovation Group, report DIG O1, Milton Keynes.

Weick, K.E., 1995, *Sensemaking in Organizations*, Sage Publications.

Wener, R.E., 1985, *The Environmental Psychology of Service Encounter*, in The Service Encounter de Czepiel, Solomon, Surprenant.

Wernerfelt, B., 1984, "A Resource Based View of the Firm," *Strategic Management Journal*, vol. 5, N1, 171–80.

Wheelwright, Clark, 1992, *Revolutionizing Product Development*, New York: The Free Press.

Whitney, Daniel E., 1988, "Manufacturing by Design," *Harvard Business Review*, July–August, 83–91.

Williamson, O., 1991, "Strategizing, Economizing and Economic Organization," *Strategic Management Journal*, vol. 12, 75–94.

Williamson, Oliver, 1999, "Strategy Research: Governance and Competence Perspective," *Strategic Management Journal*, 20(12), 1087–1108.

Woudhuysen, James, 1990, *Product design management in the European market*, Design Management Journal, Summer, vol. 1, no. 2, 32–5.

Xerox (company), 2000, "Industrial Design: Crossing the Client/Consultant Divide," *Design Management Journal*, vol. 11, no. 2, Spring, 28–34.

Yamamoto, Mel, and David R. Lambert, 1994, *The Impact of Product Aesthetics on the Evaluation of Industrial Products*, vol. 11, 309–24.

Zack, Michael, 1999, "Developing a Knowledge Strategy," *California Management Review*, vol. 41, no. 3, Spring, 125–43.

Zimmer, M.R., and L.L. Golden, 1988, "Impressions of Retail Stores: A Content Analysis of Consumer Images," *Journal of Retailing*, vol. 64, Fall, 265–93.

Zweigenhalt, R.L., 1976, "Personal Space in the Faculty Office," *Journal of Applied Psychology*, vol. 61, no. 4, 529–32.

INDEX

Books from Allworth Press

Designing for People
by Henry S. Dreyfuss (paperback with flaps, 6 3/4 x 9 1/2, 256 pages, $21.95)

The Industrial Design Reader
edited by Carma Gorman (paperback, 6 x 9, 256 pages, $19.95)

Citizen Designer: Perspectives on Design Responsibility
edited by Steven Heller and Véronique Vienne (paperback, 6 x 9, 272 pages, $19.95)

Design Issues: How Graphic Design Informs Society
edited by DK Holland (paperback, 6 3/4 x 9 7/8, 288 pages, $21.95)

The Graphic Designer's Guide to Clients:
How to Make Clients Happy and Do Great Work
by Ellen Shapiro (paperback, 6 x 9, 256 pages, $19.95)

Editing by Design: For Designers, Art Directors, and Editors:
The Classic Guide to Winning Readers
by Jan V. White (paperback, 8 1/2 x 11, 256 pages, $29.95)

Teaching Graphic Design: Course Offerings and Class Projects
from the Leading Undergraduate and Graduate Programs
edited by Steven Heller (paperback, 272 pages, $19.95)

Looking Closer 4: Critical Writings on Graphic Design
edited by Michael Bierut, William Drenttel, and Steven Heller
(paperback, 6 3/4 x 9 7/8, 304 pages, $21.95)

Looking Closer 3: Classic Writings on Graphic Design
edited by Michael Bierut, Jessica Helfand, Steven Heller, and Rick Poynor
(paperback, 6 3/4 x 9 7/8, 304 pages, $18.95)

Graphic Design History
edited by Steven Heller and Georgette Balance (6 3/4 x 9 7/8, 352 pages, $21.95)

Please write to request our free catalog. To order by credit card, call 1-800-491-2808 or send a check or money order to Allworth Press, 10 East 23rd Street, Suite 510, New York, NY 10010. Include $5 for shipping and handling for the first book ordered and $1 for each additional book. Ten dollars plus $1 for each additional book if ordering from Canada. New York State residents must add sales tax.

To see our complete catalog on the World Wide Web, or to order online, you can find us at *www.allworth.com*.